STORIES FROM
QUECHAN ORAL LITERATURE

Rosita Carr.

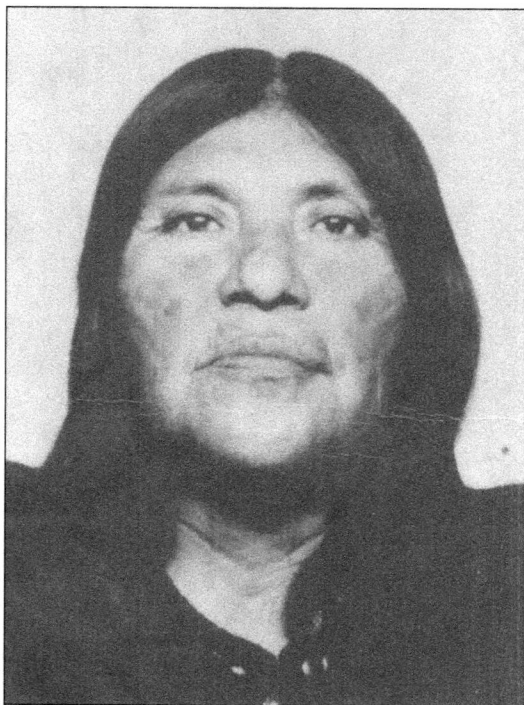

Jessie Webb Escalante in the 1970s.

Stories from Quechan Oral Literature

A.M. Halpern and Amy Miller

Told by
Rosita Carr
John Comet
Jessie Webb Escalante
Mary Kelly Escalanti
Josefa Hartt
Tom Kelly
Anonymous

Translated by
Barbara Levy
George Bryant
Millie Romero
Amy Miller

OpenBook Publishers

http://www.openbookpublishers.com

Digital material and resources associated with this volume are available at http://www.openbookpublishers.com/isbn/9781909254855#resources

This is the sixth volume in the World Oral Literature Series, published in association with the World Oral Literature Project.

ISSN: 2050-7933 (Print)
ISSN: 2050-362X (Online)

ISBN Paperback: 978-1-909254-85-5
ISBN Hardback: 978-1-909254-86-2
ISBN Digital (PDF): 978-1-909254-87-9
ISBN Digital ebook (epub): 978-1-909254-88-6
ISBN Digital ebook (mobi): 978-1-909254-89-3
DOI: 10.11647/OBP.0049

Cover image: *Picacho Peak - Early Morning*, Photo by William D. Isbell, CC BY.
Frontispiece: photographs of Rosita Carr and Jessie Webb Escalante. All rights reserved.

All paper used by Open Book Publishers is SFI (Sustainable Forestry Initiative) and PEFC (Programme for the Endorsement of Forest Certification Schemes) Certified.

Printed in the United Kingdom and United States by Lightning Source for
Open Book Publishers (Cambridge, UK)

Contents

Notes on Contributors

The storytellers who contributed to this volume were respected elders at the time the stories were recorded, in the late 1970s and early 1980s. Most had learned the stories from their own parents, grandparents, aunts, and uncles, who in turn learned them from even earlier generations. They entrusted their stories to Abe Halpern because they believed that it would be better to pass them on in the admittedly untraditional format of a book than to let them be forgotten. Had it not been for the foresight, generosity, and courage of these storytellers, it is likely that many of the stories in this volume would by now have been lost.

The translators and linguists who participated in the preparation of this volume hope to have honored the wishes of the past generation of elders by conveying their stories, and all the traditional knowledge contained within them, to present and future generations of Quechan people.

Some families prefer not to share information about relatives who are no longer living, and their wishes are respected here. Other families have chosen to share biographical information as a way of making sure that it is passed on, along with the stories themselves, to future generations. We are very grateful for the contributions of all the storytellers and translators, including those whose biographies have been withheld.

Storytellers

Anonymous. One storyteller was born in 1923 and lived into the twenty-first century. She asked to remain anonymous.

Rosita Carr was born in the spring of 1884 on Fort Yuma Indian Reservation. She passed away on May 13, 1983.

Jessie Havchat Webb Escalante Etsepoiquarque was born on Fort Yuma Reservation on September 17, 1903. She grew up in a very traditional Quechan family and was well known as an expert on stories, songs, and Quechan traditions. She was a major contributor to *Spirit Mountain: An Anthology of Yuman Story and Song*, edited by Leanne Hinton and Lucille Watahomigie (University of Arizona Press, 1984). She passed away on February 1, 1998.

Mary Kelly Escalanti was born in 1905. She was the sister of Tom Kelly and the youngest child of one of the last great Quechan medicine men. She contributed a story and songs to *Spirit Mountain: An Anthology of Yuman Story and Song*.

Tom Kelly was born late in 1891, at a time when Quechan territory extended across the border into Mexico. His family moved to the U.S. side of the border during the Mexican Revolution. He was the son of one of the last great medicine men, and he himself was a highly regarded expert on ceremonial matters and a major contributor to the book *Kar'úk: Native Accounts of the Quechan Mourning Ceremony*, by A.M. Halpern, edited by Amy Miller and Margaret Langdon (University of California Press, 1997). He passed away in 1982.

Translators and Linguists

George Bryant was born in 1921 and grew up speaking Quechan. He attended school on Fort Yuma Reservation, at Phoenix Indian School, Yuma High School, and the Sherman Institute. He joined the Marines as a young man and was awarded numerous decorations during World War II and the Korean War. Later he served on the Quechan Tribal Council and was instrumental in persuading the federal government to restore tribal lands, and in implementing many of the policies that have made the tribe successful today.

George Bryant follows a family tradition of working with linguists to preserve the Quechan language. His father and grandfather worked with Abe Halpern in the 1930s, and he himself has worked with Amy Miller since 1998. George Bryant is the primary contributor to the forthcoming *Quechan Dictionary*. His book *Xiipúktan (First of All): Three Views of the Origins of the Quechan People* was published in 2013 by Open Book Publishers.

A.M. Halpern, called Abe by his friends, was born in 1914 and received his Ph.D. in Anthropology from the University of Chicago in 1947. He began work documenting the Quechan language in 1935 and continued (with lengthy interruptions for World War II and a thirty-year career in international relations) until his death in 1985. Further information about his work among the Quechan is provided in the Introduction to this volume, and a detailed biography may be found in Halpern's book *Kar'úk: Native Accounts of the Quechan Mourning Ceremony*.

A.M. Halpern's other publications include numerous articles on anthropology and linguistics, the most famous of which are "Yuma Kinship Terms" (*American Anthropologist*, 1942) and a grammar of Quechan published as a series of articles in the *International Journal of American Linguistics* (1946-1947). He transcribed, translated, and edited the section on "Quechan Literature" in *Spirit Mountain: An Anthology of Yuman Story and Song.*

Barbara Levy grew up speaking Quechan. She learned English at school and as a student at Santa Monica City College. She also attended the American Indian Language Development Institute in 2004 and 2005. Barbara Levy is well known as an artist, doll-maker, and storyteller. After teaching the Quechan language for many years as a volunteer, she was named Director of the Quechan Language Preservation Program in 2010. Her essay "My Uncle Sam — The Storyteller" was published (under her former name, Barbara Antone) in *Circle of Motion*, edited by Kathleen Mullen Sands (Arizona Historical Society, 1990), and her story "Coyote and Hen" appears in *Behind Dazzling Mountains: Southwestern Native Verbal Arts*, edited by David Kozak (University of Nebraska Press, 2012).

Amy Miller earned her Ph.D. in linguistics from the University of California, San Diego and has devoted the past 30 years to documenting Yuman languages. In 1998 she began to work with Quechan tribal members on projects which include not only the present volume but the forthcoming *Quechan Dictionary* and George Bryant's book *Xiipúktan (First of All): Three Views of the Origins of the Quechan People*. She and her teacher Margaret Langdon completed the writing of A.M. Halpern's book *Kar'úk: Native Accounts of the Quechan Mourning Ceremony* in the decade following his death. Amy Miller's other books include *A Grammar of Jamul Tiipay* (Mouton de Gruyter, 2001) and the *Barona Inter-Tribal Dictionary* (Barona Museum Press, 2008).

Foreword

Mark Turin

New forms of collaboration have become central to the documentation, protection, and dissemination of endangered oral traditions. Indigenous communities who in the past shared their traditional knowledge with outside scholars are now exploring how to connect the narratives of their ancestors with a global public in ways that are respectful and ethical. This rich collection of Quechan oral literature is one such undertaking, and as readers, we have Quechan community members to thank for their generosity in sharing these extraordinary stories with us through this new anthology.

Collaboration is not easy, and it's rarely fast. As the 'story' of the eleven stories that came to be published in this volume demonstrates, partnerships can emerge almost accidentally, and may take half a century to be realized. When the young Abraham Halpern, under the auspices of the California State Emergency Relief Administration, visited Fort Yuma Indian Reservation for the first time in 1935 to compile a dictionary of the language, neither he nor the Quechan tribal members who entrusted their words to him could have predicted the sequence of events that would one day result in this book. With the outbreak of World War II and subsequent professional reassignments that would take Halpern in different directions, transmission of these treasures of Quechan oral literature was interrupted. Perhaps only the insightful *Kwayúu*, 'The One Who Sees,' could have foreseen the twists and turns that would one day result in this publication.

And then, in the 1970s, Halpern returned to the community. Through a second period of research and recordings, he reconnected with his earlier work, with elders, and with the oral traditions of the Quechan people of which he had become an almost accidental curator. In *Stories from Quechan Oral Literature*, Amy Miller builds powerfully on these various stages of work to make a lasting contribution to a deepening conversation between members of the Quechan community, outside scholars, and the historical archives and linguistic collections to which they have access.

Part of the complexity of collaboration is that it involves many people. As the names of the partners in this collection attest, there are many voices and contributions that must be acknowledged. As readers, we must foremost acknowledge the contributions of the many Quechan people who, over generations, have so generously shared their time, voices, and stories; organizationally, thanks go to the Tribal Council and the Language Preservation Program for their guidance and support. It is also important to recognize the translators, fieldworkers, linguists, and other partners who worked together so effectively to shape this work, and Amy Miller in particular for her passion and commitment in seeing this collection through to publication. Collaborations can be challenging because they bring many contributors into the conversation, and yet this is also why collaborations are so inherently exciting and necessary.

As readers will discover in the first few pages, the oral literature of the Quechan people is great literature and an expression of the enduring creative capacity of humanity. The depth, sophistication, and timeless quality of these stories allow them to be read by, and to, people of all ages who will be drawn in and challenged by the insights that they bring. And most importantly, the oral literature of the Quechan people is an enduring living tradition: these stories have existed and persisted through voice, in community, on cassette, and now in print. As readers, we are the richer for these stories and must show our appreciation to all those who preceded us — ancestors, elders, mentors, and scholars — for all that they have done to bring the oral literature of the Quechan people to us.

Dr Mark Turin
Director, World Oral Literature Project
Chair, First Nations Languages Program
University of British Columbia

Vancouver, Canada
September 2014

Introduction

Amy Miller

This book is a collection of eleven traditional stories from Quechan oral literature, presented in the Quechan language with English translation.

Part I of this introduction sets the stories in their cultural and cross-cultural context. Part II describes how this volume arose through the collaborative efforts of tribal elders and linguists. It explains the translation process and the format in which the stories are presented. It also outlines the Quechan writing system and the conventions used in this volume.

Summaries and notes on the stories may be found at the beginning of each chapter.

Part I: The stories and their cultural context

The Quechan are a Yuman people who have traditionally lived along the lower part of the Colorado River in California and Arizona.[1] At the time of first contact with whites, Quechan territory extended from around Needles, California to the Gulf of California (Forde 1931: 88). Today, the Quechan Indian Nation occupies a portion of the tribe's former territory along the Colorado River, on Fort Yuma Indian Reservation in Winterhaven, California and extending into Yuma, Arizona.

---

1 Bee (1981: viii) points out that Spanish records of the late seventeenth century are the first to mention the Quechan by name, but Stewart (1983: 1) cites evidence that the ancestors of the Quechan lived in the area for at least a millennium.

http://dx.doi.org/10.11647/OBP.0049.07

Traditional Quechan culture is described in detail by Forde (1931). Further information may be found in Forbes (1965), Bee (1981, 1983), Halpern (1997), and Miller (1997).

The Quechan language, also known as Kwatsáan Iiyáa or Yuma, belongs to the Yuman language family. Recent work shows that the Yuman family is older and deeper than linguists had previously recognized; see Miller (in press). Within the Yuman family, Quechan is closely related to Mojave, Maricopa (Piipaash), Hualapai, Havasupai, and Yavapai (including Tolkapaya, Northeastern Yavapai, and Southeastern Yavapai), and somewhat more distantly related to Cocopa, Ko'alh, the Kumeyaay languages (including 'Iipay, Campo/Imperial Valley, Los Conejos, Jamul Tiipay, Nejí/Ja'aa Wa, La Huerta, and San José de la Zorra), and Kiliwa.

Quechan storytelling

Until the second half of the twentieth century, storytelling was a vital part of Quechan culture. As Abraham Halpern (1980: 51) explains:

> Traditionally, stories were told always at night — never in the daytime — in an atmosphere of intimacy and affection. [One elder] recalls as a very young child being held in the arms of her maternal grandfather while he put her to sleep by telling stories. [Another] recalls that after work in the fields everybody gathered around the campfire to be amused by Coyote stories told by his maternal grandfather.

By the 1970s, storytelling was "not yet a lost art, but ... well on the way to becoming one" (Halpern 1980: 51). At that time,

> Even people in their 30s, as well as those older than that, remember with pleasure being put to sleep by tales told by their elders, and when a storyteller is now available who will narrate such tales, there are always eager listeners to hear him ... however, the number of narrators who are confident of their ability to tell the stories is small indeed.

Quechan elders in the 1970s and early 1980s were well aware that the storytelling tradition was in danger, and their oral literature along with it. They trusted Halpern with their tales, convinced that it was preferable to transmit their oral literature in the foreign format of a book than to let it vanish.

Today a few Quechan people still tell stories. However, the stories that are told today represent a small fraction of the Quechan oral tradition, and they are typically told on occasions in which the narrator is an honored guest at an educational or inter-tribal artistic gathering rather than in the traditional context of late-night familial or social interaction.

The stories in this volume are no longer widely known, even among Quechan elders. This book is intended to make them accessible in a bilingual format for the benefit of present and future generations.

The stories in this volume

Most of the stories in this volume take place at the beginning of time and are best understood in the context of the Quechan Creation myth (see for example Harrington 1908, Wilson 1984, Bryant and Miller 2013, and the 2010 film *Journey from Spirit Mountain*). Their characters are the First People, that "race of beings who occupied the world in the mythic times before humans came into existence" and who "have names that we now associate with animals, or occasionally with plants and other natural phenomena" (Bright 1993: 20). In Quechan oral literature, the First People typically have the same cognitive and communicative abilities as today's humans, and the same moral worth. Many have the characteristics that are now associated with their animal namesakes; for instance, Buzzard has wings and a taste for rotten flesh, while Spider travels down a silken thread. Some of the First People are endowed with spiritual powers which allow them to change size, form, or location at will, and some are able to use their powers to influence the actions of others and even to influence natural phenomena.

The narratives in this volume are arranged in order of increasing complexity and are divided into chapters according to topic. Chapters 1 and 2 introduce the reader to some of the themes and devices important in Quechan literature, as well as to Quechan rhetorical style and structure. They prepare the reader for the longer and more challenging stories which begin in Chapter 3.

Chapters 2, 4, and 5 are devoted to what I call "story complexes," that is, sets of narratives which share topics, characters, and events, but which are told from different perspectives and focus on different aspects of a story. Chapter 2 presents two narratives about an orphan boy who saves his community by killing a seven-headed monster. The story complex in Chapter 4 consists of three narratives, each offering a different perspective on the life and death of a giant named *Kwayúu*. The story complex in Chapter 5 similarly presents three very different narratives concerned with the twin sons of Old Lady *Sanyuuxáv*. The first half of the story of *'Aavém*

Kwasám in Chapter 6 is unlike any other in this volume, yet its second half has much in common with stories of *Kwayúu* and of Old Lady *Sanyuuxáv*, leaving the reader with an appropriate sense that much if not all Quechan oral literature is interrelated.

The stories and story complexes in this volume form just a small part of the intricate web of interconnected stories that make up Quechan oral literature. Even in the small sample presented here, it is clear that the Quechan oral tradition is enriched not just by the artistry and imagination of its storytellers, but by the diversity of perspectives from which its stories are told.

Why these stories are important

In a culture where material possessions have traditionally been burned at death, language and oral literature are among the few things that have been passed down from ancient times. Of course, language and oral literature are dynamic: they change over time, adapting to new circumstances and enriching themselves with new ideas. They nonetheless remain important repositories of the traditions, values, knowledge, and beliefs of past generations.

The stories in this volume may be appreciated on many levels. From one perspective, they are self-contained and entertaining. From another, they are instruments of what Millie Romero described as "powerful teaching": they provide information about traditional society and its values, and lessons about life and people, that stands to benefit modern readers as well as traditional listeners. As Halpern (1980: 56) observes,

> The Quechan, nowadays as well as a generation or two ago, state that stories are told with the specific intent of educating the young concerning both good and bad behavior. [...] Some have commented to the effect that the story shows the young that there are people who behave in certain ways, good or bad, but that one doesn't lecture the young concerning the meaning of the story. It is rather for the listener to reflect on the story and search out its meaning for himself. It is as if by exposing the listener to the total aspect of the human comedy one defines for him models or behavioral types, leaving it to him to choose his way in accordance with his natural gifts.

From yet another perspective, many of the stories are part of a mythology that once spread across much of southwestern North America. Certain aspects of the story *Xarathó*, for instance, parallel the "Bird Nester" myth, widespread in the American Southwest, as outlined by Bierhorst (2002: 86-91). The three stories of Old Lady *Sanyuuxáv* presented in Chapter 5 are reminiscent of the Southwestern myth known as "Flute Lure" (see Bierhorst 2002: 94-96). Within Yuman literatures, Quechan stories of Old Lady *Sanyuuxáv* are closely related to the Mojave story of Satukhota (Kroeber 1972: 99-116), the Halchidhoma story of Flute Lure (Spier 1933: 367-396), and the Kumeyaay (Diegueño) story of Chaup (DuBois 1904).

This volume contributes to Yuman and Native American literature in important ways. First, as representatives of the oral literature of the Quechan, its stories fill a tribal gap in Southwestern literature and mythology. Second, while the major studies of Yuman mythology by Kroeber (1948, 1972) and Spier (1933: 345-422) take the form of ethnographers' summaries, the stories in this volume are presented in the original language and in the storytellers' own words. Third, and perhaps uniquely, this volume presents multiple stories about certain characters and events told from a variety of perspectives, giving the reader a vivid appreciation of the complexity and interconnectedness of Quechan oral literature and also of the fact that the narratives which make up this literature are not fixed entities but are as vibrant and diverse as the Quechan people themselves.

Part II: How this volume came about

A.M. Halpern's work on Quechan language and literature

The history of this volume can be traced back to 1935, when a 21-year-old student named Abraham Halpern visited Fort Yuma Indian Reservation for the first time. "I was assigned," Halpern later wrote, "as supervisor of a project to compile a dictionary of the Quechan language by the California State Emergency Relief Administration, working with a crew of tribal members."[2] He also taught some Quechan tribal members to write their language so that they could record stories told by the elder generation.

---

2   This passage from Halpern's unpublished writings is quoted by Langdon (1997: xvi).

The project lasted only three months, however; it ended when SERA was dissolved. Halpern made a second trip to Fort Yuma Reservation in the summer of 1938, this time supported by the University of Chicago.

During these two trips, Halpern mastered the language and gathered material for a grammar which was later published as a series of articles in the *International Journal of American Linguistics* (1946-1947) and which remains one of the finest descriptive grammars ever written.

Halpern's work on Native American languages was interrupted by World War II, when he was recruited to develop intensive language courses for the military. After the war he was invited to join General MacArthur's staff as Advisor on Language Revision in Japan, and later he returned to the U.S. to pursue a career in Far Eastern political analysis, research, and teaching.

In 1976, at the urging of his wife, Katherine Spencer Halpern, Halpern returned to Fort Yuma Reservation. Many people remembered him from his visits in the 1930s. Those who were too young to remember him were impressed with his command of the language. Several people have told me how they once heard a man telling Coyote stories in the community center and how surprised they were when they entered the room and saw that the storyteller was a white man. "I thought it must be old man C—," said Barbara Levy, "but it was Halpern." Halpern also taught tribal members to sing the song cycle known as *Uuráv* (Lightning), which he had learned in the 1930s and which since that time had been forgotten by most people. A modern performance of *Uuráv* by Quechan tribal singer Preston J. Arrowweed may be seen in the film *Journey from Spirit Mountain*.

At the time of Halpern's return, many Quechan elders recognized the importance of preserving their knowledge for the benefit of future generations. Between 1976 and 1983, dozens of elders collaborated with Halpern, making tape recordings of traditional stories, songs, local history, vocabulary, and personal reminiscences. These elders included Howard Allen, Mabel Brown, Rosita Carr, Ignatius Cachora, Lorey Cachora, Pete Cachora, Amelia Caster, Henry Collins, John Comet, Lee Emerson, Jessie Webb Escalante, Mary Kelly Escalanti, Peter D. Escalanti, Josefa Hartt, Mina Hills, Stewart Homer, Preston Jefferson, Lavina Kelly, Tom Kelly, Lawrence Levy, Ethel Ortiz, Anona Quahlupe, and Isabel Rose, among others. Some of their stories, songs, and personal reminiscences have been published in *Spirit Mountain: An Anthology of Yuman Story and Song* (see Emerson 1984, Escalante 1984a,b,c, Escalanti 1984a,b,c, Caster 1984a,b, and Ortiz 1984), and some of their important teachings about Quechan culture were included in *Kar'úk: Native Accounts of the Quechan Mourning Ceremony* (Halpern 1997). The present volume represents one more installment in the ongoing effort to complete the work that Halpern and tribal elders began in 1976.

The stories in this volume were told in private homes to small, Quechan-speaking audiences which included Abe Halpern, often an interpreter, and sometimes friends and relatives of the narrator. They were recorded on cassette tape. Cats, dogs, chickens, and airplanes may be heard, and electricity generators are ubiquitous.

Since he spoke and understood Quechan very well, Halpern was able to follow most of the stories as they were being told; the depth of his understanding is made clear by the questions he asked (in Quechan or through an interpreter) at the conclusion of the story. Halpern later transcribed the stories by hand, and a study of his papers shows that he listened to recordings of the stories in the company of Quechan speakers, including Ernest Cachora, Tessy Escalante, Mina Hills, Barbara Levy, Eunice Miguel, and Millie Romero, in order to verify the accuracy of his transcriptions.[3] His transcriptions are interspersed with notes on the proper interpretation of difficult passages and glosses of words and expressions unfamiliar to him.

Halpern's command of Quechan was great enough that his annotations and glosses are relatively few, and for many of the stories — including those in this volume — he never got around to writing out full English translations. He did, however, translate passages from several for quotation in his article "Sex Differences in Quechan Narration" (Halpern 1980), and he wrote summaries of "The Man Who Bothered Ants" and "*Púk Atsé*" as well as extensive notes on the interpretation of the first half of Josefa Hartt's story "Old Lady *Sanyuuxáv*."

Halpern died in 1985, before he was able to finish his work. He was mourned by the Quechan Tribe and honored with an anniversary ceremony a year after his death. A headstone bearing his Quechan name, *Quechan Iiyáa* (Quechan Language), has been placed in the tribal cemetery.

Translation, the bilingual presentation, and the broken-line format

I came to this project armed with copies of Halpern's recordings and copies of his transcriptions. In order to translate the stories, I worked individually

---

3 Not all of Halpern's marginal notes identify the person who helped him, so it is possible that some names have been omitted.

with three fluent Quechan speakers: Barbara Levy, George Bryant, and Millie Romero. We began the translation process by listening to a story and discussing it in English. Then we returned to the beginning and the real work began: we went over the story again, this time very slowly, and I asked about each unfamiliar word and phrase and gradually came to understand the story at the morphological and syntactic levels as well as at the level of the narrative. Translation was never easy; sometimes it was necessary to repeat a passage dozens of times before its meaning became clear. I went over each story at least twice, with at least two speakers. I am grateful to Barbara Levy, George Bryant, and Millie Romero for their insights into the stories and into Quechan language and culture, and also for their patience and for the dedication and enthusiasm with which they approached the work. Without them the stories in this volume would never have been made available to an English-speaking audience.

The stories are presented here in a bilingual format, with the original Quechan story on the even-numbered pages and a line-matched English translation on the facing (odd-numbered) pages.

The Quechan text is divided into lines motivated by prosodic criteria, including melody, rhythm, and pauses, as outlined by Miller (1997). Each line of Quechan is given a coherent English translation. Since native speakers prefer to translate at the levels of the word and the theme, responsibility for translation at the level of the prosodic line fell to me, and the line-by-line translations in this volume incorporate not only the insights of Barbara Levy, George Bryant, and Millie Romero but also my own understanding of Quechan morphology, syntax, and discourse. For a detailed discussion of the process used to arrive at line-by-line translations, see Miller (1997: 19-24) and Miller (2013: 7-11).

The primary goal of the translation presented here is to convey in English the intended meaning of each line of Quechan. In some cases it was necessary to add lexical information to an English line in order to capture information conveyed either implicitly or grammatically in the corresponding Quechan. For instance, since English lacks a switch-reference system, it was sometimes necessary to add a noun phrase to the translation to help the reader keep track of reference. Since English lacks overt case markers for lexical noun phrases, it was sometimes necessary to add a verb to a line consisting solely of a postposed noun phrase in order to clarify that noun phrase's function. Added information appears between parentheses.

Groups of lines are divided into sentences based upon their intonational and/or syntactic characteristics and punctuated accordingly. Certain grammatical morphemes unambiguously indicate major syntactic boundaries, but such morphemes are relatively rare, and in order to make the English translation more readable I have divided the texts into sentences of manageable length on the basis of intonational cues. A line falling to a low pitch, for instance, is presumed to end a prosodic "sentence" and is punctuated accordingly.

Lines are also organized into groups on the basis of prosodic information; typically, a group of lines ends, and a blank line appears, whenever the narrator brings his narrative to a full stop, typically identified by a relatively long unfilled pause, audible intake of breath, and/or a fall to an especially low pitch.

The resulting broken-line format[4] is intended to allow the English translation to capture as much as possible the rhetorical structure and local organization of the oral delivery, to highlight stylistic devices such as repetition and syntactic parallelism, and to call attention to affective factors such as emphasis and uncertainty. It also regulates reading pace, encouraging the reader to give due attention to each idea as it is expressed as the story unfolds. Language learners will find that each line of English provides the key to a the corresponding line of Quechan, resulting in units of meaningful language small enough to be digested by beginners, while each text provides a model of both syntax and rhetorical structure for advanced students of language and storytelling.

How this volume was edited

The project of translating Abe Halpern's vast collection of Quechan language material has been under way since 1998. My fellow translators and I soon discovered that Halpern recorded multiple versions of certain stories. Each version offered a unique perspective on mythic events, and

---

4 This format bears a superficial resemblance to the "ethnopoetic" formats of Tedlock (1972, 1983), Hymes (1981), Luthin (1991), and several papers in Swann (1993), among others. Ethnopoetic formats are often associated with dramatic poetry or measured verse, so it is worth mentioning that the stories in this volume fall into neither category.

each was astonishingly different from other versions of the same story. Although it was generally expected that I should seek out the "best" or "most correct" narrative to represent each story, I could not bring myself to do so: not only would a great deal of valuable material be neglected, but Quechan oral literature would be misrepresented and much of its richness lost. It was clear to me that the only way to do justice to Quechan oral literature would be to allow multiple narratives on a given topic to coexist in the written volume, just as they have traditionally coexisted in the oral sphere. The concept of the "story complex" was born of this necessity.

Most of the stories in this volume were told as free-standing narratives, but Josefa Hartt's story of *Kwayúu* and John Comet's story of *Shakwatxót* were extracted from longer narrations.

Within each story, omissions are few. Omissions of just a few words are indicated with a convention of three asterisks (***), as are brief interruptions. Omissions of more than one prosodic line of material, and major interruptions, are indicated by three sets of three asterisks (*** *** ***). Pause fillers (of great frequency and usually in the form of the syllable *áa*), as well as false starts, have been omitted in order to conserve space and allow fluent reading of the narratives.

Sound system and orthography

In this volume, Quechan is written phonemically, using a practical writing system developed in consultation with tribal elders at numerous orthography sessions in 1998 and 1999 and a forum on Quechan writing at the 2004 Yuman Languages Summit in Parker, Arizona. This writing system is also used in *Xiipúktan (First of All): Three Views of the Origins of the Quechan People* (Bryant and Miller 2013), in *Kwatsáan Iiyáa Mattkuu'éeyk! (Learn the Quechan Language!)*, and in the forthcoming *Quechan Dictionary*. Symbols used in the Quechan alphabet are given in the left-hand column below, and the sound is described in a non-technical way in the right-hand column. In the middle column, each phoneme is rendered in the phonetic symbols used by Halpern (1997).

Quechan alphabet

á, à	/a/	like the *a* in *about*.
aa	/a·/	a longer sound, like the *a* in *father*.
a	/ə/	unaccented *a* represents the "disappearing vowel"; its pronunciation is discussed below.
e	/e/	like the *e* in *pet*.
ee	/e /	the same sound, but held for a longer time. For some speakers, in some contexts, *ee* is lowered and sounds almost like the *a* in *mad*, only held for a longer time.
ə	/ə/	this symbol represents the "disappearing vowel" in post-stress position; see below.
f	/f/	like English *f*. This sound is found only in loan words.
g	/g/	like English *g*. This sound is found only in loan words.
i	/i/	like the *i* in *pit*.
ii	/i·/	like the *i* in *machine*, but held for a longer time.
k	/k/	like the *k* in *sky*.
kw	/kʷ/	the same sound, but made with rounded lips. It sounds like the *kw* in *backward*.
ky	/kʸ/	like the *ky* in *backyard*.
l	/l/	is like English *l* as in *list*.
ll	/ɬ/	this sound is not found in English and is rare in Quechan. To make it, touch the tip of your tongue to your upper teeth, and blow air out along the sides of your tongue.
lly	/ɬʸ/	this sound is not found in English and is rare in Quechan. To make it, touch the tip of your tongue to your lower teeth, and blow air out along the sides of your tongue.
ly	/lʸ/	like the *lli* in *million*.
m	/m/	like the *m* in *mom*.
n	/n/	like Spanish *n*, as in *bonito*.
ng	/ŋ/	like the *ng* in sing. This sound is rare in spoken Quechan but found in many song words.
ny	/nʸ/	like the *ny* in *canyon*.
o	/o/	like Spanish *o*; somewhere between the sound of *o* in *gone* and the sound of *o* in *poke*.
oo	/o·/	the same sound, but held for a longer time.

p	/p/	like the English *p* in *spin*.
q	/q/	similar to *k*, but pronounced further back in the mouth.
qw	/qʷ/	the same sound, but made with rounded lips.
r	/r/	a tapped or slightly trilled *r*, like the *r* in Spanish *María*.
s	/s/	like Spanish *s*, as in *peso*.
sh	/ṣ/	this sound is not like English *sh*; instead, it is a "whistling sound" made with the tip of the tongue at the roots of the teeth and slightly curled back.
t	/t/	like Spanish *t*, as in *bonito*. This sound is made with the tip of the tongue touching the upper front teeth or even between the teeth.
th	/ð/	like the *th* in English *this*.
ts	/c/	like the *ts* in *outside*, but a single sound rather than a sequence of two sounds.
tt	/ṭ/	like English *t*, as in *stuck*, or slightly farther back in the mouth.
ty	/tʸ/	like the *ty* in *got ya!*
u	/u/	like Spanish *u*; somewhere between the *u* of *put* and the *oo* of *hoop*.
uu	/u·/	like the *oo* in *moon*, but held for a longer time.
v	/v/	like the *v* in *very*.
w	/w/	like the *w* in *wet*.
x	/x/	like the *ch* in German *ach* or the *j* in Spanish *joya*.
xw	/xʷ/	the same sound, but made with rounded lips.
y	/y/	like the *y* in *yes*.
'	/ʔ/	this sound, known as "glottal stop," is actually a brief period of silence made by closing the vocal cords. In English it is found in the negative expression *uh-uh* and the warning *uh-oh*.

Notes on pronunciation and spelling

For many speakers, particularly those of the older generation, a vowel at the beginning of a word is preceded by aspiration (a puff of air, which some people think of as a little *h*). Aspiration disappears when the word is prefixed; for instance, while aspiration may be heard at the beginning of *av'áak* ('he walked'), it is not heard in *nyaav'áak* ('when he walked').

In the 1930s, Halpern (1946a: 31) determined that unaccented *ee* and *oo* were allophones (variants conditioned by their surroundings) of *ii* and *uu* respectively, and his orthography reflects this analysis. Halpern assumed that his analysis holds true for the 1970s, and the spelling in this volume reflects his assumption. For many Quechan speakers of the present generation, unstressed *ee* and *oo* are phonemically distinct from unstressed *ii* and *uu*, and consequently there are slight differences in spelling between the modern versions of certain words and the older versions presented in this volume.

The vowels *á* and *à* are pronounced like the *a* in *about*. Unaccented *a*, on the other hand, represents an inorganic vowel: that is, a vowel which may disappear or be relocated when prefixes are added to or subtracted from a given word. Illustrative examples may be found in *Kwatsáan Iiyáa Mattkuu'éeyk!*. The pronunciation of an inorganic vowel depends upon the consonants that surround it. For instance, when followed by *y* or between palatal consonants, unaccented *a* may be pronounced like the *i* in *pit*; when followed by *w* it is usually pronounced like the *u* in *put*; and when followed by glottal stop (') and an accented vowel, it may echo the sound of the accented vowel.

The symbol *ə* represents the inorganic vowel in post-stress position.

When an accented vowel is followed by *y* or *w*, the sounds are pronounced sequentially. When pronouncing the sequence *áay*, for instance, first pronounce the *aa* sound (like the *a* in *father*), then pronounce the *y* sound (as in *yes*). The resulting sequence will sound something like the English word *eye*, but held for a longer time. When pronouncing the sequence *éw*, first pronounce the *e* (like the *e* in *pet*) and then the *w* (as in *wet*).

Quechan grammar

The phonology and morphology of Quechan are described in detail by Halpern (1946, 1947). Further information may be found in Langdon (1977) and Miller (1997).

Conventions

The following conventions are used in this volume:
- Each line of Quechan text represents a prosodically motivated unit.
- Each line of English presents a translation of the corresponding line of Quechan.

- If a prosodic line is too long to fit within a graphic line, it is continued on a second graphic line. The second graphic line is indented.
- A prosodically motivated paragraph is followed by a blank line.
- A series of three asterisks (***) indicates a brief interruption or the omission of a word or two.
- Three series of three asterisks (*** *** ***) indicates a more lengthy omission or a major interruption.
- When the symbol *t* or the symbol *tt* (each of which represents a distinct sound, as described above) is followed by the symbol *t* or the symbol *ts*, a hyphen is used to separate the relevant symbols.

Acknowledgments

This volume is the result of a collaborative effort involving many people. Barbara Levy, George Bryant, and Millie Romero worked with me for years on the translation of the stories. Their talent and dedication have made this volume possible, and their friendship has made the project a pleasure.

I am grateful to the families of the storytellers for their support. I am also grateful to the family of Abraham M. Halpern for giving me the opportunity to finish Abe's work, and to Katherine Spencer Halpern and Margaret Langdon for accompanying me on my first trip to Fort Yuma Reservation in 1998 and introducing me to the Quechan Culture Committee and members of the Quechan community.

I thank the many Quechan people who have taught me about their language, including Myra Andrews, Preston J. Arrow-weed, George Bryant, Muriel Bryant, Ila Dunzweiler, Arlie Emerson, Perdius Escalante, Tessy Escalante, Della Escalanti, Frank Escalanti, Pearl Escalanti, Cora Hill, Phylis Jones, Bertha José, Olivia José, Shirley Kelly, Barbara Levy, Arnold Millard, Faith Millard, Dorothy Montague, John Norton, Judith Osborne, Linda Rivera, Millie Romero, and Vernon Smith.

The Quechan Language Preservation Program was instrumental in getting this book published, and I thank its director, Barbara Levy, as well as Quechan language teachers Ila Dunzweiler, Arlie Emerson, Della Escalanti, and Judith Osborne for their assistance. Some of the work for this volume was done at the Quechan Elderly Nutrition Site, and I thank the past and present staff of the Site, including the late Betty Robles, for their hospitality and assistance.

I am grateful to Quechan Tribal Council member Emilio Escalanti for arranging numerous orthography sessions with tribal elders in 1998 and 1999 and for moral support throughout the past sixteen years. I am grateful to Quechan Tribal Council member Juliana Comet for special assistance. The Quechan Tribe's grants writer, Cliff O'Neill, did much to facilitate the publication of this book, and Quechan Newsletter Coordinator William Isbell provided the cover photo. I thank them both. Special thanks to Della Escalanti and Perdius Escalante for contributing photos for use in the frontispiece.

An anonymous reviewer for Open Book Publishers made numerous helpful comments on the manuscript, and this book has benefitted from his suggestions. Additional helpful comments were provided by Benjamin Hanser, Matthew Hanser, and Alessandra Tosi. Bianca Gualandi took special care in designing and typesetting this book. I thank all of them.

The English translation of the anonymous story of Old Lady *Sanyuuxáv* is an updated version of that published in *Voices from Four Directions: Contemporary Translations of the Native Literatures of North America*, edited by Brian Swann (© 2004 by the Board of Regents of the University of Nebraska). It is used with the permission of the University of Nebraska Press.

The material in this volume is based upon work supported by the National Science Foundation under grants no. SBR-9728976, BNS-9910654, and BCS-0317783. Any opinions, findings, conclusions, or recommendations expressed in this material are those of the authors and do not necessarily reflect the views of the National Science Foundation. I thank John R. Johnson and Diane Wondolowski of the Santa Barbara Museum of Natural History for administering the National Science Foundation grants from 1997 to 2008.

Publication of this book is made possible by the Institute of Museum and Library Services Native American / Native Hawaiian Museum Services Program grant no. MN-00-13-025-13. I thank the Quechan Tribal Council for prompt approval of the grant budget.

I am especially grateful to Dr. Alessandra Tosi of Open Book Publishers and Dr. Mark Turin of the World Oral Literature Project for making the publication of this book possible.

References

Bee, Robert L. 1983. Quechan. *Handbook of the Indians of North America, Volume 10: Southwest*, ed. Alfonso Ortiz. Washington: Smithsonian Institution. pp. 86-98.

— 1981. *Crosscurrents Along the Colorado.* Tucson: University of Arizona Press.

Bright, William. 1993. *A Coyote Reader.* Berkeley, Los Angeles and London: University of California Press.

Bryant, George and Amy Miller. 2013. *Xiipúktan (First of All): Three Views of the Origins of the Quechan People.* Cambridge: Open Book Publishers. http://dx.doi.org/10.11647/OBP.0037

Bierhorst, John. 2002. *The Mythology of North America.* New York: Oxford University Press.

Cadic, Francois. 2013. Georgik and Merlin. *The Golden Age of Fairy Tales: From the Brothers Grimm to Andrew Lang*, ed. Jack Zipes. Indianapolis: Hackett Publishing. pp. 444-452.

Caster, Amelia. 1984a. "Childhood Reminiscences." In Hinton and Watahomigie (eds), pp. 320-330.

— 1984b. "Salt Song." In Hinton and Watahomigie (eds), pp. 320-330.

DuBois, Constance Goddard. 1904. "The Story of Chaup: A Myth of the Diegueños." *Journal of American Folklore* 17: 217-242. http://dx.doi.org/10.2307/534223

Emerson, Lee. 1984. "A Snake Bit Me and an Old Lady Cured Me." In Hinton and Watahomigie (eds), pp. 314-319.

— and A.M. Halpern. 1978. "Coyote and Quail." *Coyote Stories*, ed. William Bright. *International Journal of American Linguistics Native American Texts Series*, pp. 145-169.

Escalante, Jessie Webb. 1984a. "Coyote Fishes." In Hinton and Watahomigie (eds), pp. 303-305

— 1984b. "Coyote Travels." In Hinton and Watahomigie (eds), pp. 306-311.

— 1984c. "Stubborn." In Hinton and Watahomigie (eds), pp. 306-311.

Escalanti, Mary Kelly. 1984a. "Coyote and Mud Hens." In Hinton and Watahomigie (eds), pp. 312-313.

— 1984b. "Amo: Mountain Sheep Songs." In Hinton and Watahomigie (eds), pp. 331-332.

— 1984c. "Lullabye." In Hinton and Watahomigie (eds), p. 333.

Forbes, Jack D. 1965. *Warriors of the Colorado: The Yumas of the Quechan Nation and Their Neighbors.* Norman: University of Oklahoma Press.

Forde, C. Daryll. 1931. *Ethnography of the Yuma Indians.* University of California Publications in American Archaeology and Ethnology 28.4: 83-278.

Halpern, A.M. 1946a. "Yuma I: Phonemics." *International Journal of American Linguistics* 12.1: 25-33. http://dx.doi.org/10.1086/463884

— 1946b. "Yuma II: Morphophonemics." *International Journal of American Linguistics* 12.3: 147-151. http://dx.doi.org/10.1086/463905

— 1946c. "Yuma III: Grammatical Processes and the Moun." *International Journal of American Linguistics* 12.4: 204-212. http://dx.doi.org/10.1086/463915

— 1947a. "Yuma IV: Verb Themes." *International Journal of American Linguistics* 13.1: 18-30. http://dx.doi.org/10.1086/463926

— 1947b. "Yuma V: Conjugation of the Verb Theme." *International Journal of American Linguistics* 13.2: 92-107. http://dx.doi.org/10.1086/463933

— 1947c. "Yuma VI: Miscellaneous Morphemes." *International Journal of American Linguistics* 13.3: 147-166. http://dx.doi.org/10.1086/463945

— 1976. "Kukumat Becomes Sick — a Yuma Text." *Yuman Texts*, ed. Margaret Langdon. *International Journal of American Linguistics. Native American Texts Series* 1.3: 5-25. Chicago: University of Chicago Press.

— 1980. "Sex Differences in Yuma Narration." *Journal of California and Great Basin Anthropology* 2: 51-19.

— 1984. "Quechan Literature." In *Spirit Mountain: An Anthology of Yuman Story and Song*, ed. Leanne Hinton and Lucille J. Watahomigie. Tucson: University of Arizona Press.

— 1997. *Kar'úk: Native Accounts of the Quechan Mourning Ceremony*, ed. Amy Miller and Margaret Langdon. Berkeley and Los Angeles: University of California Publications in Linguistics 128.

Harrington, John Peabody. 1908. "A Yuma Account of Origins." *Journal of American Folklore* 21.82: 324-348. http://dx.doi.org/10.2307/534581

Hinton, Leanne and Lucille Watahomigie, eds. 1984. *Spirit Mountain: An Anthology of Yuman Story and Song*. Tucson: University of Arizona Press.

Hymes, Dell. 1981. *In Vain I Tried to Tell You: Essays in Native American Ethnopoetics.* Philadelphia: University of Pennsylvania Press.

Journey from Spirit Mountain. 2010. Dir. Daniel Golding, perf. Preston J. Arrow-weed. Ahmut Pipa Foundation and Hokan Media Productions.

Kroeber, A.L. 1948. *Seven Mohave Myths*. Anthropological Records 11.1. Berkeley, Los Angeles, and London: University of California Press.

— 1972. *More Mohave Myths*. Anthropological Records 27. Berkeley, Los Angeles, and London: University of California Press.

Langdon, Margaret. 1977. "Yuma (Kwtsaan) After 40 Years." *Proceedings of the 1976 Hokan-Yuman Languages Workshop*, ed. James E. Redden. Carbondale: University of Southern Illinois University Museum Studies 11: 43-51.

— 1997. "Biography of A.M. Halpern (1914-1985)." In Halpern (1997), pp. xv-xix.

Luthin, Herbert William. 1991. *Restoring the Voice in Yanan Traditional Narrative: Prosody, Performance, and Presentational Form*. Ph.D. dissertation, University of California, Berkeley.

Miller, Amy. in press. "Phonological Developments in Delta-California Yuman." *International Journal of American Linguistics.*

— 2013. "Introduction." In Bryant and Miller, pp. 3-18. http://dx.doi.org/10.11647/OBP.0037.04

— 1997. "Introduction." In *Kar'úk: Native Accounts of the Quechan Mourning Ceremony*, by A.M. Halpern, ed. Amy Miller and Margaret Langdon. Berkeley and Los Angeles: University of California Publications in Linguisitcs 128: 3-38.

Ortiz, Ethel. 1984. "Locust Songs." In Hinton and Watahomigie (eds), p. 332.

Quechan Language Preservation Program. in prep. *Kwatsáan Iiyáa Mattkuu'éeyk!*

Spier, Leslie. 1933. *Yuman Tribes of the Gila River.* Chicago: University of Chicago Press. Reprinted by Dover Publications Inc., 1978.

Stewart, Kenneth M. 1983. "Yumans: Introduction." In *Handbook of the Indians of North America, Volume 10: Southwest,* ed. Alfonso Ortiz. Washington: Smithsonian Institution, pp. 1-3.

Swann, Brian. 1992. *On the Translation of Native American Literatures.* Washington: Smithsonian Institution.

Tedlock, Dennis. 1983. *The Spoken Word and the Work of Interpretation.* Philadelphia: University of Pennsylvania Press.

— 1972. *Finding the Center: Narrative Poetry of the Zuni Indians.* New York: Dial Publishing.

Wilson, William. 1984. "Exerpts from the Lightning Song." In *Spirit Mountain: An Anthology of Yuman Story and Song.* Tucson: University of Arizona Press, pp. 335-344.

1. The Man Who Bothered Ants

Told by Jessie Webb Escalante

Translated by Barbara Levy,
George Bryant, and Amy Miller

http://dx.doi.org/10.11647/OBP.0049.01

Notes and synopsis

This story was told to Abe Halpern by Jessie Webb Escalante on April 22, 1980. Halpern later reviewed his transcript of the story with Ernest Cachora.

The main character in this story is a person who has a habit of annoying ants by poking their nest with a stick. Eventually an angry ant pulls both the man and his horse into the nest. Man and horse are held captive for such a long time that the man's family and friends begin to mourn his death. Finally, the man and his horse are released and return home. The horse, once pure white, is now covered with red spots which are the handprints of ants.

In some ways, this is a simple story explaining a fact of nature: how the appaloosa got his spots. At a deeper level, however, the story is revealing about Quechan literature, culture, and worldview. It takes place at the beginning of time, and its characters are among the First People. It features a theme favored in Quechan oral literature: the main character's love of his home and people. No explanation is given for the man's behavior, and none is needed: in Quechan culture, people are the way they are, and others around them accept this. In the end, the man understands that what has happened to him is the consequence of his own actions.

The Man Who Bothered Ants

Told by Jessie Webb Escalante

Pa'iipáats suuváat.
Pa'iipáats nyaváyk suuváa.

Pa'iipáats 'atáyk nyaváyk viivák,
athúus
athótk
aváts 'ashéntək alyuuváapətəka.
Tsam'athúlyəm éevtək uuváat.

'Anyáayk viithíim,
amanək,
tsam'athúly nyaványa,
tsam'athúly kéek a'ét.
'Anyétsəts nyuu'ítsk.

Tsam'athúly kéek uuváak.
Nyaványa ka'ák viiwáam
uukakyáav.

Awétk uuváat.

Nyáavəm éevtək,
'ashéntək alyuuváak awétk uuváa.

Tsam'athúly 'avá xalykwáak awétk,
uuváat.

Vuuváam,
uuyóov va'árək,
tsam'athúlyavats,
uuyóovk vuunóotsáa,
nyamuuév aly'émətək vuunóo.

Someone was over there.
Someone was living over there.

A lot of people were living here,
but
it happened
that this (person) was the only one (who did it).
He bothered ants.

When the sun came up,
he got up,
and as for the ants' nest,
he was going to stir up the ants.
We say that.

He went about stirring up the ants.
He went along kicking their nest,
going all around it.

That's what he was doing.

He bothered these (ants),
and he was the only one who did.

He looked for ants' nests, and so,
there he was.

Here he was,
and they always watched him,
those ants,
they watched him, but
they didn't bother him.

Vuunóom,
vuuváatk,
vatháts,
'anyáa atspák viithíim,
nyáanyəm éevtək,
nyáanyəm éevtək uuváat.

Uuyóovt,
avuuváak,
nyáavəts,
'axátt-ts siiv'áwəm,
atháwk alyvák viiyáa.

Makyéely aakwíink aváatk a'étk athúm.

Xátt xamáaly nyiipáq kwa'ítsənyts.

Uuváak,
kór alynyaayémək uuváa.

Nyaawínyəm'áshk viiyáak.

Viiyáaxáyəm,
tsam'athúlyənyts atspákəta.
Ayúutka.

Siiv'áwt.
Aváts 'axáttəny alyta'ór alyaskyíik a'éxaym,
nyiiv'áwtk viiv'áwt.

"Móo,
maapa'iipáa,
máanyts mawíi va'árək viimuuváak,
ammawíim,
'ayúutk 'awétkítya,"
a'íi,
a'ávəks,
a'étk uu'áv lyavíitəm,
a'ávək siiv'áw.

Here they were,
and here he was,
this (person),
and the sun came up,
and he bothered them,
he kept on bothering them.

They watched him,
and there he was,
this (person),
and there was a horse over there,
and he took it and went riding on it.

He was planning to turn around somewhere and come back.

It was a pure white horse.

There he was,
he was there for a long time.

He went along doing it once again.

He went along, and suddenly,
an ant came out, they say.
And he saw him.

He stood there.
This (man) was still on top of the horse, and suddenly
(the ant) was standing there.

"Okay,
you person,
you are the one who is always doing that,
that's what you do,
I've seen it,"
he said,
and (the man) heard it, or
he heard something like that,
and he stood there listening.

Kórəly nyaa'ím,
'axáttəny ayáak nyiktaxpályk,
nyavály alyaakxávət.
Tsam'athúly nyavály alyaakxávək,
iiwáa.

Nyaaiiwáamk,
vanyaawáam,
'avá alyaakxáva.
'Amátt maxák aakxávətəm.
Nyaváyapátk siivák athúm,
alyaakxáv.

Ayúutk siiv'áwət.
'Amáttənyts 'axwétt-tək.
Pa'iipáavəts 'axwétt-tək athótəm,
ayúutk siiv'áw.

Pa'iipáats athót,
'axwéttk,
pa'iipáanyanyts.

Athúm,
pa'iipáanyts vaathíik apák,
'axáttəny uuyóovək vuuv'ótsk,
séx a'étk vuuv'ótst.

'Axáttənyts xamáaly nyiipáq a'étum.

Viithíik,
'axáttəny apásk a'áv.

'Axátt-ts athótəm ayúutk,
apásk a'ávək a'étk uuváat.
Tsam'athúly 'ashéntəts nyiivapáay.

Iisháalya —
athúts,
nyiitsáam.

After a while,
(the ant) went after the horse and pulled him,
and he took them into the nest.
He took them into the ants' nest,
all by himself.

All by himself,
he took them away,
and he brought them into the nest.
He took them under the ground.
(Other ants) were living there too, and so,
he took them in.

(The man) stood there looking.
The ground was red.
The (ant) people were red, and so,
he stood there looking.

They were people,
and they were red,
those people (were).

So,
those (ant) people came,
and they stood there looking at the horse,
they stood there in a crowd.

The horse was pure white.

(One of them) came,
and he touched the horse with the palm of his hand.

He saw that it was a horse,
and he wanted to touch it.
One of the ants leaned on it.

His hands —
he did it,
he put them down there.

Axtátt nyiitsáam,
sharéq,
avík atsáam,
awím,
awétk suuváat.

Suuváam,
vatháts ayúuk suuváa.
'Amáttəvats xáam athúum ayúuk suuváatk,
amétk suuváat,
kaathóm takuuvékxats athúulyemtəm.

Suuváam,
pa'iipáanyənyts shataméevək vuunóok.

"Pa'iipáanyts kaathómtan 'anyéwk athómúm?"
a'étk vuunóo.

Uuyóov alyém,
shatmatháav.

"Apúykəm athótkitya,"
a'étk vuunóo.

Matsats'étk vuunóot.
Apúyk a'étk awítya.
Matsats'íi vuunóo.

Vuunóok,
kór alynyaayémən,
pa'iipáats 'atáytan mattaaévk,
matsats'íim viitháwk,
níimtək viitháw.

"Móo,
nyamáam,
apúytək athútya,"
a'ét.
"Kaathómək uuváaxats athúulyəmk,"
a'étk viitíiv.

He put them down on the (horse's) back,
he took hold of him,
he put (his hands) down there,
and so,
he went about doing it.

There he was,
and this (man) was watching.
He saw that the place was different,
and he was weeping,
(because) there was no way he could return.

There he was,
and the people (back home) were missing him.

"How could that person have disappeared?"
they were saying.

They didn't see him,
and they didn't know what had happened to him.

"It must be that he has died,"
they were saying.

They were weeping.
They thought he was dead.
They were weeping.

There they were.
and after a while,
a lot of people got together,
and they were weeping,
and they got through it.

"Okay,
that's all,
he is dead,"
they said.
"There's no way he will be here again,"
they were saying.

'Anyáats vanyaathík,
kór alynyaayémk,
vanyaatháwəm,
takavék —
uukavék.
Tsam'athúlyənyts atháwk uukavék.

"Móo,
nyamáam.
Kayémk," a'ét.

Uukavék vuuthíik,
nyavány 'avuuyáanyəm shapíittk awét.

Atspákt.
'Axáttəny uunaxwíly alyaskyíik atspákt.

Atspák,
avathíim.
'axáttənya
tsam'athúly nyiisháalya nyiitháawətk,
'axwéttk,
'axwéttk athót,
xamáalyətk 'axwétt.

Takavék viithíit.

Vatháts apúyk a'étk athúm,
nyaashtamatháavk viitíivt.
Viitíivxayəm,
nyiiv'áw a'ét.

"Ta'axánək athúuk kaathúu?" aaly'étk,
ayóovxayəm,
ta'axánək —
aváaмək athót!

Ayóovət,
matsats'étk siitháw.

Time lay here,
a long time passed,
and while they were there,
he came back —
they brought him back.
The ants took him and brought him back.

"Okay,
that's all.
Go on back," they said.

They brought him back,
and they closed the door of their house.

He reappeared.
Still leading the horse, he reappeared.

He reappeared,
he came (back),
and as for the horse,
the ants' handprints were here and there on his back,
and they were red,
they were red, and so,
(the horse) was white and red.

He came back.

They thought he was dead, and so,
they sat here without recognizing him.
They sat here, and suddenly
he was standing there.

"Could it really be him?" they wondered,
and they looked, and suddenly
it really was him —
he was back!

They looked at him,
and they were weeping.

'Axáttəny láw a'ím ayúuxayəm;
'axwéttk,
iisháalya nyiitháaw,
'axwéttk,
'axwéttk a'ét.
Ayúutk viiv'áw.

Anák,
mattkanáavək vuunóot.

Vatháts pa'iipáava xalykwáak vuunóok,
aaéevək vuunóok.
'Atáytank viivám,
nyuukanáavək vuunóot.

" 'Anyáats 'athúu 'ayáaxayəm,
tsam'athúlyəm 'éevək 'uuváam,
vanyawítsəm 'athúum nya'thúuva," a'í.
'Atsuuyúuny kanáavək vuunóot.

'Axáttəny atháw,
tasháttk uuyóovək vuunóot.

'Axwéttk.

Axtátt nyiitháaw,
'axwéttk athót,
iisháalyənyts.

Athúum,
uuyóovək vuunóo.

Móo,
nyamáam.
Takavék aváak a'étk.

Vuunóok athúuk a'étk,
nyaamáam.
Apáyəx.

They turned their heads and looked at the horse;
they were red,
the handprints were here and there,
and they were red,
they were red, they say.
(The people) stood there looking.

He sat down,
and he went about telling his story.

This one went looking for people,
and he gathered them together.
A lot (of people) were here,
and (the man) went about telling them.

"I went along doing (that),
I bothered ants,
and this is what they did to me," he said.
He went about explaining what he had seen.

They took the horse,
they stood it there and looked it over.

It was (marked with) red.

They were here and there on its back,
and they were red,
the handprints.

So,
they were looking at it.

Well,
that's all.
He came back, they say.

Here they were, and so,
that's all.
That will be the end.

2. Two Stories About the Orphan Boy and the Monster

'Aréey

Told by an anonymous Quechan elder

*Translated by Millie Romero,
Barbara Levy, and Amy Miller*

Tsakwshá Kwapaaxkyée (Seven Heads)

Told by John Comet

*Translated by Barbara Levy,
George Bryant, and Amy Miller*

http://dx.doi.org/10.11647/OBP.0049.02

This chapter presents two narratives about an orphan boy and a seven-headed monster. These stories appear to have been influenced by European folklore (as discussed below), yet they are nonetheless very much Quechan stories. For readers who are unfamiliar with Quechan literature, they provide a relatively simple plot while introducing Quechan themes, literary devices, and rhetorical style. Readers who are already expert in Quechan oral literature will appreciate the ingenuity with which these stories integrate European and traditional Quechan ideas.

The two narratives in this chapter focus on different events: 'Aréey on the difficult journey the boy must make in order to reach the monster, and Tsakwsha Kwapaaxkyée on the details of the fight between the two main characters and the events which unfold after the monster is killed.

Notes and synopsis: 'Aréey

This story was told to Halpern on March 14, 1979 by a Quechan elder (born in 1923) who asked to remain anonymous. The elder's niece, Millie Romero, was also present, and explained that the story had been told to the elder by her parents as a bedtime story. Halpern later reviewed his transcript of the story with Millie Romero.

The main character is an orphan boy who lives under the authority of a character called 'Aréey (see below for the significance of this name). 'Aréey mistreats and imprisons the boy. Eventually a monster threatens the population, and everyone who tries to kill the monster fails. The orphan boy volunteers for the job, but his offer is rejected with scorn. He uses his spiritual powers to escape from confinement, overcome tremendous obstacles, and kill the monster. He returns home with the monster's seven tongues to prove that he has done the deed.

The seven-headed monster in this story is referred to as 'Aavém Kwasám but bears no resemblence to the character of the same name in Chapter 6.

Notes and synopsis: *Tsakwshá Kwapaaxkyée* (Seven Heads)

John Comet told the story *Tsakwshá Kwapaaxkyée* to Abe Halpern on January 31, 1981.

In this story, a village is besieged by an unknown predator. Sheep and other domestic animals are being killed and eaten at night, and no-one can figure out who the predator is or how to stop him. Finally an orphan boy who lives in the village discovers that the monster Seven Heads is responsible. He seeks out Seven Heads and, against all odds, succeeds in killing him. He cuts off the monster's seven tongues and carries them home, where his cat swallows them.

Soon another person finds the body of Seven Heads and takes credit for killing the monster. The orphan boy's cat regurgitates the monster's seven tongues, and everyone realizes that the true hero is the orphan boy. The man who made the false claim is cruelly punished, and the people have a feast to celebrate the death of the monster.

European influence and the significance of these stories in the study of oral literature

Both of the narratives in this chapter involve an orphan boy who kills a seven-headed monster and cuts out his tongues. A similar monster meets a similar fate in some European fairy tales; see for example the story of Georgik and Merlin (Cadic 2013). In the story of Georgik and Merlin, just as in *Tsakwshá Kwapaaxkyée*, a dishonest person takes credit for killing the monster and is revealed as an impostor when the monster's severed tongues are found. It should be noted that apart from these shared points of plot, the stories in Chapter 2 are very different from the fairy tale of Georgik and Merlin.

Other details provide further suggestion of European influence. In the story called *'Aréey*, the name of the title character is borrowed from the Spanish word *rey* ('king'), and the character has much in common with royal antagonists in European fairy tales. The fact that the monster has seven heads is another revealing detail. Seven is a significant number in European culture. In traditional Quechan culture, on the other hand, the ritual number is four: events of ritual significance are performed four times or last for four days (see chapters 3-6 of this volume, Halpern 1997, and

Bryant and Miller 2013), and in the Creation story, Sky Snake had four heads (see Bryant and Miller 2013). Third, both of the stories in this chapter depict acts of cruelty — for instance, in one story, *'Aréey* imprisons the orphan boy, and in the other, the guilty impostor is tied to a mule and dragged to death — which may have been inspired by the behavior of whites toward Native Americans.

In spite of European influence, the two stories in Chapter 2 are rich in traditional Quechan elements. For instance, in the story called *'Aréey*, the orphan boy protagonist has spiritual powers which allow him to change form at will. Thanks to these powers, he is able to complete a dangerous journey at which ordinary people have failed. In the story *Tsakwshá Kwapaaxkyée*, the Quechan ritual number four coexists alongside the Western significant number seven: the monster Seven Heads breaks four knives, and it is after the fourth knife is finally broken that the orphan boy manages to kill him.

Since it evidently arose after contact with Europeans, the story complex of the orphan boy and the seven-headed monster constitutes a relatively new addition to Quechan oral literature. It provides a window onto the process by which an oral literature might adapt, expand, and enrich itself with new ideas. It also serves as a case study of a story complex in the early stages of development, its narratives already diversifying thanks to the imagination, resourcefulness, and diverse perspectives of Quechan storytellers.

'Aréey

Told by an anonymous Quechan elder

Xuumár xatál vatháts uuváakitya.
Maxáyt.
Vanyuuváak,
'Aréeyts atháwkitya.
Xwaatháwk.

***
Nyaatháwk awím,
aataruuxáarək —
apúy.
Apúyk ayáatənyk uuváakitya.

Vanyuuvám,
'Aréeyənyts a'ím.
Xuumár kwxatáləny a'ím,
" 'Anytsuutsétsəny matháwk,
maas'úlyk,
xamáalyk,
aaráar a'ím,
muukavék matakxávəxa."

'Aréeyənyts a'ím
xuumárəny —
kwaxatáləny a'ím.

A'ím,
nyaa'ávək,
xuumár kwxatálənyts
nyatsuutsétsəny nyaatháwk,
vanyaayáakəm
xaasa'íly kwa'úurəm.
Nyaaváamək aas'úlyk,
aas'úly kuu'éeyk uuváa.

This orphan child was around, they say.
He was a boy.
There he was,
and 'Aréey took him, they say.
He took him as an enemy prisoner.

***

He took him, and so,
he put him to work —
and (the boy) was dead tired.
He was going along dead tired, they say.

There he was,
and 'Aréey said it.
He said to the orphan child,
"Take my blanket,
and wash it
(so that) it's white,
pure white,
and bring it back inside."

'Aréey said it
to the child —
he said it to the orphan.

He said it,
and when he heard him,
the orphan child,
he took the blanket,
and he went along
to the edge of the ocean.
When he got there he washed it,
he did his best to wash it, poor thing.

Xamáaly ly'émǝk iikwévǝm,
nyaayúuk,
amíim siiv'áwt.
Nyaxátt-ts xavík.
Nyaxátt-ts nyíily tík a'ím.
Nyaxáttǝntim nyiivák,
ayúuk uuvá.

Xátt kwanyíilyǝnyts ayúuk avathík a'ím,
"Kamíi alyka'émǝk.
Avány,
tsuutsétsnya,
nyaakata'ámǝk,
shaly'áyǝny awím,
vaawée
vaawée
vaawée
vaawé.
Kawíim kuunóok,
katkavéekǝm,
aváts xamáalytan,
páq a'ím,
aaráar a'ím.
Matakxávtǝxa."

"Xottk."

A'ím,
nyaatháwk,
viiwáak,
'aréeyǝny áayk.
'Aréeyǝny nya-áayǝm,
tsuutsétsk vuunóok;
"Nyáava xuumár 'uuxéerxats,
vathány."

Xatálǝk a'ím.
Sáa
xuumár vatháts kwasuuthíiny matt-tsapéek.

It wasn't white at all,
and when he saw it,
he stood there crying.
His dog was with him.
His dog was pitch black.
(The boy) kept him as a pet, and there he was,
and he was watching.

The black dog lay there watching and said,
"Don't cry.
As for that,
the blanket,
put it face down,
and use the sand,
like this
and like this
and like this
and like this.
Keep doing it,
and then turn it over,
and it will be really white,
perfectly white,
pure white.
(Then) you can take it back in."

"All right."

So,
he took it,
he went along,
and he gave it to 'Aréey.
He gave it to 'Aréey,
and he went about spreading the blanket out;
"This is a child I must imprison,
this one."

He was an orphan, they say.
But
this child had great powers.

Uuváas athótk,
mattuuxatálək vanyuuváakəm,
axéerək nyaatsaváwtsəm.
***

Nyaatsaváwtsəm,
siivám,
nyáanyəm pa'iipáa nyaaéev,
'atsuumáav a'ím vuunóokəm.
Pa'iipáanyts apáмək vuunóom,
vathány axéertsəm alyvák viivák.
Nyavály avák siivá.

A'ávək uuvátəm,
a'ávək uuváxáyəm,
pa'iipáanyəny 'Aréeyənyts a'ím,
pa'iipáanya nyiitskakwék,
"Máam,
pa'iipáa maamakyípəts alymavák
'Aavém Kwasám matapúy mayáam?
Matapúyxa maaly'íim?"

A'éxáyəm,
pa'iipáanyəny,
pa'iipáa 'ashént alyav'áwk
kayáak viiyáany,
nyiikwévəm,
takavék aváa.

Xáyəm,
nya'ashéntits ayáanys,
nyiikwévəm,
pílyəm púyk,
takavék aváa.

Vanyuuváak,
xuumár kwxatál aváts siiv'áwk,
'Aréeyəny a'ím,
" 'Anyáa 'ayáaxa."

There he was,
he was acting like an orphan,
and they tied him up and put him away.
***

They put him away,
and there he was,
and at that point they got the people together,
and they were going to have a feast.
The people were arriving,
and he was in here (where) they had tied him up.
There he was in the house.

He was listening,
he was listening, and suddenly,
'Aréey said to the people,
he asked the people,
"Well,
which one of you people in here
is going to kill 'Aavém Kwasám?
Do you think you can kill him?"

He said it, and suddenly
a person,
one person was among them,
and he went straight off to do it,
(but) it was no use,
and he came back.

Right away,
another one went, but
it was no use,
he was exhausted from the heat,
and he came back.

Then,
that orphan child was standing over there,
and he said to 'Aréey,
"I will go."

"Maxuumárək nyiimakwévək,
kaawíts maxwíivək mawíyúm,"
a'étəm.

" 'Anyáa 'ayáak" a'ét.
" 'Anyáa 'ayáak,
'Aavém Kwasám 'atapúyxa.
'Akamíim,
muuyúumxá."

A'ím,
pa'iipáanyənyts aatsxwáaaar a'étəm,
makyík xalypámk.

Xalypámk a'ím,
aatsxwáar a'ítsəm a'ávək viivákəm;
as'ílytsəm,
uukavék 'avá alyashpétt-tsəm,
siivátum.

Siivákəm,
'axátt —
'axáttəny atskuunáavək uuvát,
'axátt kwanyíily.
Nyaxáttəny atskuunáavək uuváak.
A'ím,
vathám,
"Tiinyáaməm,
vi'nayémxa,"
a'étəma.
Nyaxáttəny a'ím.

" 'Axóttk."
'Axáttənyts " 'Axóttk," a'éta.
" 'Awétsxa."

Nyaatiinyáam nya-áaməm,
xuumárənyts kwaskyíi atháwk,
alytsayóq vuunóonyk vuunóonyk vuunóok,
nyaavíirəm,
nyaavíirəm,
"Vatháts 'anyép aly'tsuuyóqənyts.

"You are an incompetent child,
you are not strong enough to do anything,"
he said.

"I will go," (the boy) said.
"I will go,
and I will kill 'Aavém Kwasám.
I will bring him back,
and you will see."

So,
the people laughed,
they didn't believe him at all.

They didn't believe him, and so,
he heard them laughing at him;
they didn't let him do it,
they took him back and shut him up in the house,
and there he was.

There he was,
and the dog —
he was talking to the dog,
the black dog.
He was talking to his dog.
So,
at this (point),
"Tonight,
we will leave,"
he said.
He said it to his dog.

"All right."
The dog said, "All right.
We'll go."

When it started getting dark,
the child took a dish,
and he went about spitting into it, on and on and on,
and when he finished,
when he finished,
"This is my spittle.

Tsaqwérək vaa'íim viivám,
nyaatók va'tháwk aaly'íim,
aaly'ítsxá,"
a'éta.

"Xóttk,"
'xáttənyts.

A'ím,
'xátt tsoqtsóqənyts siiv'áwk.

Nyaav'áwk,
uutspám,
shóx a'ét.
Nyaayúuny —
ankúpk kwalyvíik uuvám,
nyamaxávək,
nyamuupúuk viiwétsk.

Pa'iipáa 'ashéntəts uuvám,
nyáany uukanáavək a'ím,
" 'Atspáqəts xavíkəm nyaav'óom;
'ashéntəts xamáalyk,
'ashéntəts 'axwéttk awím,
'anyáats av'ayáaxas,
nya'púyəm,
kaxamáaly aváts apúyəm mayúuxa.

" 'Íis,
nya'a'xóttəm,
xóttk nya'thúum,
vatháts xuuvíkəly 'axóttəm,
'atkavék 'aváaxa."

Nyaa'íim,
" 'Axóttk.
'Ayóovxa,"
nyaa'ítsəm,
vatháts,
'axáttənyts xuumárəny nyaaxavík viiwéts.

It will be here talking like this,
and they will mistakenly think we are still here inside,
they will think so,"
he said.

"All right,"
the dog (said).

Saying (that),
the dog stood up.

He stood up,
and they went out,
they went out swiftly.
That thing —
there was something like a little hole there,
and they went into it,
they went through it and off they went.

A person was there,
and (the boy) told him,
"There are two flowers standing there;
one is white,
and one is red, and so,
I will go, but
if I die,
you will see this white one die.

"But,
if we're all right,
if we're all right, then,
both of these (flowers) will be all right,
and I will come back."

When he said it,
"All right.
We will watch them,"
(the person) said,
and this one,
the dog was with the child and off they went.

'Amátt nyáava nayémək,
viiwétsk
viiwétsk
viiwétsk,
kwaxatsúurənyts xiipúkəm,
nyáanyəm,
'áw aráa mattiitsóowk,
vanyaawétsk,
naxakyíik.

Amák kwathíkənyts 'uupílyəny matt-tsapéem,
suuv'óok,
ayúuk siiv'áwk,
suuv'óony,
suuv'óok.
Suuv'óony,
xanapáats mattnyiitsóowəntik
vanyuuv'óookəm,
naxkyíik viiwétsk,
viiwétsk,
viiwéts.

Vanyaawétsk,
nyamáam,
nyáasi nyaakatánəm,
nyuuv'óok uuv'óok.

Nyuuv'óook athúm,
shaly'áyts viithíkəntim,
naxkyíintik,
'uupílyəny matt-tsapéesət.
Xanapáats nyáany mattnyiitsóowk,
nyaanaxkyíik siiwétsk
***
'anyáa kwatspáasily katánəm.
Xaasa'íily kwa'úur uuv'óok suuv'óom,
"Ka'thóm 'anaxkyíik?
'Aavém Kwasáməny a'étəm,
matapúy ma'íim ma'ítyənká?"
a'étəma.
'Axáttənyts a'íim.
Xuumárəny tsakkwék.

They headed away from this place,
and they went on,
and on,
and on,
and cold weather was the first (problem they encountered),
and at that (point),
they turned themselves into a blazing fire,
and they went on,
they went across it.

What lay beyond it was extremely hot,
and they stood there,
(the boy) stood there watching,
they stood there,
and they stood there.
They stood there, until
this time they changed themselves into ice,
and they stood there,
and they went across it and went on,
and on,
and on.

They went on,
and finally,
they reached that distant (place),
and they stood there and stood there.

They stood there, and so,
this time there were sand dunes,
and they crossed these too,
even though it was extremely hot.
They changed themselves into ice,
and they went across and kept going on,
***
and in the emerging day they got there.
They stood there at the edge of the ocean, and
"How will we get across?
This so-called 'Aavém Kwasam,
how are you going to kill him?"
he said.
The dog said it.
He asked the child.

A'éxayəm,
" 'Ayáak 'atapúyxa."

Nyaa'íim,
"Kamathóm maaxkyéev ma'íim ma'ítyənkáa?
Xaasa'ílyəny,
vuulyéwəny nyiináam
nyammav'áwk."

" 'Aaxkyéevxa."

"Kamathóm mathúu ma'ím ma'ím?"
a'í;
suunóo.

Siiv'áwxay,
kúur nyaa'íim,
xártsampúk mattiitsóowk.
Shaly'áynyi tsamíim,
pónənənən,
xaasa'íly aaxkyéev.

Xaasa'íly nyaaxkyéevkəm,
suuv'óom —
'Aavém Kwasám nyaványənyts suuvám —
ayúuk siiv'áw.

'Uuméeny matt-tsapéek,
'avíinyts 'amáy tan alyvám,
ayúuk viiv'áwk.

"Kamathóm makúlyxanká?"
a'étəm.

"Náq ka'íim.
'Awétsxa.
Mashqwíivək!"
" 'Axuulyóoyəny nyiináamək 'uuv'óok nya'athúuva.
Nyiiny'ávək amántəxa."

As soon as he said it,
"I'll go and kill him," (said the boy).

Then,
"How are you going to get across?
The ocean
is extremely wide,
from where you are standing."

"I'll get across."

"How are you going to do it?"
he said;
there they were.

(The boy) stood there, and suddenly,
after a little while,
they turned themselves into tiny brown ants.
They were placed on the sand,
and dust rose up in a cloud,
and they crossed the ocean (by tunneling under it).

They crossed the ocean,
and they stood there —
'Aavém Kwasám's house was there —
and (the boy) stood there looking.

It was extraordinarily high,
the rock (where he lived) was at the very top,
and (the boy) stood here looking.

"How are you going to climb it?"
(the dog) said.

"Be quiet.
We will go.
You're being noisy!" (the boy said).
"Here we are, (giving off) our distinctive odor.
He will smell us and wake up."

Uuv'óok vaa'íim,
'amáy tayáamək ayóovək uuv'óom.
Vaa'íim,
xalytótt mattiitsóowk,
líiiip!,
'amáy alykatán.

***
Kúp kwalaxúytantum.
Tskwashányəny paaxkyée kwa'átsk viitháwm,
ayóovək suuv'óom;
nyaayúu tsanpéevəm,
takxávək ayúuk siiv'áw.

Uuvák,
axwíivəm a'ávək athúm,
mattapéek uuváakəm,
páa tsakyíw a'ím.

Nyuuváats,
'atsaayúu,
xalytótt mattiitsóowətk awím,
ayúuk uuvátk.

Uuvák,
viitháwk viitháwk,
viitháwxaym,
kaawémtək vuunóom,
ashmáam.

Ashmáam,
nyaayúuk,
uupúuvək viiwéts.

'Aavém Kwasámənyts uuvák,
Pa'iipáa asóok vuunóo,
***
nyatsasháakəny tavéerək viiyém.

Pa'iipáanyts tapúy a'ím aváamək,
uuváanym,
nyáany asóok alytakxávək awétk,

They stood there like this,
they stood there looking way up to the top.
They went like this,
they made themselves into spiders,
and up they went (on the spider's silken thread),
and they got to the top.

***

There was a hole going right through.
Those seven heads were there, just as they had said,
and (the boy and the dog) stood there watching;
(the hole) was a small thing,
and he took (the dog) in and stood there watching.

(The monster) was there,
and he smelled the odor they gave off, and so,
it was pretty strong,
and he felt like biting someone.

(The boy) was there,
well,
he had turned himself into a spider, and so,
he was watching him.

There he was,
and they stayed and stayed,
they stayed, and suddenly,
they managed to do something,
and (the monster) went to sleep.

He went to sleep,
and when they saw this,
they went on in.

'Aavém Kwasám was there.
He had been eating people,
***
and he had piled up their bones and left.

People had arrived, intending to kill him,
and there they were,
and he had let those (people) in, in order to eat them, and so,

asóok alytakxávək awétk,
vuunóom —
matt-tsapéek,
nyatsasháakányts.

Nyaayúuk siivák,
suuv'óokəm,
nyuuv'óokəm.
xalytótt nyáany mattiitsóowətk athúm,
líiiip a'ím,
máam,
axwíivəm a'ávkəm,
'iipáyk uuváam,
ayúuk uuvá.

Xuumára kwasuuthíits nyiináam,
viiv'áwk awétk awím,
'aavény tashmátsk,
miipúkəny tatkyéttk aavíirk,
awíik a'étəma.

Nyaavíirkəm,
" 'Anyáats nya'aavíirkəm."
"Kamawém ammawíim?
Tskwashány muukamnáwxamká?
'Uunéxəny mattapéem,"
a'ím.
Xáttənyts siivány tskuunáav,
nyáasim.
tsaqwérək uuváakitya,
'axáttənyts.

***

Nyuuvám,
tskuunáavək a'ím;
"Kaawémk?
Tskwashá kwavatáyəny viimawáak
pa'iipáany maatsuuyóoyxanka?"

"Nyáanyts athúulya'émǝxa.
Nyaayúu kwanymé 'awíim.
'Awíim,

he had let them in, in order to eat them, and so,
he went on doing this —
and there were a lot of them,
the bones.

(The boy) saw this,
and they stood there in the distance,
and as they stood there,
they had turned themselves into those spiders, and so,
up they went (on the spider's silken thread),
and that's all,
(the monster) smelled the odor they gave off,
and he came to life and there he was,
and they were watching him.

The child's powers were extraordinary,
and he stood there and used them, and so,
he put the snake to sleep,
and he chopped through its necks and finished,
he did, they say.

When he finished,
"I have finished," he said.
"How will you manage it?
How will you carry his heads?
They're terribly heavy,"
(the dog) said.
The dogs that were there could talk,
in those (days),
and he was speaking (to the boy), they say,
the dog (was).

***

He sat there,
and (the dog) was talking to him;
"How will it happen?
How will you bring these great big heads
and show them to people?"

"It won't be those heads.
I will do something else.
I will do it,

pa'iipáanyənyts uuyóovxa
'Aavém Kwasám 'atapúyəm."
"Xóttk."

Xaym,
iipály aakyéttk vuunóok;
paaxkyéek viitháw 'etəm.

Viitháwm awim,
axéerək vuunóok,
nyaavíirək,
a'íim,
"Móo,
máam,
'Aavém Kwasám 'atapúyk 'av'áwtk 'athúm.
Iipály 'aatskyéttk va'uunóok,
'aavíirəm,
máany manyíilyqxa,"
a'étəma.
'Axáttəny a'ím.

"Manyíilyqəm,
'awétsxa."

A'ím,
suuv'óom,
kúur a'ím,
"Nyamáam,
'Avém Kwasámts apúyk,"
a'íim.

Nyatsasháakənyts,
iimák —
sél sél sél sél sél! —
xalakúyk.

Nyuunóom,
nyaayúukəm,
amáam,
aatspáatsk,
'Aavém Kwasám tapúyk nyaa'íim.

and the people will see
that I have killed 'Aavém Kwasam."
"All right."

Right away,
he went about cutting off the tongues;
there were seven of them, they say.

There they were, and so,
he went about tying them up,
and when he finished,
he said,
"Okay,
that's all,
I have killed 'Aavém Kwasám.
I have been cutting off his tongues,
and I have finished,
and you will swallow them,"
he said.
He said it to the dog.

"You swallow them,
and we will go."

He said it,
and they stood there,
and in a little while,
"Finally,
'Aavém Kwasám is dead,"
he said.

The bones,
they danced —
rattle-rattle-rattle-rattle-rattle! —
they were rejoicing.

(The spirits) were there,
and when they saw it,
at last,
they came out,
when he told them he had killed 'Aavém Kwasam.

Xuumárənyts vinathíik,
nyaanakavék vanyaanathíik katánək
'Aréeyəny.
'Aréeyəny nyaanakavék nyaakatánk,
"Makyíts 'Aavém Kwasáməny tapúy?"

" 'Anyáats 'atapúyk 'av'áwk."

"Kaawíts maxwíivək mawépək muuváak ma'íim,"
a'ítsəm.

Siiv'áwk kuu'éeyk,
xuumár kwxatáləny.

A'ím,
aatsxwáaar a'ím.

"Xatál,
xuumár kwxatáləny.
Kaawíts axwíivkəm.
Mawíim muuváak ma'ím!"

A'ím,
aatsxwáaar a'ítsk suunóotsəm,
siiv'áw kuu'éeyk,
'axóttk athúm.

Nyaxáttənyts av'áwəm;
"Kayóqəm uuyóom."

A'ím,
'axátənyts ayóqxayəm,
'Aavém Kwasám iipályəny nyaayúu nyiitháwəm,
uuyóov.

Nyaanymáam.
Xuumár kwxatáləny,
nyáanyi amánk 'axóttk athúuk a'étəma.

The child (and the dog) came this way,
they came back and arrived
at 'Aréey's (place).
When they arrived back at 'Aréey's (place),
"Who has killed 'Aavém Kwasám?" (someone said).

"I killed him," (said the boy).

"You are not strong enough to have done it,"
they said.

He stood there, the poor thing,
the orphan child (did).

And so,
they laughed.

"He's an orphan,
he's an orphan child.
He is not strong enough.
And you say that you did it!"

And so,
they were all laughing, over there,
and he stood there, the poor thing,
(but) it was all right.

His dog stood there;
"Throw up, so they can see them," (said the boy).

And so,
the dog threw up, and suddenly
'Aavém Kwasám's tongues and things were there,
and they saw them.

That's all.
As for the orphan child,
from then on he was just fine, they say.

Tsakwshá Kwapaaxkyée (Seven Heads)

Told by John Comet

Tsakwshá Kwapaaxkyée uu'ítsənyts,
suuváak 'eta.
Piipáa 'aláayts.

Suuvám;
piipáa nyaváyk,
'atáyk nyaváyk siitháwm,
nyuuváak suuváakitya.
Tsakwshá Kwapaaxkyéenya.

Sanyuuváak,
tiinyáam kwashíintənyəm,
nyaayúu tapúyk uuváatk:
'amó awétk,
kaawíts,
nyatsxáatt avkwathík avány,
tapúyk.

Tiinyáam aváatkəm,
nyáany tapúyk asóok awét.
Awíim uuváak athúuk 'eta.

Uuváam,
piipáa kwanyváyənyts,
uuyóovəsáa,
shtamatháav awíis,
piipáany,
iimáattəny uuyóov alya'émtum.
Shtamatháavəm,
avawétk uuváat.
Tiinyáam nyaashmáts aváak awét.

"Kaawítstants aváak awíim?"
aaly'íim.
Uuyóovət.

The one called Seven Heads,
he was there, they say.
He was a bad person.

There he was;
people were living there,
a lot of them were living there,
and there he was, they say.
Seven Heads.

There he was,
and each night,
he went about killing things:
he did it to sheep,
or whatever,
the domestic animals that were there,
he killed them.

Night came,
and he killed those (animals) and ate them.
He was doing it, they say.

There he was,
and the people who lived there,
they watched, but
they didn't know (what was going on),
the people,
they didn't see the bodies.
They didn't know (what was going on),
and he kept doing it.
At night while they were sleeping he came and did it.

"What on earth is coming and doing (this)?"
they wondered.
They watched.

Taxalyuukwáats vuunóonyk,
uuyóov alya'émk 'eta.

Sanyuuváak;
"Kaawíts suuváak,
'ayúuxa 'aaly'íim,"
siiyáak,
xalykwáak suuváanyk;
"Kaváarək.
'Ats'ayúulyəm."

Matt-tsakakwék athúm;
piipáanyts mattaaéev.
Piipáa nyavány apák,
mattaaéev.
Mattuukanáavəs athót.
"Kaawíts uuváak athóxa maaly'íim?"
a'étəm;
"Áa-áa,
'ashmathíika."

Avawíi kwa'átsk uuváatəs,
tiinyáam aváak awét.
Tiinyáam aváak awét,
uuváak awét.
'Ayúusáa,
'uuyóov aly'émtəm,
awétk uuváat."
A'íikəta.

A'íim,
matt-tsakakwék.
Piipáa nyavá siitháwət.

Tiinyáam vaa'íim aváak,
awét.
Vaawét tapúyt.

Awétk vuunóok awíikitya.
Nyaqwalayéwəm uuyóovət.

They went on searching,
but they didn't see him, they say.

There he was;
"Something is there,
I think I might see him," (someone) said,
and he went along,
he went hunting for him.
"No.
I don't see anything."

They asked each other;
the people had a meeting.
They got to someone's house,
and they had a meeting.
They told each other about it.
"What do you think is there?"
they said;
"Well,
I don't know."

"He is doing it, just as they said, but
he gets here at night and does it.
He gets here at night and does it,
he hangs around and does it.
We've watched, but
we haven't seen anything,
and he keeps on doing it,"
They said it, they say.

So,
they asked each other.
There they were in someone's house.

He got there at night, like this,
and he did it.
He killed them like this.

He kept on doing it, they say.
In the morning they looked.

Ayóov,
ayóov;
nyatsuuxáattəny awétk.
Namák alya'émk vuunóot.

Vuunóom,
siitháwm,
piipáa xatálvəts suuváakitya.
Suuváak.
Shuupóowkitya.
"Kaawíts avuuváatk awítya,"
aaly'íim suuváakəta.
Xuumár kwxatálv 'éta.

Suuváak;
" 'Ayúuxa 'aaly'íim,"
suuvát.

A'ím,
piipáats nyuuváyapatk uuváak,
nyáanyts ayúuxa a'étk,
siiyáak,
uuváat,
nyiirísh 'ét.
Tapúy kamúlyk a'ét.
Nyaakwawítsəny xalykwáatsk,
nyiirísh a'ét.

Suuváany,
aváts,
xuumárənyts,
siiyáatapatk,
ayúutk,
takavéktək uuváat.
"Kaawíts nyaawíim,
'ayúuxa 'aaly'ét."

Nya'ím
nyatiinyáam,
nyaawínyəməshtəka.
Nyaawínyəmáshk,
tapúy.

They looked,
and they looked;
he had done it to their animals.
He kept at it without stopping.

He kept at it,
and there they were,
and there was an orphan there, they say.
He was there.
He knew (what was going on), they say.
"Something is around here doing this,"
he was thinking, they say.
He was an orphan child, they say.

There he was;
"I think I will watch," (he said),
and there he was.

So,
(another) person was living there too,
and he said he would watch,
and he went,
and there he was,
(but) there was nothing there.
He pretended he was going to kill him.
He went looking for the one who had done it,
(but) there was nothing there.

He was there,
and this one,
the child,
he went along too,
and he watched,
and he came back and there he was.
"When he does something,
I think I will see him," he said.

Then,
at night,
(the killer) did it again.
He did it again,
he killed (something).

Asóok vuunóok,
nyiinamák viiyém.

Siitháwnyək,
piipáanyts.
"Kaawítstants uuváak awíim 'ityá?"
a'ét.

"Tiinyáam awétk,
'anyáam awíilyəm,
tiinyáaməm awétk awét.
Awétəm,
'uuyóov aly'émtəm 'itya."
a'étk;
mattuukanáavək vuunóot.

Mattaaéevəm'ashk,
mattuukanáavək vuunóot.

Nyáanyi,
xuumárənyts,
viiyáak ayúutəs —
ayúum:
kaawíts nyaatapúytəm'ashk avathíkəm,
ayúuk siiv'áwkəta.

Ee'ée,
kaawíts suuváak awét.
Tsakwshány uukyéttk alytáptək,
asóotk awét.

Áa,
aváanyək,
viiyáantik 'eta.
Xuumárənyts nyaayáantik,
ayúuk awítya!
Ayúut.

Nyaawíntik,
suuváam,
nyamatspámək ayúukəta.

He went on eating it,
and he left (the remains) there and went off.

There they were,
the people.
"What on earth can be around (here) doing (this)?"
they said.

"He does it at night,
he doesn't do it in the daytime,
he does it at night.
He does it,
and we don't see him,"
they said;
they were telling each other about it.

They had another meeting,
and they were telling each other about it.

At that (point),
the child,
he went along and he might have seen it —
he saw it:
once again (the killer) had killed something,
and (the child) stood there looking, they say.

Yes,
he had been there and done something.
He had cut the head off and thrown it away,
and eaten (the rest).

Well,
(the child) got there,
he went along again, they say.
The child went along again,
and he saw him!
He saw him.

He was doing it again,
there he was,
and (the child) came out and saw him, they say.

Ayúum,
awím,
vaa'íim:
"Piipáa avány,
makyény tuupúy kaa'áamts," a'éta.
"Tsakwshá Kwapaaxkyéenya.
Páa 'aláay."

Awétk awíim,
xuumárənyts,
nyáasi,
xatáltək uuváasáa,
nyaayúu uuthúts aspérətk uuváatk,
iimáatt nyaayúu tsáamts aspérətk viiwáatk.
Nyáasi tsáam manyúuvəkəta.
Awét.

Tsakwshá Kwapaaxkyée uu'ítsənyts —
'asháakts vaa'íim vathályavíim,
atháwkəm;
aatskyítt 'íikəta.
Tapúy 'ím,
xuumára.

Tapúy 'ím.
Nyaa xuumár,
nyáalyavíim atháwapatk awím,
mattaatskyíttkəta.

Mattaatskyíttk
mattaatsxámək vuunóonyək.

Nyaayúu,
Tsakwshá Kwapaaxkyée nyasháak nyuuwítsənyts,
alyéshkəta.

Alyéshtəm,
kwanymé atháwəntikəta.
" 'Anymatsaváamúm!" a'íikəta.
Kwanymé atháwtəntík,

He saw him,
and so,
he said this:
"That person
is someone that can never be killed," he said.
"Seven Heads.
A bad person."

He did it, and so,
the child,
over there,
he was an orphan, but
he was strong in the things that he did,
his body and everything were strong.
Over there, he fought everything, they say.
He did.

The one called Seven Heads —
there was a knife like this,
and he picked it up;
he was going to cut (the child) up, they say.
He was going to kill him,
the child.

He was going to kill him.
That one, the child,
he picked up (something) similar, and so,
they cut each other up, they say.

They cut each other up,
they kept on striking each other.

Well,
the knife that Seven Heads had,
it broke, they say.

It broke,
and he picked up another one, they say.
"You can't do it to me!" he said, they say.
He picked up another one,

awítsəntík,
awítsk viitháwk viitháwk viitháaaaw tanək,
uulyéshəntikəta.

Tsakwshá Kwapaaxkyée nyasháakəny uulyéshəntik.
Xavíkəm uulyésh.

" 'Anymatsaváamúm!"
'Ashént atháwəntik athútya.

Awítsk vuunóonyk vuunóonyk,
mattkaawém alya'ém,
vuunóonyk vuunóooootan,
nyamáam,
nyuulyéshəntík.

Nyuulyéshk.

Vuunóok,
uulyéshəny,
nyaatsuumpáp amáam,
Tsakwshá Kwapaaxkyéeny miipúk tatkyéttkəta.

Xuumárənyts.

Nyáanyá,
xáam vathány uukyéttk —
táq a'ím —
viitápk awítya.

Nyaatápm,
nyamáam,
apúyk a'íikəta.

Nyaapúyəm,
xuumárənyts alynyiithúutsk siiv'áwnyək.
"Vathány,
'atapúyk 'anamákxaym,
piipáats suuváak aváak,
' 'Anyáats 'awíim nya'thúuva,' a'éxa."
Aaly'íim siiv'áwkitya.
Iiwáaly alynyiithúutsk.

and they did it again,
they really did it, going on and on and on,
and he broke this one too, they say.

Seven Heads had broken a knife again.
He had broken two.

"You can't do it to me!"
He picked up another one.

They did it again, going on and on,
and they weren't able to do anything to each other,
they really went on and on,
and finally,
he broke another.

He broke it.

They went on,
and as for breaking (knives),
the fourth (time that it happened), that was all,
he chopped through Seven Heads's necks, they say.

The child (did).

As for that,
he chopped through them on this side —
they were cut clean through —
and he threw (the heads) down here.

When he threw them down,
that was all,
(the monster) was dead, they say.

He was dead,
and the child stood there thinking about it.
"As for this,
if I kill him and leave him here,
someone might come along,
and he might say 'I did this.'"
(The child) stood there thinking, they say.
He thought about it in his heart.

Nyaav'áwk;
" Iipály avány 'aakyíttk,
'atháwxa,"
'íikəta.

Iiwáam alynyiithúutsk.
A'ím,
iipályəny aakyíttkəta.
Iipály vaawíim.
Iipáalyəny aakyíttk atháwt.

A'ím,
aas'úuttk,
vathány nyaavíirək,
atháwk,
ta'úlyk,
viithíikəta.
Aváts apúyk siithík.

Nyaanamák,
vanyáathíik,
nyaványi aváakəta.
Nyaaváak,
kanáav alya'émkəta,
tuupúya.

Kanáav alya'émk.

Póosh nyaxátt-ts siithíkəm,
aqásəm,
aváatkəta.

Nyaaváam,
iipályəny ashóok nyaavíirkəm,
póoshəny áayəm a'ítya.
"Kanyíilyqəm!"
Anyíilyəqətá,
póoshənyts.

Anyíilyq.

He stood there;
"I'll cut off those tongues,
and I'll take them,"
he said, they say.

He thought about it in his heart.
And so,
he cut off the tongues, they say.
He did this to the tongues.
He cut off the tongues and took them.

So,
he wrapped them,
and when he finished this,
he picked them up,
and he carried them,
and he came this way, they say.
And that (monster) lay there dead.

He left him,
and he came this way,
and he got to his house, they say.
When he got there,
he didn't tell anyone, they say,
about the killing.

He didn't tell anyone.

His pet cat was there,
and he called it,
and it came, they say.

It came,
and he finished unwrapping the tongues,
and he gave them to the cat, they say.
"Swallow them!" (he said).
It swallowed them, they say.
the cat (did).

It swallowed them.

Nyamáam,
siithíkəta,
xuumárənyts.
Apátk siithík.

A'ím,
piipáanyts nyuuváak uuváak,
nyáanyts:
qwalayéwəm siiyáak,
ayúu va'ár kwa'átsk,
viiyáanyk —
apúyk avathíkəta,
nyaayúunyts!

Tsakwshá Kwapaaxkyée!

Apúyk viithíkəm,
kamúly,
nyáanyts awíi kamúly a'étkəm;
'asháak atháwkəm,
aakyítt
aakyítt
aakyítt,
awíikəta.
Iimáatta.

Awíim.
Iimáatt kwaxwáattəny vathí nyamalúuk,
vathí nyamalúuk awíikəta.
Iimáattnya.

Ava'íim,
suuváanyək,
takavék viithíikəta.

Viithíik,
nyaaváak,
"Móo!
Tsakwshá Kwapaaxkyée 'atapúyk!" a'íikəta.
Piipáanyts a'íim.
Kwayúunyənyts.

That's all,
there he was, they say.
the child.
He lay down and there he was.

So,
the (other) person was hanging around and hanging around,
and he was the one:
the next day he went along,
he was always looking for him, just as he had said,
and he went along —
and it was lying there dead,
that thing!

Seven Heads!

(Seven Heads) was lying there dead,
and (the person) pretended,
he pretended that he was the one who had done it;
he picked up a knife,
and he cut it
and he cut it
and he cut it,
he did (that), they say.
To the body.

He did it.
He rubbed the blood here on his body,
he rubbed it on here, they say.
On his body.

He did that,
he went about doing it,
and he came back, they say.

He came,
and he got there;
"Well!
I have killed Seven Heads!" he said, they say.
The person said it.
The one who had seen (the body).

'Íis,
xuumárənyts vathík takavék nyaaváak,
viithíktək;
" 'Anyáats 'atapúytək 'athúm."
Aváak viithík;
kanáav alya'émək viithík.

Saváts awítsəm.
" 'Eey!"
'íikəta.

"Piipáa nyamaayáak muuyóov awítsəm,
maayáak!"
Piipáany apéetk,
avaayáakəta.
'Atáyk iináam.

Vaayáak,
apámək,
uuyóovəm;
apúy kwa'átsk athúuk 'eta.
Aaíim makyí iisháaly nyaakyéttk,
nyaakyéttk,
nyaakyétt.
Púyk avathíkəta.

"Ee'é," a'ím,
"Awíi kwa'áts,
vatháts."

Aakavék vaathíik,
nyaványi apák 'eta.
Apák.

" 'Anyáats 'awíim nya'athúuva,"
'íikəta.

A'íim,
a'ávək siithíkəta,
xuumáranyts.
Avathík.

But,
the child came back here,
and here he was;
"I am the one who killed him."
He got here and here he was;
he was here and he didn't tell anyone about it.

That (other) one did.
"Hey!"
he said, they say.

"You people go and look,
you go!"
There were a great many people,
and they went, they say.
There were a whole lot of them.

They went,
and they got there,
and they looked;
he was dead, just as (the person) had said, they say.
Somewhere on his hand he had been cut,
and cut,
and cut.
He was lying there dead, they say.

"Well," they said,
"He did it, just as he said he did,
this (person)."

They came back,
and they got to his house, they say.
They got there.

"I am the one who did it,"
he said, they say.

(The person) said it,
and he heard him, they say,
the child (did).
There he was.

A'ím,
"Piipáa makanáavək,
kwanyváy vathány tsáaməly makanáavəm
mattaaéevəm.
'Uuwíts nyáany uuyóov alynayémxa."
Piipáats siiyáak,
'aváats kanáavək viiwáakəta.

"Piipáats tapúy!
Piipáa kwa'aláayəny tapúy viithík!

"Maayáak muuyóov a'ítsəm athúuva!"
a'ítsəm.
Piipáats "Áa," nyaa'étk,
viiyémk vuunóokəta.

***

Siivám,
mattnyaaéevək,
vuunóok,
'atáytank,
nyaatsaamánək saayáak 'eta.
Uuyóov a'ím.

Nyaayóov;
vaayáak apámək uuyóov.
Apúy kwa'átsk avathík,
a'éta.

A'ím,
piipáavats awíilyəs awétk,
awíi kamúlyk a'ítsk,
iimáatt nyaakyíttk uunóom,
aaíim 'axwáatt mattapée avathíkəta.

"Ée!
Awíi kwa'átsk!
Nyaathík!" a'ím 'íikəta.

So,
"You tell people,
you tell all these (people) who live here
that they (should) get together.
They should go and see what I did."
Someone went along,
he went from house to house telling about it, they say.

"Someone has killed him!
He has killed the bad person!

"They said for you to go and see!"
they said.
People said, "All right,"
and they went, they say.

***

There he was,
and they got together,
and there they were,
there were a lot of them,
and they started from there and went along, they say.
They were going to look.

They looked;
they went along and got there and looked.
He was lying there dead, just as (the person) had said,
they say.

So,
this person wished he had done it,
and he pretended to have done it,
he had gone about cutting the (monster's) body,
and (the monster) had just bled (on him), they say.

"Yes!
He did it, just as he said he did!
There it is!" they said, they say.

Nyaathíi —
"Ée'é," nyaa'étk,
aakavék vanyaathíik,
'aványi apák,
mattaaéevəkəta.

'Aványi apák,
mattaaéevək avatháwm,
"Áa-aá,
mawíim," a'ét.
 "Áa,
'awésh," 'ét.

A'ím,
nyaa'ávək,
siithíkəta,
xuumárənyts.

Xuumár amúlya
Xalyiipíitt amúlyk a'éta.
Amúlyənyts.

Áa,
xuumár kwatapúyətánənyts.

Siithíkəm,
"Ée'é,
Tsakwshá Kwapaaxkyée uu'ítsəny athúu kwa'átsk.
Piipáa 'aláayts nyuuváa kwa'áts,
amáam.
'Anyáa 'atapúyəm viithíkitya!"
a'íikəta,
xuumáranyts.

A'íikəta.
A'étkəm athúm,
piipáa uu'ítsəny 'atskuunáts.
"Iipályvətək athúuk athutya,"
a'íikəta.
"A'étəm,

They came —
"Okay," they said,
and they came back,
and they got to the house,
and they had a meeting, they say.

They got to the house,
and they were having a meeting,
"Yes,
you did it," they said.
"Yes,
I did it," he said.

So,
when he heard it,
he was over there, they say,
the child (was).

As for the child's name,
he was named Xalyiipíitt, they say.
It was his name.

Yes,
he was the child who had really killed (the monster).

He was over there,
"Okay,
it was the one called Seven Heads, just as he said.
There was a bad person here, just as he said,
that's all.
(But) I am the one who killed him, and there he is!"
he said, they say,
the child (did).

He said it, they say.
He said it, and so,
what he said to the people was a request.
"(Seven Heads) had tongues,"
he said, they say.
"And so,

nyaamawétsk,
mayóov
iipályənyts nyiirísh avathíkxa,"
a'íikəta.
Xuumár a'éta.

A'ítsəm,
"Maayáak,
muuyóovxa,"
nyaa'íntikəta.

A'ím,
" 'Anyáats 'awíim nya'athúuva,"
a'étk uuváa,
piipáa 'ashént —
kwawítsəny,
nyaamák kawítsənyts,
kwaatskyíttənyts.
" 'Anyáats 'awét av'áar," a'ét.

" 'Amáttk mayáak muuyóovəly," a'ítsk,
vanyaayáantik 'ét.
Aakavék.
Xuumárənyts nyiiv'áwk viiyáakəta.
Xalyiipíittənyts.
Kwatapúytanányts.

Vaayáak apámk awéta.

Apámk,
awíim,
iiyáany uutáq,
uutsalyáq nyaa'ím,
iipályənyts nyiirísh a'ím!
Akyítt-təm nyiirísh a'íikəta.

"Mayúukəm?"
uuyóovk vuunóokəta.
"Vatháts,
piipáa lyavíik,
iipályvtək athúukəta.
Vathány iipály nyiirísh a'ét!

if you go,
you (will) see
that the tongues are gone,"
he said, they say.
The child said it.

Then,
"You should go
and see, "
he said it again, they say.

And so,
"I am the one who did it,"
he kept saying,
one person —
the one who had done it,
the one who had done it afterwards,
the one who had cut him up.
"I have always been the one who did it," he said.

"I wish you would go to the place and see," (the child) said,
and they went (there) again, they say.
They went back.
The child stood up and went along, they say.
Xalyiipíitt (did).
The one who really had killed (the monster).

They went along and got there.

They got there,
and so,
they opened his mouth,
they propped it open,
and there was no tongue!
He had cut it out and there was nothing there, they say.

"Do you see?" (he said),
and they went on looking, they say.
"This (monster),
he's like a person,
he is supposed to have a tongue.
This one's tongue is not there!

" 'Anyáats 'awíim 'athúuvəta!
Sáa
nyammatkavékəm,
nyaatsuuyóoyxa,"
'íikəta.

Nyaa'íim,
viithíikəta.
Aakavék nyaathíintikəta.

Vanyaathíik,
'aványi apák.

Nyaapákəm,
póosh nyaxáttəny aqásk 'eta.

Póosh aqásəm,
nyaxátt nyaaqásk,
"Kathíik!" a'étəm,
aváakəta.

Aváam.
"Kayóqəm
uuyóo a'ím!"
Póoshənyts ayóqəta.

Ayóqəm,
iipályənyts alyavákəta.
"Muuyóov," 'íikəta.

"Nyáany
Tsakwshá Kwapaaxkyée iipály athúuva!" 'íikəta.

"Ée,
avathúu kwa'átsk," a'íikəta.
"Máany matsanyáayəm ma'éta!"
a'ítskəta.
Piipáa avány a'íts.

"I am the one who did it!
But
when you go back,
I will show it to you,"
he said, they say.

Saying this,
he came this way, they say.
They came back too, they say.

They came this way,
and they got to his house.

When they got there,
he called his pet cat, they say.

He called his cat,
he called his pet,
"Come!" he said,
and it got there, they say.

It got there.
"Throw up,
so that they can see!" (he said).
The cat threw up, they say.

It threw up,
and the tongues were in there, they say.
"You see them," he said, they say.

"Those
are the tongues of Seven Heads!" he said, they say.

"Yes,
they are, just as he said," they said, they say.
"You have lied to us!"
they said, they say.
They said it to that (other) person.

Nyaa'íim,
"Móo,
amáam.
Piipáa uu'its tsanyáayta.
Matapúytəxá,"
a'ítskəta.

Piipáa kwatáyəny nyiikanátskəta.
"Avány,
tsanyáaytəm apúytk.

Xalyiipíitt tán tapúy kwa'átsəsh,"
a'ítskəta.

"Iipály lyavíi kwa'áts.
Nyavám," a'íikəta.

"Savány,
matapúytəxa,
tsanyáay a'ítsəm," nyaa'étk.
" 'Axóttk," nyaa'étk a'ím.

Piipáa tsuumpákəm
'iipáava nyaatháwk,
viiwáakəta,
kwatsanyáaya.

Nyaatháwk,
nyaawáak,
nyuukwév iimény axíirək,
nyaavíirək.

Nyaayúu,
múul yaakapétt siiv'áwm,
nyáany malyaqény axérək vuunóok,
nyaavíirək 'íikəta.

Nyaavíir,
athúm,
múuləny aatsqwíttk,

Having said it,
"Well,
that's all.
That (other) person has lied in what he said.
You will kill him,"
they said, they say.

They summoned a lot of people, they say.
"This one,
because he lied, he dies.

"Xalyiipíitt is the one who killed (the monster), just as he said,"
they said, they say.

"It appears to be tongues, just as he said.
There they are," they said, they say.

"That one,
you will kill him,
because he lied," they said.
"All right," they said.

Four people
took the man,
and they brought him along, they say,
the one who had lied.

They took him,
they brought him along,
and they tied his legs with a rope,
and they finished.

Well,
there was a crazy mule there,
and they went about tying the rope around its neck,
and they finished, they say.

They finished,
and so,
they whipped the mule,

amáam,
avéshk,
piipáany uunaxwíily,
athúu kathómk athúm.

Apúyk athúm
uunaxwílyk viiwáa.

Athúukəta.

Athúm,
"Móo,
máam,
nyaamawíi kwa'átsk," 'et.
Nyáasi,
amáam,
nyaayúunyts apúyk,
nyáasəts xalakúyk aaíimk suunóokəta.

Xaltakóoyk suunóok,
nyáasəts.
'Ats'uumáavəxa,"
a'íikəta.

Máam,
apúyts amáam,
'atsuumáavxa a'ím.
Xalakúyk viitháwk.

A'ím,
'atsaamáats kamíim,
awíiyum.
Mattapéem,
piipáa kwatáyənyts uumáav awéta.

Uumáavək,
amáam,
iiwáanyts 'axótt-tan amaamáam.
Matt-taxmakyépk vaawíim,
suunóokitya.

and that's all,
it ran,
and it dragged the person,
and I don't know what happened.

He must have died
(as) it dragged him along.

It happened, they say.

So,
"Well,
that's all,
you did it, just as you said," they said.
Over there,
that's all,
the creature was dead,
and those (people) just went about rejoicing, they say.

They were rejoicing,
those (people).
"Let's have a feast,"
they said, they say.

That's all,
his death was over,
and they were going to have a feast.
They were rejoicing.

So,
they brought food,
and they were going to do it.
There was a lot of it.
and many people ate.

They ate,
and that's all,
they were happy, that's all.
They hugged each other like this,
and there they were, they say.

Nyamáam.
Piipáa nyaapúyəm,
piipáa kwaláay.

Awíikəta.

A'íim,
nyáavəm áamtəka.
Vuunoony.

That's all.
The person was dead,
the bad person.

He did it, they say.

So,
that's all.
There they were.

3. Xarathó

Told by Jessie Webb Escalante

Translated by Barbara Levy,
George Bryant, and Amy Miller

http://dx.doi.org/10.11647/OBP.0049.03

Jessie Webb Escalante told the story *Xarathó* on March 14, 1979 to an audience which included her daughter Tessy Escalante as well as Abe Halpern. Tessy Escalante later helped Halpern to review his transcript of the story.

Notes and synopsis

The main character of this story is *Xwetsxwéts* (Oriole), who lives happily with his two beautiful wives and their children. One day, Coyote bewitches Oriole, with the result that Oriole suddenly finds himself alone in a cold place high above the four levels of heaven. He is taken in by an old blind man (who happens to be the title character, *Xarathó*, although his name is not mentioned in this telling of the story) and his two daughters. Oriole teaches the family to eat deer meat and introduces them to corn, melons, beans, and pumpkins (which of course are staples of the traditional Quechan diet).

Oriole misses his home. His weeping is noticed by Buzzard. In exchange for a nice rotten deer, Buzzard carries Oriole home on his back and leaves him near his home with the instruction that he must lie face down for four days before returning to his family. Oriole tries to do as he is told, but when he sees that Coyote has taken over his family and is mistreating his wives and children, he jumps up in anger — and finds himself instantly transported back to the cold place above the four levels of heaven.

Eventually Oriole is carried to his home again, this time on Spider's silken thread. Spider likewise instructs him to lie face down for four days. This time Oriole manages to do as he is told. After four days he gets up to find his wives and children abused and starving. The wives are pregnant with Coyote's children. Oriole causes his wives to miscarry and cooks the fetuses into a porridge. Leaving the porridge for Coyote to eat, Oriole and his family dig a tunnel and escape. They travel across the ocean and settle on the other side.

Coyote tracks them down. He is now in bad shape himself: he is very thin, and food goes right through him. Oriole sews up Coyote's anus so that he may retain what he eats, and he allows him to remain with the family.

This story is rich in traditional Quechan themes. The spiritual powers of the First People are vividly on display throughout. Characters love their home and are homesick when separated from it. The ritual number four occurs often in this story, as it does throughout traditional Quechan literature (see Bryant and Miller 2013 and chapters 1 and 4-6 of this volume). Even the practice of sewing up the anus occurs in several Quechan stories, including "Kukumat Became Sick" (Halpern 1976).

The character of Coyote is famous in Quechan literature (see, for instance, Emerson and Halpern 1978, Escalante 1984a,b,c, Escalanti 1984) and throughout Native America (see Bright 1993). Some say that Coyote is a symbol of mankind (Bright 1993: 22), and in the story *Xarathó* we see some of Coyote's most human characteristics: he can be greedy and treacherous, yet he is also vulnerable. In the story *Xarathó*, Coyote is eventually forgiven — a twist not found in every Coyote story.

Xarathó

Told by Jessie Webb Escalante

Nyaayúuts nyaváyk siivá.
Xwetsxwéts.

Nyaváyk siivák,
athúm,
'anyáa atspák viithíim,
nyaayúu mattxalykwáayk viiyáa.

Nya'iipá nya'uutíish ashtúum,
viiyáa.

Viiyáak,
'aqwáaq akyáam,
awím,
kamíim.
Nyaatsavéts xavíkəm nyaatsavétsk —
pa'iipáa 'iixán nyiikwanáaməts,
uuváak,
sanyts'áak 'axúutt-tan xavíkəm nyaatsavétsk viivá.

Viivák,
athúm,
kamíim,
nyuumáayk nyuutara'úyk,
nyuusóoy.

'Anyáayk viithíim,
athúum,
vuuváat,
nyiimán.

Uuváam,
aváts viitháawk,
'avák atháawk viitháw,

A creature was living over there.
It was Oriole.

He lived over there,
and so,
when the sun was coming up,
he went hunting for things.

He picked up his bow and his arrows,
and he went along.

He went along,
and he shot a deer,
and so,
he brought it back.
He had two wives —
he was an extraordinarily handsome person,
there he was,
and he had two very beautiful women as his wives.

Here he was,
and so,
he brought back (meat),
and he fed them and took care of them,
he fed them meat.

It was getting light,
and so,
he was here,
and he got up.

Here he was,
and these (two wives) were here,
they were here at the house,

'axá ayáak,
'a'íi xalykwáak,
athúm,
viitháw.

Kamíim,
alyúlyk,
asóotsk,
athótk vuunóot.

Nyaayáantik,
viiyáat.
'Anyáa atspák,
viiyáak,
nya'uutíish 'iipá tsa'úlyk viiyáa.

Viiyáaxáyəm,
nyaayúuts siithíitapat.
Xatalwéts!

Siithíik,
láw a'étk ayúut.
"Móo,
nyáav manyváyk ammavák mathútya?"
a'ét.

"Mm,
nyáav 'anyváyk,"
 a'ím.

"Nyi'mánək va'uuváak 'athótk'ash,"
a'ét.
" 'Anyáa atspák avathíim,
nyaayúu 'xalykwáak.

"Va'athótk.
'Anyváyk.
'Axóttk,
sanyts'áakts xavík nyiitháawk athúm.
Xuumáarəts nyiitháwəntik athúm.

and they went after water.
and they looked for wood,
and so,
here they were.

He brought (meat),
and they cooked it,
and they ate it,
(that's how) they were.

When he went along this time,
he went along.
The sun came up,
and he went along,
he carried his bow and his arrow and he went along.

He going along, when suddenly
a creature was coming along there in the distance.
It was Coyote!

He came along in the distance,
and he turned his head and looked.
"Well,
is this where you live?"
he said.

"Mm,
this is where I live,"
(Oriole) said.

"I come from (here),"
he said.
"When the sun comes up,
I hunt for things.

"This is what I do.
I live (here).
It's good,
there are two women there.
There are children there too.

"Nyi'mánǝk va'uuváak 'athósh,"
a'ét.

Xatalwéts a'ávǝk viiv'áwk;
"Áa-áa,
xóttǝm," a'ét.
"Nyiinyaatuuqwérǝly 'aaly'étk 'av'áw 'athútya,"
a'ét.

"Móo,
'axóttk.
'Aváts nyáasiivák siivám;
nyáasi mayém,
nyaamayúuk,
nyáasi.

"Maváam,
mayúuxa.
'Anyaatsavéts nyáasi atháwk siitháwm,"
a'ét.

Av'áwk viiv'áwk.
Xatalwényanyts —
iithónyǝnyts —
thó kwaly'iimée vathí tsamíim,
vaawée awétk —
atháwk,
ta'ora'órǝk vaawé 'étk atáp!

'Aqwés 'ora'órǝts athót!

Tuupák anák;
viivát.

Láw 'étk ayúut.
Nya'uutíish nya'iipá nyuutháwk,
vaawíim,
viiyáa.

"I come from (here),"
he said.

Coyote stood listening;
"Yes,
all right," he said.
"I think I would like to stay with you,"
he said.

"Well,
all right.
There is a house over there;
(if) you go over there,
you'll see it
over there.

"You'll get there
and you'll see it.
My wives are over there,"
(Oriole) said.

He was standing here.
That Coyote —
his face —
he put his forehead here,
and he went like this —
he took it,
and he rolled it into a ball like this and threw it!

It was a yellow warbler!

It sat on a post;
here it was.

(Oriole) turned his head and looked.
He aimed his bow and arrow,
like this,
and he went along.

Viiyáatəm,
Xatalwényts ayúuk viiv'áw.

Véem véem a'íik aaly'éxáyk,
'amáy athík aatsuumpáp!
Alyav'áw a'étk alyav'áw —
viiv'áwk!

Láw a'étk ayúum —
'amátt-ts xáam athúum —
ayúuk viiv'áw.

Nyiiv'áwk,
"Ka'thómtanək 'athóm?"
a'étk uuvá.
Anák siivát.

A'ávək siivám;
'a'áwəts axwíivəm,
a'áv.

Kwataráats axwíivəm a'áv.
Siivát;
"Makyímtan a'émam?"
aaly'étk a'ávək siivát.

Nyaav'áwk,
nyamkanyók viiyáatk,
axwíivany a'ávək viiyáa,
viiyáa.

'Aváts siivám aváam.

Nyaayúu,
'aványts xanapáatsk vuunóony,
nyiikwév.

Xanapáatsk 'uuy'úuy a'étk,
nyiikwévəm,
nyáavily aakxávək aashmátstəka.

He went along,
and Coyote stood here watching him.

He took a step and another step, and suddenly,
it was the four levels of heaven!
He was standing in one (level) after another —
(and then) he was standing here!

He turned his head and looked —
the place was different —
and he stood here looking.

He stood there,
"Where exactly am I?"
he was saying.
He sat down and stayed there.

He sat there smelling it;
a fire gave off an odor,
and he smelled it.

The burning gave off an odor and he smelled it.
He sat there;
"Where exactly could it be?"
he wondered as he sat there smelling (the fire).

He stood up,
and he went following it,
he went along smelling its odor,
he went along.

He came to a house over there in the distance.

Well,
the house was iced over,
it was terrible.

It was iced over and glassy,
it was terrible,
and they had gone into it and gone to sleep.

Kwara'ák tasínyməts alythík,
'aaxwíirək aapáayk alythík,
xanapáats.

Mashtxáats xavík alytháawkəm,
uushmáam nyiitháawəntik athúm.

"Móo,
pa'iipáats aváak," a'ím.
Kwara'ákənyts a'ávək avathík.

"Kaakxávəm,
ashmáawú,"
a'ét.

Atháwk,
aakxáv.
Xanapáats nyiipáam,
qatsíiiwsh a'étk uuváat.

Apáa alya'émətək uuváat,
xatsúurtəm athúm,
qatsíiiwsh a'étk viiyém
viithíit a'étk uuváa.

"Ka'áv!
Pa'iipáa kwaváany alyuunéxəmpiny!"
a'ét.

"Katháwk,
atók katsamíim,
ashmáawú,"
a'ét.
Mashtxáany a'íim.

Atháwk,
iisháaly taxuupályk viiwáamk,
atók tsamíim.
Alythík viithíkət.

An old blind man lay in there,
he lay propped up in a corner,
(against) the ice.

There were two girls in there,
they were sleeping there too.

"Well, now,
someone is here!" he said.
The old man had been listening.

"Bring him in,
so he can sleep,"
he said.

They got him,
and they brought him in.
He lay there on the ice,
and he was slipping and sliding.

He didn't lie down,
(because) it was (so) cold,
and he went slipping and sliding off
as he tried to come this way.

"Listen to him!
The new person is restless!"
(the old man) said.

"Get him,
and put him in the middle,
so he can sleep,"
he said.
He said it to the girls.

They got him,
they went along pulling him by the arms,
and they put him in the middle.
He lay here.

Ashmáa kwa'átsk viithík.

Viithík,
'anyáayk viithíim,
amánək.
Atspámk.
'Atsayúut,
láwaláw 'étk uuváat.

Nyaayúuny —
'aqwáaqənyts viithíik,
'aványi uunóok vuunóo.
'Aqwáaq 'uupályəny nyiináam,
matt-tsapéek,
'aqwáaqányts.

Ayúutk uuváat.

Vanyuuváak,
'ashént atháwk tapúy.
Matsáat avuuváakəm,
'ashént atháwk tapúy.
Kamíim,
ayóovək viitháw.
Mashtxáanyts ayóovək viitháw.

"Kaa'émk a'ím uuváak,
mattatéeyəny.
Tapúyk vuuthíik awím,"
a'ét.

Nyáany asóotsk athúulya'émək,
'qwáaqa.
Shatmatháavək.

Xaalyíists a'íim,
'amátt nyiipáam viithík,
xavashúuk viithíkəm,
nyáava ashtúum alyúlyk amátst,
nyaanymáamtəka.
Vuunóot.

He lay here sleeping, just as (the old man) had said he would.

He lay here,
and when it was getting light,
he got up.
He went out.
He saw things,
he kept turning his head (to look).

Creatures —
deer were coming,
and they were hanging around the house.
The number of deer was extraordinary,
they were numerous,
the deer.

He was watching them.

Here he was,
and he got one and killed it.
He was hungry, and so,
he got one and killed it.
He brought it back,
and they were watching him.
The girls were watching him.

"I wonder why he is doing this
to a friend.
He has killed him, brought him here,"
they said.

They didn't eat that,
deer meat.
They didn't know about it.

(There was a plant) called xaalyíis,
it was lying on the ground,
it was green,
and this is what they gathered and boiled and ate,
that's all.
Here they were.

Vanyuunóok,
'aqwáaq avány kamíim,
alyúlyk vuunóo.
Uushák nyiinyáay:
'a'íi atháwk,
uushák vaawíim,
avány áayk,
avány áayk awíma.

Amáam a'ávəny,
manyéem a'áv.

Vathány vaawétk uuváat.

'Anyáa atspák avathíim,
nyáany ayáak.
Tapúyk,
kamíim,
alyúly,
nyuusóoyk awétk vuunóot.

Nyamáam,
manyéem uu'áav.
Kwara'ákəts siithík alyaskyíim,
'a'íim uushák áaytsəm,
asóok a'áv.

"Pa'iipáa kwaváanyts mattatéeyəny awépatəm;
ka'ávək" a'í,
aaíim áaytsəm asóok a'áv.
Mattkwiisháayəm a'ávk 'ét.
Manyéetanək 'ét.

Viithíkt.

Uuváak,
viiyáak,
'amáttəny láw 'ím ayúum;
'amáttənyts mattkwiisháay.
'Atsnyiitsuuváwxats athúum.

Here they were,
and he brought that deer,
and he went about cooking it.
He pierced a piece and gave it to them:
he picked up a stick,
and he pierced it like this,
and he gave it to that one,
and he gave it to that one.

They ate it and tasted it,
and it tasted good.

This is what he was doing.

The sun was came up,
and he went after that (deer).
He killed it,
and he brought it,
and he cooked it,
and he went about feeding it to them.

That's all.
They found that it tasted good.
The old man was still lying there,
and (Oriole) pierced it with a stick and gave it to him,
and he ate it and tasted it.

"The new person has done it to our friend;
taste it," they said,
and they just gave it to him and he ate it and tasted it.
It tasted delicious, they say.
It was really good, they say.

He lay here.

(Oriole) was there,
he went along,
and he turned his head and looked at the land;
the land was wonderful.
It was a place where he could plant things.

Ayúuk viiv'áw.

Siiv'áwk,
nyáasi aa'ámpək.
Nyáasi athík,
amétk siithíkt.

"Kaathomtank av'uuváak?" a'étk,
athók aaly'étk,
amétk,
siithíkt.

Siithík,
kór alynyaayémək suuváa.
'Anyáa atspák viithíim,
viiyáak,
nyáasi athík amétk athótk,
uuváat.

Kór alynyaayémək,
vanyuuváam,
nyaayúuts ayúuk suuváa.
'Aqáaq.
Ayúuk suuváa.
'Amáyəm áamək ayúuk uuváa.

"Athótk,
kaawítstanəts athúum
'atsaváwəm 'axóttxas athósh?"
a'íim,
alynyiithúutsk siithík.

Vanyaayáantim,
'amáyəm áamək —
ayóqt.

Ayóq.
Tathíts ayóq.

Nyaayúu xáam kwuuthúts tsáamək awét,
áay.
'Amáttəny aapáx.

He stood here looking at it.

He stood there,
and he fell face down, over there.
He lay there,
he lay there weeping.

"Why am I here?" he said,
and he thought about what had happened,
and he wept,
lying there.

He lay there,
he stayed there for a long time.
The sun came up,
and he went along,
and he lay there in the distance and wept,
there he was.

A long time passed,
and as he was here,
a creature was watching him.
(It was) Crow.
He was watching him.
He was passing by overhead and watching him.

"So,
just what is it
that would be good for me to plant?"
(Oriole) said,
and he lay there thinking.

As he went along again,
(Crow) passed by overhead —
and he threw up.

He threw up.
He threw up corn.

He did it with all different kinds of things,
he gave them (to Oriole).
He dropped them on the ground.

Tathíts athótk,
tsam'iitóts athótk,
'axmátts athótk athót.

Ashtúum,
'amáttnyi,
awíim amánək ashtúum tsaváwk uuvát.
'Amáttəny axwélyk alyaapáx aapáx awétk,
viiwáam.

Uuváatk uutara'úytək.
'Anyáa atspák avathíim,
nyáasily uuváak,
'anyáaxáv,
nyáasily athík,
amétk siithíktək.
Uuváa.

Uuváak,
kór alynyaayém,
'atsaamáatsənyts nyamáam lyavíik.
Tathítsənyts nyamáam athíitsk 'ét.

Tsam'iitóny nyamáam 'axwéttk,
'axmáts athúum,
nyáalyvíik athót.
Ayúutk suuváa.

Tathítsəny xiipúk ashtúu vuuthíitk kamíim.
Aatsuuyóoyəm ayúuk.
Shatmatháavət,
pa'iipáanyanyts.
Mashtxáanyts shatmatháavət.

"Kaawíts athúum mawíim mawéməm?"
a'étk;
ayóovxa.

Alyúlyək vuunóok,
taamáatsk nyuumáay.
Kwara'ák kwatasínym180ny áayk awím.

There was corn,
there were melons,
and there were pumpkins.

He gathered them up,
off the ground,
he got up and gathered them and went about planting them.
He dug in the ground and dropped them in,
he went along (doing it).

He stayed there and took care of (the crops).
The sun came up,
and there he was in that distant place,
and the sun set,
and he lay there,
he lay there weeping.
There he was.

There he was,
and a long time went by,
and the food was finally ready.
The corn had finally gone to seed, they say.

The melons were finally red,
and there were pumpkins,
and they were ready.
He stood there looking at them.

Corn was the first thing he gathered and brought back.
He showed it to them and they saw it.
They didn't know about it,
these people.
The girls didn't know about it.

"What is it you've managed to do?"
they said;
they were going to look.

He went about boiling it,
he got it ready to eat and fed it to them.
He gave some to the blind old man.

'Axótt-təm a'ávək,
amátst.
'Ashíintəm awétk vuunóot.
Tsam'iitó awétk,
matuuqwés awétk,
awétk vuunóot.
Nyiáayəm amátst.
'Axmáts a'íim awíim,
maaríikts a'íim awíim,
awét.

Vuunóom;
siitháaw,
nyaamáam shatuupáwk siitháaw.
"Móo,
'anyáa vathám,
'aayáam mayúuxa,"
a'ét.

Nyiishtúum viitsawé.
Kwapárək tsatssháattk nyaatsuuyóoyəm.
"Kayúuk!
Vatháts athúum!

"Vathány kashtúum,
kamáam!"
a'ím.
"Vathány vakawíim,"
a'ím,
aatsuuyóoyəm,
ayúuk viiv'áw.

"Xwóott!
Mattkwiisháay kwa'átsk,"
a'ím,
ashtúum,
uukyéttk ashtúum,
'avá tsakayáak.

Vuunóo.
Nyáava athótk uuváat.

It tasted good,
and they ate.
He went on (introducing the foods), one by one.
He did melon,
he did canteloupe,
he went on doing it.
He gave it to them and they ate it.
He did what's called pumpkin,
he did what's called beans,
he did.

He kept at it;
there they were,
and they finally came to know about these things.
"Well,
today,
we will go and you will see,"
he said.

He gathered them and took them.
He stood them at the edge (of the field) and showed them.
"Look!
This is it!

"Gather this up,
and eat it!"
he said.
"Do it like this,"
he said,
and he showed them,
and they stood there watching.

"Oh, my!
It's delicious, just as you said,"
they said,
and they gathered it up,
they picked it and gathered it up,
and they took it home.

Here they were.
This (is what) he was doing.

"Vathány vamawíim muunóo.
Vatháts nyaarúvəm,
mashtúum,
matsáam.

"Muukavék mashtúum,
'amátt matsakxávəm,
atspáam,
nyáalyavíitəntim mayúuxa,"
a'íim,
nyuukanáavək vuunóom,
a'ávətsək siitháw.

Siitháwk.
Kór alynyaayéməm,
nyáamínyəm'áshk uuváa.

Nyaayúuts siiv'áwm,
nyáany maxák athík,
amétk suunóot.

Amétk vuunóo,
'anyáanyts axávət,
'anyáanyts axávtək uuváa.

'Anyáa axávəm,
'avá kayáak viithíik a'étk awím.

Uuváak,
kór alynyaayémk,
uuváam,
ayúuk.

'Ashéets 'amáy alyuuváak,
ayúuk uuváat.
Aakwíin.
Aa'óoyvək uuváa.

Uuváak,
kór alynyaayém.

"Keep on doing this like this.
When this is dry,
you gather it up,
and you put it away.

"You will pick it up again later,
and put it back in the ground,
and it will grow,
and you'll see it like this again,"
he said,
he went on explaining it to them,
and they sat there listening.

There they were.
A long time passed,
and once again he was weeping.

A creature was standing there in the distance,
and (Oriole) lay under that (thing),
and he was weeping.

He went on weeping,
and the sun set,
the sun went on setting (each day).

The sun set,
and he came straight back to the house.

There he was,
a long time passed,
and there he was,
and (someone) saw him.

Buzzard was up in the sky,
and he was watching.
He made a turn.
He went circling around.

He stayed there,
and a long time passed.

"Móo,
pa'iipáa vatháts,
nyáaviithík viithíkəm,
'uuyúuny 'uuyúuny
kór alynyaayémt.

Apúyk nyaathúum,
asháxəm 'a'ávxa 'aaly'íim 'uuváany,
nyiiríish a'étk viithík.
'Ayúutk 'uuváat," a'ét.
Suuváat.

Atsénək viithíik,
makórəny ta'úur a'étk
anákt.

"Móo,
Pa'iipáa!
Máanyts nyáavəm mathík ammathík.
Mapúyk nyaama'íim,
masháxəm 'a'ávxa 'aaly'íim.
'Ayúuk 'uuváa.
Nyiiríiish a'étəm 'a'áv.
'Uuváa.
Va'thíik 'athótk'ash," a'ét.

"Kaawítstan kamathómək viimuuváak,
nyiimamán mathúum?"
a'étəm.

"Áa-á,
'anyáats matt'akanáavəm ma'ávxa."

" 'Anyáats nyáavi 'anyváyk,
'a'axóttk,
nyáasi 'uuváak sa'uuváatk 'athútya.

" 'Uuváak.
Xuumáar 'awíim nyi'tsáam.
'Anyaatsavéts xavíkəm;
'anyaatsavétsk 'athúm.

"Well,
this person,
he lies here and lies here,
and I have been seeing him and seeing him
for a long time.

If he were dead,
I would smell him rotting, I think,
(but) he has been lying here (doing) nothing.
I have been watching him," (Buzzard) said.
There he was.

He came down,
he landed right on top of him,
and he sat down.

"Well, now,
Person!
You have been lying here.
If you were dead,
I would smell you rotting, I think.
I have been watching you.
I have noticed nothing.
(Here) I am.
That's why I came here," (Buzzard) said.

"Why are you doing here,
if you come from there?"
(Buzzard) said.

"All right,
I will explain myself and you'll hear it," (said Oriole).

"I live here,
and I'm all right,
but I (used to be) over there.

"I was there.
I had children.
And two wives;
I had wives.

"Sa'uuváak 'athótəny,
pa'iipáats aváamk,
vaawítsəm.

"Nyaayúu nyaatsuuyóoyk,
awíik a'étk,
awítstəm;
láw 'a'étk 'ayúuxayk,
avíly 'av'áw 'a'étk,
av'uuváat.

"Av'uuváatk,
'atkuuvékxəny,
nyam'uuthíitxəny,
'ashmathíitk 'uuváak 'athótk'ash,"
a'ét.

"Nyáava 'iiwáanyts 'alyáaytəm 'athótk'ash,"
a'ét.

" 'Axótt-ta,
muu'ítsa.
'A'ávək 'avák."

*** *** ***

'Ashéenyts aváamək ayúuk,
vaa'íim,
mattkanáavək vuunóok,
pa'iipáany.

Kanáavək vuunóom nyaa'ávək,
" 'Anyáats 'a'íim ma'ávxa,"
a'ím.

"Máanyts,
'aqwáaq katapúyk avík katsamíim.
Viithík viithík,
asháx ta'axánək,
'amaa'íilykəv ta'axánəm
'aváak.

"There I was,
and someone came along,
and he did this.

"He showed me something,
he was going to do it,
and he did it;
I turned my head and looked, and all of a sudden
I found myself standing here,
and here I am.

"Here I am,
and as for returning home some day,
as for going home some day,
I (just) don't know how to do it,"
he said.

"This is what I am sad about,"
he said.

"It is good,
what you said.
I heard it," said Buzzard.

*** *** ***

Buzzard got there and watched him,
and he went like this,
he went about explaining his idea
to the person.

He went about explaining it to him, and he heard it;
"I will say it and you will hear it,"
he said.

"You,
kill a deer and lay it here.
It will lie here and lie here,
and get good and rotten,
it will be really wormy
(by the time) I get there.

" 'Aallyéerəqək va'uunóok,
'atóo ta'axánək,
 nyáava,
'a'íim ma'ávxa,"
a'ét.

"Xóttk,"
a'íim.

A'íim,
 ayáa kwa'átsk,
'aqwáaqəny ayáak.
Tapúyk,
 kamíim,
 nyiitsamíim,
 viithík.

Shamáts tsuumpáp táx nyaa'íim,
 asháxk 'amaa'ílyk kwa'átsəm,
 matt-tsapéem a'áv.
Uuváak,
'Ashéenyts 'amáyəny uuváak,
 aa'óoyk uuváa.

Vanyuuváak,
 atsénək vanyaathíik,
 nyiináak a'ét.

Nyiináak a'étk awím,
 asóo kwa'átsk uuváa.
Vuunóony vuunóok,
 atsáavək,
 nyiinyép.

Anák,
 malyxóny 'amáyly tséek,
 llyép llyép llyép llyép a'étk vanyaawét.

Uuváam ayúuk awím.

"I will slurp it up,
and get really full,
and at that (point),
I will say (something) for you to hear,"
he said.

"All right,"
(Oriole) said.

So,
he went after it, just as he had been told,
he went after a deer.
He killed it,
and he brought it back,
and he put it down,
and there it was.

When it was exactly four nights (later),
it was rotten and wormy, just as he had said,
and (the smell) was overwhelming.
There he was,
Buzzard was up in the sky,
and he was circling.

There he was,
and he came down,
and he settled there, they say.

He settled there, they say, and so,
he was eating it, just as he had said.
He went on and on,
and he ate it up,
and it was all gone.

He sat up,
and he raised up his wings,
and he went flap-flap-flap-flap like this.

There he was, and Oriole saw him.

"Móo,"
a'ét,
vanyaathíik aváak.
Nyaamínym'áshk siithík a'ím.

"Kayúukíi!
Máanyts,
kamánək nyaakayúuk!
'Iisháalyəny matt'aashlíilək,
'awíim,
nyáanyəm katslyuuvévək,
miimény 'aa'ártsəm katslyuuvévək kawíim.
Kuunóok,
kaavíirək,
alykathíkəm nyatháwk,
nyatatsénú,"
a'ét.

"Xóttk,"
athúu kwa'átsk.

Axtáttəly nyaa'órək alythík kwa'átsk,
iisháalyəm nyamtsalyuuvévək.
Atháwk vuuthíik,
ayérək yáash a'étk,
tatsénk vuuthíit.

Aakwíiin aakwíiin a'étk,
vuuthíi.

Vuuthíik,
nyavá 'avuumáktan shátt awét.

Láwaláw a'étk ayúuny.

Nyaványts viivát.

Apéttk nyiithíkəm.

"Móo,
nyáavi mathík viimathíktəxa," a'ét.

"Well,"
(Buzzard) said,
and he came back and got there.
(Oriole) was lying there weeping again.

"Look!
You,
get up and look!
I'll let my arms hang down,
and so,
you line (yours) up even with them,
and make your legs even with my tail.
Go on doing it,
and finish,
lie there and I will take you,
I will take you down,"
he said.

"All right," (he said),
and he did it, just as he had been told.

He lay on top of (Buzzard's) back, just as he had been told,
and he made his arms even (with Buzzard's arms).
(Buzzard) brought him this way,
he flew downward through the air,
and he brought him down.

He went around and around in circles,
and he brought him this way.

He brought him this way,
and precisely in back of his house he set him down.

(Oriole) turned his head from side to side and looked.

His house was there.

He was lying in the brush.

"Well, now,
you must lie here," (Buzzard) said.

"Nyáavi kaa'ámpǝk viikathík.
Máan ka'íilyka'ém.
Nyáavi kathík viikathíkǝny,
viikathík.
Shamáts tsuumpáp táx a'íim,
nyamáam,
mamán,
manyvány makayáamma.

"Nyaayúuts anáwǝm ma'ávǝs,
mamán alyma'émǝtǝxa.
Viimáthíktǝxa.
Máan ma'éxayk,
matkavéktǝxa."
A'íim vuunóok aavíirǝm,
a'áv.

" 'Athóxa."

Vuunóok aavíirǝm,
aa'ámpǝtk aa'ámp,
nyaayúuk,
takavék viithíit.

Siithík kwa'átsk,
'anyáa nyamnyaaxávǝm,
Xatalwényts aváak avuuváak.

Nyaayúu 'anyóyǝm awíim.

Viiyém —
'atsxalykwáak athúuk a'ím,
viiyémǝk,
nyaayúu,
xam'aqatháashk awétk,
'atsíi apúy awétk a'ím,
'aavée apúy awétk,
xam'aavíir,
kaawíts viikwáam tsáam,
xamuulól.

"Lie here, face down.
Don't get up.
Lie here, and lie here,
and lie here.
In exactly four nights,
finally,
you may get up
and go straight to your house.

"You might hear something make noise, but
you must not get up.
You must lie here.
If you were to get up, then
you would go back to where you were."
He went on saying it and he finished,
and (Oriole) heard him.

"I will do it."

He went on and he finished,
and (Oriole) lay there and lay there, face down,
and (Buzzard) watched him
and he turned around and went back.

(Oriole) lay there, just as he had been told,
and when the sun set,
Coyote arrived and hung around.

He did unpleasant things.

He went off —
he was going to hunt for things,
and off he went,
well,
he did water beetles,
he did dead fish, and so,
he did dead mice,
a gopher snake,
everything that was in the area,
(even) crickets.

Ashtúum,
kamíim,
sanyts'áakəny a'ím,
"Muká,
kamátsk!"
a'éta.

Amáts alya'émt.
Xuumáar uumáay,
amáa alya'émək athót.

Masharáy.
'A'íi atháwk,
nyiaatsqwíttk uuváa,
Xatalwényányts.
"Kamátsk!
kamátsk!" a'étk uuváa,
nyiitatavíirək vuunóo.

Xuumáarənyts aatsqwéttk viiwém,
'aványm uukatskwénək vuunóo.
Tsavakyév matsats'íim,
viiwáamək,
nyuuthíik.

Vatháts 'avuumák aa'ámpək viithík,
xalyapántan nakwíin.
Xalyapántan nakwíinək vuunóotk,
a'ávək avathík.

"Móo,
'ayáak,
'a'íim a'ávxa," a'étk,
máan a'ét.

Iiwáa atháam,
máan a'étk,
athúuk a'étk:
'amáyəly av'áw a'ét —
takavék!

He gathered them,
and he brought them,
and he said to the women,
"Now,
eat!"
he said.

They didn't eat.
He fed the children,
and they didn't eat.

He got angry.
He picked up a stick,
and he went along beating them,
Coyote (did).
"Eat!
Eat!" he kept saying,
and he was chasing them around.

He went along beating the children,
he went around and around the house.
They ran weeping,
going,
and coming.

This (Oriole) was lying face down in back of the house,
and they made a turn right next to him.
They were making a turn right next to him,
and he lay there listening.

"Okay,
I will go after him,
and I will say (a thing or two) for him to hear," he said,
and he got up suddenly.

He was angry,
and he got up suddenly,
and it happened, they say:
he was standing in the heavens, they say —
he went back!

Takavék aváamtək.

Siithíkt,
nyuuthík vanyaathíkəm'ashk amétk siithík.
'Anyáa atspák viithíi.

"Kamathóm maváalyma'émətəm?
'Ayúutk av'atháwəny,"
a'ét.

"Áa,
av'uuváas 'athótk," a'ét.
Kanáav alya'émtək.

Xanapáats matt-tsapéem,
alynyaathúun,
nyaashmányəm'ashtək siithíkt.

Tók tsamítsəm,
nyiithík ashmátk siithík.

'Anyáa atspákəm,
amán.
***
Nyuuthík siiyémək,
amétk suunóo,
'anyáa nyaaxáv —
nyaathúnym'ashtək uuváat.

Aváamək ayúut.
'Ashéenyts aváamək ayúut.
"Nyuukanáapa ma'ám!
'Anyáats ammathóxa 'a'íim!
Nyuukanáav 'awét!
Nyaamáamtək athútya!
'Awíntixats alyathómək," a'ét.

A'ávək,
amétk siithík.

He went back and got there.

He lay there,
once again he lay weeping in his bed.
The sun came up.

"Why weren't you here?
We were looking,"
(the girls) said.

"Oh,
I might have been around," he said.
He didn't tell them (what had happened).

The ice was overwhelming,
and they slipped him inside,
and once again he slept.

They put him in the middle,
and he lay there sleeping.

The sun came up,
and he got up.
***
He left his bed,
and he went around weeping,
and when the sun set,
it happened again.

He got there and looked.
Buzzard got there and looked.
"You heard what I told you!
I said what would happen to you!
I told you!
That's all!
I can't do it again," (Buzzard) said.

He heard him,
and he lay there weeping.

Siithík,
'akór alynyaayémək,
suuváa.

Suuváam,
nyaayúuts aváamək ayúut.

Xalytótt-ts.
Aváamək ayúut.

"Móo,
kaawíts kamathúum?" a'íim.
"Aví kamathúum?"
a'étəm.

Kanáavək vuunóot.
"Nyáasi 'amánək va'thúum va'thíiny.

" 'Atkuuvékxany 'ashmathíik,
nyáavi 'uuváatk va'uuváatk 'athót,"
a'ét.

"Nyayúuk va'uuváak.
Ammathúum nyayúuk va'uuváakəm,
nyáavəm mathíkəm 'ayúutəntik,
nyáavəm mathíkəm 'ayúutəntik va'uunóo,
'a'étka,"
a'ét.

"Xóttk nyaathúm.
'Anyáa atspák viithíim,
'aváaxá.
Va'thíik 'aváak.
Nyatháwk nyatatsénxa.
'Anyáats."

"Xóttk."

Nyaawíi kwa'átsk:
aváam,
nyiinákəm,

He lay there,
and a long time passed,
and there he was.

There he was,
and a creature got there and saw him.

It was Spider.
He got there and saw him.

"Well,
what is it you are doing?" he said.
"What are you doing here?"
he said.

(Oriole) told him (what had happened).
"I started out over there and I came here.

"I don't know how to get back,
that's why I'm staying here,"
he said.

"I've been watching you.
I've been watching what you do,
I've watched you lying here again,
I've been watching you lie here again,
and I (have something to) say,"
(Spider) said.

"It's all right.
When the sun comes up,
I will get here.
I will come and get here.
I will take you down (to your home).
I am the one."

"All right."

He did it, just as he said he would:
he got there,
he sat down,

axtáttəny taxpíly,
atháwk,
lóoooq awétk vuuthíit.
Uukwíiiin uukwíiiin a'étk vuuthíit,
nyavá 'avuumák shátt awét.

"Móo,
nyáavi kathík viikathík.
Viikathík,
shamáts tsuumpáp táx a'ím,
nyamáam,
mamánək,
manyvá makayáamma,"
a'ét.

"Xóttk,"
nyaa'ét.
Nyavá 'avuumák nyaathíkəm'ashk siithíkt.

Nyaawínyəm'ashtək vuunóok,
aatsqwíttk vuuthíik,
viiwáak vuunóot.

A'ávək siithík.

Siithík,
siithík,
uumánxa matt-tsapéem a'ávəs athótk
alyathík,
alyaskyíik siithík.

Siithík,
shamáts nyaatsuumpápəm,
"Móo,
nyamáam!"
a'ét.

Máan a'étk,
amánək a'áv.
Takavékəntik kaathúu aaly'étk viithíixayk,

and (Oriole) clung to his back,
and he took him,
and he brought him down (on his spider's thread).
He took him around and around in circles,
and in back of his house he set him upright.

"Well,
lie here and lie here.
Lie here,
and in exactly four nights,
that's all,
you may get up,
and go straight to your home,"
he said.

"All right,"
(Oriole) said.
Once again he lay there in back of his house.

Once again, (Coyote) was doing things,
he was beating them,
he was going along.

(Oriole) lay there listening.

He lay there,
and he lay there,
he felt an overwhelming (desire) to get up, but
he lay there,
he was still lying there.

He lay there,
and (after) four nights,
"Well,
at last!"
he said.

He got up suddenly,
he got up and (tried to) be careful.
He came this way, thinking that he might go back again,

xótt-təm,
vanyaathíik vanyaathíik,
nyavá aváat.

Nyaayúuny,
nyaatsavétsənyts,
akwérvək vuunóonyk nyiikwévək,
iimáatt tsanályk vuunóony nyiikwévtan.

Nyiitháwk viitháw;
matsáam apóoy.

Matsats'étk siitháw.

Xuumáarəts nyaalyvéek athót.
Ayúut siiv'áw.

'Avásnyənyts —
'atsíipúy kwashént,
kaawíts xam'aavíir,
kaawíts viikwáam,
kwasháxənyts kaa'éepəm,
ayóovək siiv'áw.

Siiv'áw.
"Xwóott, " aaly'étk,
ayúuk siiv'áw.

'Atsaayúu nyaaxalykwáantik viiyém,
viitháawəm,
ayúmək a'ét.
Xatalwévəts.

Nyiiríish a'étəm ayóov,
sanyts'áakəts avatháwəm ayóov.
Ayúuk siiv'áw.
"Kamuuvíly ta'axánk!
Tathíts katawáam!"

Tathíts tawáam vuunóo.
Xuuvíkəly awítsk suunóokəm,
aavíir.

(but) it was all right,
he came came and came this way,
and he got to his house.

When he saw them,
his wives,
they were terribly thin,
they had been losing weight just terribly.

There they were;
they were starving.

They were weeping.

The children were the same.
He stood there looking.

That house —
a dead fish was the only thing (there),
a gopher snake or something,
whatever was in the area,
and the stench was overwhelming,
and he stood there looking.

He stood there.
"Oh my," he thought,
and he stood there looking.

(Coyote) went off hunting for things again;
here they were,
and he intended to keep an eye on them.
This Coyote (did).

(Oriole) saw that (Coyote) was gone,
and he saw that the women were there.
He stood there looking.
"Hurry up!
Grind corn!" (he said).

They went about grinding corn.
Both of them went about doing it,
and they finished.

Tashkyén atháwk nyiitáp.
"Alykashuuvíik!"
alyshuuvíik vuunóo.

Xuumár ayóov a'étk viitháawk athót,
xuuvíkəly,
Xatalwé nyaxuumáar.

Uutóoyətk uuvát,
xuuvíkəly.
Ayúuk siiv'áw.

"Móo,
avík kakav'órək!
Avík kakav'órək kathúum!
a'étəm,
avík kav'órək,
avík kav'órək,
shuuvíiny.

Axtáttəny sqám sqám awétəm,
xuumáarənyts alyanály.
Llyóq a'étk anályvəm.
Aváts avány avawíntik vuunóok,
aavíirək awét.

Alyshuuvíik vuunóok vuunóok vuunóok,
aavíirək,
nyiiyápk anamák.
"Móo,
nyamáam,
'astuukyáany!"
nyaa'ét.

Nyiinyaashtúum,
'avá kwaaxwíirək,
axwélyk vuunóok,
nyáanyəm uupúuv.

He took a pot and put it down there.
"Make it into porridge!" (he said),
   and they went about making porridge.

They were expecting children,
   both of them,
   Coyote's children.

They were pregnant,
   both of them.
He stood there looking.

"Well,
   step in there!
Step in there!"
   he said,
and (one of the women) stepped in there,
and (the other one) stepped in there,
   in the porridge.

He went pound! pound! on his wife's back,
   and the child fell out.
It disengaged and fell out.
He did it again to that (other wife),
   and he finished.

He cooked them in the porridge, going on and on and on,
   and he finished,
   and he threw it down there and left it.
"Well,
   that's all,
   let's get out of here!"
   he said.

He gathered up his wives,
   and in a corner of the house,
   he went about digging a tunnel,
   and they went into it.

Uupúuvək,
nyaayúu nyamtsapéttk vuunóok,
aavíirək,
viiwétsk,
maxák náamək viiwéts.
Axwílyk vanyaawéts.

'Atátt a'ím tsapéttk.

Nyaayúu nyamtsapéttk,
'amátt kaawíts nyamtsapéttk,
viiwétsənyk,
viiwéts,
'akór nyayémtan,
nyáasily uutspám.

Vanyaawétsk,
xaasa'íly katánmək,
uuv'óok suuv'óo.

Suuv'óok,
amáam,
'axá nanák viiwétsk.

Vatháts 'anyáa nyamaxávəm nyaaváak,
ayúuny,
nyiirísh a'étəm ayúut.

Shuuvíivats viivám atháwk,
amáam vuunóony,
atsáav.

Nyaxuutsamáarəny,
alyshuuvíik vuunóok kwavíirəny,
amáam vuunóok,
atsáav.
Nyáany atsáavəntik awét.

Nyaamáam,
nyiixalykwáak,
axwíitsk awáamək,
nyaayúuny axwíits aaly'étk suuváa.

They went in,
and they went about covering it with something,
and they finished,
and they went along,
they went along under (the ground).
They went digging their way along.

They covered it with what are called thorns.

They covered it with things,
they covered it with dirt or whatever,
and they went this way,
they went this way,
and after a really long time,
they came out over there in the distance.

They went along,
and they reached the ocean,
and they stood there and stood there.

They stood there,
and finally,
they went floating on the water.

When this (Coyote) got home at sundown,
he looked,
and he saw that they were gone.

He took this porridge that was sitting there,
and he went about eating it,
and he ate it up.

His children,
the ones that had been made into porridge,
he went about eating them,
and he ate them up.
That's what he ate.

At last,
he looked for them,
he went sniffing for them,
and he thought he smelled something.

"Vathám axávəta,"
a'ét.
"Vathám ayémta,"
a'ét.
Viiyáat.

Vanyaayáak,
vanyaayáak,
vanyaayáak,
xaasa'íly vakamée a'étk siiv'áw.
Nyiiríish a'étəm ayúuk.

Aváts'axá nanák viiwétsk,
xaasa'íly 'axkyéely nyaváytsək,
siitháw.

'Aqwáaq nyaayáanyəm'áshk awím,
ashílyk,
alyúlyk,
asóotsk siitháw.

Vatháts,
Xatalwényts,
nyiixalykwáak uuváak.

'Axá tuunák viiyáak,
alyvák,
iixúuny tsatspátsk;
alyvák,
kó kó kó kó kó awíi viiyáany.
'Anyaaxávíi,
qwalayéwíi,
'anyaxávíi a'étk viiyáa.

Vatháts,
'aqwáaq wée qalyamáa atháwk,
'a'áw atápəm,
axwíivək.

"They went through here,"
he said.
"They went this way,"
he said.
He went after them.

He went,
and he went,
and he went,
and he stood there at the edge of the ocean.
He saw that they were gone.

They had travelled over the water,
and they were living on the other side of the ocean,
there they were.

(Oriole) went after a deer again, and so,
and they fried it,
they cooked it,
and they sat there eating it.

This one,
Coyote,
he was looking for them.

He went travelling over the water;
he sat in something,
and he stuck his nose out;
he sat in it,
and he went paddle-paddle-paddle-paddle-paddle.
Maybe it was sunset,
maybe it was dawn,
maybe it was sunset, but (still) he went along.

This (Oriole),
he took some deer gut,
and he threw it in the fire,
and it gave off an odor.

Xatalwéva aqásk,
awíim,
iixúuny aapáayv a'étəm,
a'ávək;
axwíivəts.

"Viitháwəta!
Nyáavik atháwk viitháwəta!"
a'ét.

'Ashúts nyáavik nyaváyk viiváta,"
a'étk,
iixúu nyiktathómpək a'áv.
Viiyáat.

Vanyaayáak,
'axá sa'íly atónyi avák,
amíim vuunóot.

Amíim,
"Wóoow," a'étk vuunóo.

"Móo,
aviithíit!
Ka'áv!"
a'ét.

"Avathíita!"
a'étk,
siitháw.

A'áv a'ím awétk awím,
nyaayúu,
'aqwáaq wée xalyamáany 'a'áw atápəm,
kwaxwíivənyts iixúusily aváam,
a'ávək siiyáak,
nyáanyi.

Kanyótk siiyáat.

Nyaayáak aváam.

He summoned this Coyote,
and so,
with his nose up at an angle,
Coyote smelled it;
(the deer gut) gave off an odor.

"Here they are!
Here they are, right here!"
he said.

"My little brother is living here,"
he said,
and with his nose facing that way he smelled them.
And he went after them.

As he went along,
he was sitting in the middle of the ocean,
and he was weeping.

He was weeping,
he was saying "Wóooow."

"Well,
he's coming!
Listen!"
(Oriole) said.

"He's coming!"
they said,
there they were.

He did it so that Coyote would smell them,
well,
he threw the deer guts on the fire,
and the smell reached Coyote's nose,
and he smelled it, as he went along,
there.

He went along following (the odor).

He went along and got there.

Nyiináak a'ét.

" 'Aváak,
matt'aaxavík," a'étəm;
"Áa"
a'ét.

Ayúutəm,
siivát,
akwérpak vuunóony,
pa'iipáats alyathóm,
iithóony,
nyiikwalaxúyk nyiikwévəm,
siivát.

Siivám,
nyaayúu uutáap,
áaytsəm,
tsapóxtək siivá.

'Aqwáaq awím,
áaytsəm,
amáam —
asóok siivák.

Av'áwxaym,
llyóq a'étk anályta.
" 'Uunyíi 'atsanályəm athósh,"
a'ét.

Tuuwámp a'étk atháwk,
amátk athótk siivát.

Ayúutk siivát,
Xwetsxwéts aváts ayúuk siivák.
"Móo,
kamathúum muuváam?
'Atsmuumátsənyts análytək,
análytək athótəm 'ayúut.
'Ashkwílyt 'a'íi 'avák 'athútya,"

He settled down there.

"I have come,
my friend," he said;
"Oh,"
(Oriole) said.

He saw him,
there he was,
he was very thin,
he wasn't even human,
and as for his eyes,
they were terrible empty holes,
there he was.

There he was,
and they threw him something,
they gave it to him,
and he sat there munching it.

They used deer meat,
they gave it to him,
and he ate it —
he was eating meat.

And as soon as he stood up,
it disengaged and fell out.
"It's because I've lost a sister-in-law,"
he said.

He took what are called leftovers,
and he sat there eating them.

He sat there looking,
that Oriole sat there looking.
"Well,
what is the matter with you?
The things you eat fall out,
I've seen them fall out.
Maybe I'll sew it up,"

a'étəm;
" 'Axóttk,"
a'étəm.

Aa'ámpəm,
shakwílyk vuunóok aavíirtsəm,
siivát.

Nyuuváatk suuváat.
"Móo,
ma'axótt-tanək,
'anymaataqwérək muuváaxa,
vathí amán,"
a'ét.

"Kuutara'úy ta'axánəm,
nyaayúu 'awítsk,
nyaa'uunóok 'uunóowa,"
a'ét.

"Áa,
'athóxa."

A'étk,
siivák athúuk a'étk.

he said.
"All right,"
(Coyote) said.

He bent over,
and (Oriole) sewed him up and finished,
and there he was.

He stayed there.
"Well,
if you are really good,
you may keep company with us,
from here on,"
he said.

"Behave yourself,
and we'll do things together,
now that we're here,"
he said.

"Yes,
I'll do it."

And so,
there they were, they say.

4. Three Stories About Kwayúu

Kwayúu

Told by Mary K. Escalanti

Kwayúu

Told by Josefa Hartt

Púk Atsé

Told by Rosita Carr

All three stories translated by Barbara Levy,
George Bryant, and Amy Miller

http://dx.doi.org/10.11647/OBP.0049.04

Kwayúu (The One Who Sees) is a giant who gets his name from his tremendous size and the view which it affords him. The narratives in this chapter tell about *Kwayúu* from three radically different perspectives.

Notes and synopsis: Mary Kelly Escalanti's story of *Kwayúu*

Mary Kelly Escalanti told her story of *Kwayúu* to Abe Halpern on September 15, 1978. Halpern later reviewed his transcript of the narrative with Barbara Levy.

This story focuses on two boys whose parents have been eaten by *Kwayúu*. The boys are raised by their grandmother. Eventually they decide to avenge their parents' death by killing the giant. Ignoring their grandmother's warnings, they make a difficult journey through the four levels of heaven to where the monster lives among the bones of his victims.

The journey is made on foot, and one of the boys sings of the pain caused by his shoe. The lines of the song,

'*Ányxámarúy akáamawépetik aléeletíi*
alíiláalaláa alíiláalaláa

are heard, under comparable circumstances, in Tom Kelly's story '*Aavém Kwasám* in Chapter 6.

When they reach the home of *Kwayúu*, the boys find that he is blind, and they tease him. Somehow *Kwayúu* manages to catch them, and he instructs his wife to cook them. The boys use their spiritual powers to summon rain, so that the wife is unable to light a fire. Instead of cooking the boys, she makes *shuuvíi* (a term which may be translated either as 'porridge' or 'gravy'). When *Kwayúu* eats it, his insides are cut apart by sharp objects which the boys have placed in the *shuuvíi*, and he dies.

The boys watch him die. They sing a song which puts the spirits of his victims to rest, and then they go home and tell the news to their grandmother.

Notes and synopsis: Josefa Hartt's story of Kwayúu

Josefa Hartt's story of *Kwayúu* has been extracted from a longer narrative which was recorded on February 12, 1981. Halpern reviewed his transcript of the story with Eunice Miguel.

Josefa Hartt's story begins with the family of *Kwayúu*. This family has four sons, the youngest and smallest of whom grows to an extraordinary size and becomes known as *Kwayúu*.

Kwayúu kills and eats people. His older brother, living at the bottom of the ocean, finds out what is happening. He goes to *Kwayúu* and orders him to stop. *Kwayúu* hears him, but he is blind, so he cannot see who is speaking, and he pays no attention. Relatives warn him that someone is coming for him, but he ignores the warnings and just lies there.

The brother tries to drag *Kwayúu* into the water. This is difficult, because *Kwayúu* is so big. Finally, *Kwayúu* grows wings and tries to escape by flying. When he beats his wings, the wings leave an imprint in the wet ground which may still be seen today. He struggles, walks, and sits down, and the imprint left by his buttocks may likewise be seen today.

Eventually the brother succeeds in pulling *Kwayúu* into the water. When *Kwayúu* is finally dead, someone pulls his wing feathers into the shape of a teepee.

The Creator, who has been watching, denounces both *Kwayúu* and the brother who killed him. Dark clouds gather. The brother uses lightning to destroy himself and everything around him.

Notes and synopsis: Rosita Carr's story Púk Atsé

Rosita Carr told the story *Puk Atsé* to Abe Halpern on February 1, 1978. Halpern later reviewed his transcript of the story with Mina Hills.

This story begins with a murder. *Púk Atsé*'s daughter is killed by strangers. Her body is found by Roadrunner, who hurries to the woman's home to notify her family. The people there do not understand Roadrunner's language, and one interpreter after another fails to decipher his message. (This passage is very funny: the storyteller laughs, her audience laughs, and everyone who listens to the recording laughs as well.) Finally *Púk Atsé* himself appears. He is able to understand Roadrunner, and he learns that his daughter is dead.

The daughter's body is brought home, and the people from *Púk Atsé*'s household avenge her death by killing the enemy.

A young woman from the enemy camp survives and is taken home by *Púk Atsé*. A baby and an old woman also survive. The baby becomes the main character of the story. Even as an infant, he has extraordinary spiritual powers. *Púk Atsé*'s colleagues try to shoot him, burn him, and drown him in the rain, but his powers protect him, and their attempts fail. Finally he is left to starve — and of course this fails as well. Although he is still a baby, he manages to heal the old woman, who has been shot with an arrow, and she takes care of him. He hunts and provides food for them both.

The baby grows into a boy and has a series of adventures. He manages to escape from Old Lady Flesh-Ripper, from a monster called *Iiyáam Kwakáap*, who swallows him, and from Eagle, who tries to feed him to her chicks. Eventually he sets off to find and kill the giant *Kwayúu*. This time, he is not so lucky: *Kwayúu* catches him and takes him beyond the four levels of heaven. When *Kwayúu*'s four wives try to roast him, he summons rain to extinguish their cooking fire. He adds sharp rocks to the meal which the wives are preparing. *Kwayúu* gulps his food, and the sharp rocks cut his throat. Once *Kwayúu* is dead, the boy brings the four wives down to the first level of heaven. He turns himself into an arrow and returns to his home to visit the old woman who raised him.

The boy remains at home and grows up. Eventually he turns himself into a newly hatched dove and begins another adventure. He is recognized and caught. He is taken to an old man (who might be *Púk Atsé*), but he manages to escape, and there the story ends.

Comparative note

A monster known as *Kwayúu* is also found in Mojave literature. According to Kroeber (1948:48), his name "means a meteor or fireball, usually conceived of as a monster or man-eater." His four wives are the daughters of the sun (Kroeber 1948:12).

Kwayúu

Told by Mary Kelly Escalanti

Xuumáarəts vuunóok,
xavík vuunóok,
'aankóoyəts viivám.
Namáawk a'ím.

Viivám,
nyáava,
nyáavəts xatáləm,
ayóovək vanyuunóok.
Maawíik.

Antáy nyáany,
nyakónya,
giant nyáanyts,
asóo—
amáa—
asóok nyiitsáavək a'ét.
Pa'iipáa,
pa'iipáa avawétk vuunóotk.
'Amáyvi alythík,
avawétk vuunóot.

Vanyuunóok,
kaathóm ta'axánək,
Kwayúu a'ím amúlyk viithíkəm,
a'éməm.

" 'Aaly'étk vany'uunóok.
'Awétstanək 'ayóov.
'Ayóov
'attapóoytxa!"
a'ét.

Tapúyúm a'ím.

There were children,
there two of them there,
and there was a little old lady.
They called her Grandmother, they say.

There she was,
and these (children),
these (children) were orphans,
and (someone) was watching them.
She was a relative.

That mother of theirs,
and their father,
that giant
had eaten—
had eaten—
he had eaten them up, they say.
People,
he had been doing that to people.
He was up in a high place,
and he had been doing that.

He was around here,
he really was doing whatever it was,
and he was named Kwayúu,
they might have said.

"I've been thinking.
We will go and take a look.
We will watch him
and we will kill him!"
(one of boys) said.

He was going to kill him, they say.

'Aakóoyənyts vanyaavák a'ím,
"Makaváarək!
Matsaváamúm.
Pa'iipáa nyiikwanáaməts nyaathúuva.
Matsaváam.
Matapúy a'ím."

 'Awítsxa.
'Ayóovxa."

" 'Amáyvi athík viithíkəm,
matsaváam alyma'émúm.
Mapóoyúm!"

A'áv alya'ém.
" 'Awétsk 'ayóovxa,"
nyaa'étka.

Iiwáa vathíly tsaváw,
viiwétsk.
'Amáyvi nathómk,
viiwétsəm.
Nyiináamts athótk,
nyaayúu tsáaməly,
'axótt alya'éməm,
viiwéts.
Uuv'áak viiwéts.

'Akórəm,
'amáy athík aatsuumpápəm,
a'éta.
Xalyavíim.

Tsuumpápəm,
nakayáamək viiwétsk.
Viiwétsk uuv'óok;
nyaapóoyk uuv'óok.

Viiwétsk viiwétsəm;
nyiináam,

The old woman was sitting here, and she said,
"You are mistaken!
You won't be able to do it.
He is a dangerous person.
You can't do it.
He is going to kill you."

"We will do it.
We will take a look."

"He is up in a high place,
and there's not a chance you'll able to do it.
You are going to die!"

They didn't listen.
"We'll go and take a look,"
they said.

They set their hearts on it,
and they went.
They headed towards the high place,
and they went.
It was dangerous,
everything (was),
it wasn't good,
(but) they went.
They went walking.

Long ago,
there were four levels of heaven,
they say.
There might have been.

There were four of them,
and (the boys) went heading straight toward them.
They went along and they stopped;
when they were exhausted, they stopped.

They went and went;
it was dangerous,

nyaayúu tsáaməly aspér tanəm nyamnayémək.
Matxáts amíim.
Kaawíts stones awíim,
tsakyévək vaawíim,
nyiitsamíim,
nyamuupúuvt.
Kaawíts awíim,
nyamuupúuv vanyaawéts,
tsuumpáp.

Makyí nyaawéts,
nyáanyi,
iiményts arávta,
uuv'áak vuuwétsəny.
Iiményts aráv.

'Ashénta,
nyaxmanyéwəts,
xamanyéwəts arávəm,
amíim siivám.

    " 'Ányxámarúy akáamawépetik aléeletíi?
    Alíiláalaláa alíiláalaláa,"

a'étk siivá.

A'íim,
siivá.
Kaa'émək a'íim:
"Xamanyéw avány,
kamawéməm?
Arávək!" a'ím,
"Íim," a'ím,
amíim siivát.

A'íim,
siivák,
amíim suunóo.
Nyaaxóttəm,
viiwétst.

they went through all (kinds of) very powerful things.
The wind howled.
He had used some kind of stones,
he had put them together like this,
and put them down there,
and (the boys) went through that.
He had done something (else),
and they went through that and went on,
(through) four (levels).

Somewhere, as they went along,
at that (point),
their feet hurt,
because of (all) their walking.
Their feet hurt.

One of them,
his shoe,
the shoe hurt him,
and he sat there crying.

 "My shoe, what have you done to it?
 Fire is burning, fire is burning,"

he went on saying.

So,
there he was.
He said something:
"That shoe,
what did you do to it?
It hurts!" he said,
"It's all over," he said,
and he sat there crying.

So,
there he was,
and he was crying.
When it was better,
they went on.

Viiwétsk viiwétsk viiwéts,
nyamáam,
nyaakatánəmək,
ayóovək vuunóo.

Kwayúunyts sanyaathík,
siivák.
Tasínymək,
'atsayúu alya'émk,
siivák athúum.

Vanyaavák.
Xuumáarənyts katánmək vuunóony;
'avány nakwíinək ayóovək vuunóo.

Nyamuuéevtək vuunóo.

Iisháalyva —
tasínymək,
iisháaly vaawéemtiyum.
Atháw,
nyiishtúu a'étk vaawétk awím.

Tsakaváarəs.
Tsakavár apóoy a'étk nakwíinək vuunóo.

Vuunóom,
suunóonykəm,
kaawémək vanyaavák,
nyiishtót!
Xuuvíkəly!
Nyiishtúum.

Nyiishtúum siitháwəm;
"Móo."

Nyaavéets,
viivák,
nyáanyts.

They went and went and went,
and finally,
they got there,
and they watched for him.

Kwayúu was over there,
there he was.
He was blind,
he couldn't see anything,
and there he was.

There he was.
The children got there, and there they were;
they went around the house looking.

They played tricks on him.

This arm of his —
he was blind,
and he waved his arm around like this.
He (wanted to) get them,
and he tried to catch them, like this.

They laughed.
They went around laughing fit to die.

There they were,
and he was around there,
he was doing something,
and he caught them!
Both of them!
He caught them.

He caught them and there they were;
"Well, now," (he said).

His wife,
here she was,
that one.

"Móo,
'aakóoy!
'Aakóoyey!
Kayúuk kakawémǝm,
'amáawú!"
a'ét.

"Áa-á,
'awéxá,"
a'ím.

Tashkyénǝts viivám,
nyáany alytsáam.
Alyúly a'íim uunóo.

Uunóom,
xuumáarǝnyts viitháwǝny.
Xuumáarǝva,
shatuumáts nyiikwanáam,
viitháwk athúm.

" 'Awíim 'a'ávxa,"
a'íim viitháwk awím,
uuv'áw a'érǝk.
Uuv'áwk,
a'érǝm.

'Amátǝnyts 'axáyk,
'a'íinyts 'axáykǝm,
taráalya'ém nyiikwév.
Apóm alya'ém.

***

Athúum,
viitháw.
Viitháwm,
awétǝntim,
athúnti alya'ém;
taráa alya'ém.

"Well, now,
old woman!
Old woman!
Go and do something
so that I may eat!"
he said.

"Yes,
I will do it,"
she said.

There was a pot there,
and she put those (boys) in it.
She was getting ready to cook them.

She went on,
and the children were here.
These children,
(they had) powerful dreams,
there they were.

"I will try to do it,"
they were saying, and so,
they used their power to make it rain.
It rained,
(because) they used their power.

The earth got wet,
and the wood got wet,
and she couldn't get it to burn at all.
It wouldn't burn.

***

So,
here they were.
Here they were,
and she did it again,
and once again it didn't happen;
she couldn't get it to burn.

Vuunóonyk,
nyaatsaváamǝk,
nyaa,
'aakóoyǝnyts uukanáav alya'émǝxayk,
nyaayúu kwanymé awét.

Shuuvíik,
a'éta.
Shuuvíik.

Pa'iipáa uu'ítsapatǝnyts:
shuuvíik a'étǝm.
Awíim vuunóok.

Kwara'ákǝnya,
shamathíi kuu'éyk,
ayúulya'émkǝm.

"Móo,
nyaamaavíirkǝm?"
"Áa,
'aavíirǝk.
Mamáxa," a'ím.

Xuumáarǝnyts a'áavǝk ayóovǝk avatháw,
vuunóok awím.

Nyaatápǝm,
'apílyk iináamǝm,
aví tsaváwǝm.
Kwayúunyts aváak awím,
atháwk,
***
amáam.

" 'Apílyk," a'ét.
" 'Apílyk.
'Anóqǝm 'apílyk," a'ét.

She went on,
and when she found it impossible,
well,
the old woman didn't tell him,
she did something else (instead).

She made gravy,
they say.
She made gravy.

That's what people say:
she made gravy, they say.
She went about doing it.

As for the old man,
he didn't know, poor thing,
because he couldn't see.

"Well, now,
have you finished?"
"Yes,
I'm finished.
You may eat," she said.

The children were watching and listening.
there they were.

She put (the food) down,
and it was very hot,
and she put it there.
Kwayúu got there, and so,
he took it,
***
and he ate it.

"It's hot," he said.
"It's hot.
It's a little bit hot," he said.

Xuumáarənyts
kaawíts,
mattnamíilək uuváak,
kaawíts 'asháak athóoyvtanəm alytsamíim.
Tsuumpápk viitháw.
Awím.

Axúupxayəm,
vathíly vaawé awét,
maxákəly.
Aakyéttk,
vaawé.
" 'Apílyk!" a'ét.

" 'Ook,
'apílypaa!"
a'étk,
kanáavək siivát.

Yeah,
a'étk,
viivám,
nyaa'ávkəm —
viitháwk,
aviitháwk a'ávtanək.

Nyaawíntim,
nyaawíntim,
'anóqəm vaa'ée a'é ta'axánəm a'áv.
"Xwóott!
'Uupílyəny!"
a'ét.

Viitháwk,
viitháwk,
nyaawíntim,
" 'Apíly ta'axánək,"
a'étk;
viivá.

The children
(had done) something,
they had used their powers,
and they had put some kind of very sharp bones in it.
There were four (bones).
They had done it.

He slurped it down, and all of a sudden,
it went like this, right in here,
inside him.
It cut him,
like this.
"It's hot!" he said.

"Ooh,
it's so hot!"
he said,
and he sat there telling her about it.

Yeah,
and so,
here he was,
and when they heard him —
here they were,
they were right there and they heard him.

When he did it again,
when he did it again,
he really did go like this a little, and they heard him.
"Oh, my!
How hot it is!"
he said.

There they were,
there they were,
and when he did it again,
"It's really hot,"
he said;
here he was.

Tsapéetanəm.
"Áaaa!"
a'ét,
nyamáam,
aakyítt achémtəm,
maxákəly.
Nyaawíim,
viivák.

Nyaawíntik,
nyamáam,
nyaaxúupəntim,
nyamáam,
nyuupáyəm;
axúp vaawée.

'Uupílyəny matt-tsapéek.

Avíly aakyéttkəm áam.
Vaa'é.
Apúy.

A'étəm,
nyiiyóovək.
Viitháwk,
'atsakavártanək viitháw.

"Móo."
'Aakóoyənyts ayúuk suuváa.
"Móo," nyaa'íim.
Nyaapúyəm ayóovək.
Uuv'óok vuunóok.

Nyaayúu tsáaməly ayóovək vuunóony.

Pa'iipáa nyatsasháakənyts,
tsáam vathá lyavíik,
nyáany lyavíik,
kaawítsənyts,
matt-tsapéetan.

It was overwhelming.
"Ahhhh!"
he said,
and that's all;
it had almost cut right through him,
(from) the inside.
Then,
here he was.

He did it again,
and that's all,
when he slurped it up again,
that's all,
it was all gone;
he had slurped it up, like this.

It was overwhelmingly hot.

It had cut through, here (inside him).
He went like this.
And he died.

So,
they were watching.
Here they were,
and they were really laughing.

"Well, now."
The old woman was watching, over there.
"Well, now," she said.
They watched him die.
They were standing there.

All the things were watching.

People's bones,
all of them were like this,
they were like that,
whatever (they were),
there were a whole lot of them.

Ayóovək vuunóok vuunóok,
nyuuv'óok.

Nyuuv'óok a'ím,
aashtuuvárət:

    "Eemévəts,
    iisháaly,
    akwetsəts awétsəts,
    awék oonóonóon,
    awék oonóonóo.
    Awék oonóonóon,
    awék oonóonóo.
    Eemévəts,
    iisháaly,
    akwétsəts awétsəts,
    awék oonóonóon,
    awék,"

a'étk suunóok.

Aanáaly a'ím —
iisháalya,
iimé vatháts,
iisháalyəva,
alykwatháw tsuuétsəts —
nyaa'ím.

Íim,
kanáavka,
aashtuuvár.

Nyaayúu tsáaməly,
nyáanyts athótkəm viitháwəsh.
Íim aashtuuvárək.

Amíim siiv'áwk a'íikəta.

"Móo,
vany'uunóok,

They were watching, on and on,
they stood there.

They stood there, and so,
they sang:

> "This foot of his,
>   his hand,
>   they did it, they did it,
>   they were doing it,
>   they were doing it.
>   They were doing it,
>   they were doing it,
>   This foot of his,
>   his hand,
>   they did it, they did it,
>   they were doing it,
>   they did it,"

they were saying it.

They moved aside —
a hand,
this foot,
this hand,
these bones that were there —
(that's what) it says.

It came to an end,
and they told about it,
they sang about it.

All those things,
those (things) were there.
It came to an end and they sang.

(The boys) stood there crying, they say.

"Okay,
  here we are,

'ayóovkəm áam,
'atatapóoyt.
'Ankavék.''

'Aakóoyəny —
namáawk a'étəma —
nyáanya,
ayóovək
uukanáav a'ím.

'Avíi natsén a'ím viinathíis,
matt-tsapéek,
nuutsénəxany,
'uukórəny matt-tsapéem,
vanyuuv'óok.
''Ka'thútsk 'ankavék av'úuv'óok 'athómúm,''
nyaa'íima.

Uuv'óok uuv'óok,
awím,
arrow mattatséwk.
Arrow.
'Iipá.
***

'Iipá
'iipá mattatséwk,
nyáanya.
Natsénək vinathíik,
shóx a'étk,
'avuumák uuv'óok.

Ayúum.
Xatalwéts avuuváak;
Xatalwé uu'ítsəny,
'uuláayəny!
Nyaayúu tsáaməly athúu a'étum!
Ayúum uuváak,
nyáanyts,
'aakóoyəny vasháwk a'étk;
vuuváak.

we have seen him,
and we have killed him.
We're going back."

The old woman —
they called her their grandmother, they say —
that one,
they were going to see her
and tell her about it.

They came this way, intending to go down the mountain, but
it was overwhelming,
the way they were to come down,
the distance was overwhelming,
and they stood there.
"I wonder how we might get back,"
they said.

They stood there and stood there,
and so,
they turned themselves into arrows.
Arrows.
Arrows.
***

Arrows,
they turned themselves into arrows,
those (boys).
They came down,
swiftly,
and they stood behind the house.

He was watching them.
Coyote was there;
the one they call Coyote,
how bad he was!
He always wanted to do everything!
He was watching them,
he was the one,
he was supposed to be taking care of the old woman;
here he was.

'Aláaytanəm ayóov.
'Aláayəm nyaayóov,
"Xwóott," a'ím,
vathí uuv'óok,
matsats'íim uuv'óok
ayóov.

Uuv'óok awím,
uupúuv.

***
Xatalwényts,
'atsaráv kamúly a'étk viithík.

"Ka'thóməly," aaly'étk uuváam,
ayóovək.

"Móo,
'atatapóoyta.
'Akatánk."

"Makyí makwíivəm,
nyiirísh a'íika 'aaly'íim,
'amétk 'avát,"
'aakóoyənyts a'íim.

" 'Attapóoyvək nya'thúuva,"
a'íim nyuuv'óok.

A'étəm,
'a'ávək,
nyáamáamta.

They saw that he was bad.
When they saw that he was bad,
"Oh, my," they said,
and they stood here,
they stood there crying,
and they watched.

They stood there, and so,
they went in.

***

That Coyote,
he was lying there pretending to be sick.

"What shall I do?" he was wondering,
and they looked at him.

"Okay,
we've killed him.
We have returned," they said.

"Somehow you left (home),
and I thought you were gone (for good),
and I cried,"
the old woman said.

"We killed him,"
they stood there saying it.

They said it,
and I heard it,
and that's all.

Kwayúu

Told by Josefa Hartt

Nyáava,
'iipáats,
sanya'ákəm xavík nyiitháwk viitháwk,
awím,
nyáava,
xuuméey 'iipátsanyts tsuumpápk a'étəma.

Tsuumpápk,
tsuumpápk viitháwəm.

Viitháwəm,
a'ím,
ashíitk.
"Máanyts,
ma'xóttk,
mav'áak,
nyaayúu mathúum.
Maxalykwáaxa,"
a'íim.

Nya'íim,
***
nyiivántim,
a'ím,
"Máanyts,
vanyaamayáak,
xaasa'íly tó ta'axán,
maxákəly manyváyk.
Nyaayúu 'ats'iipáyəts alyuuváak,
viikwuuváa vathány.
Mayúuk mavasháwk viimathíkxa,"
a'íik a'étəntima.

A'íim,
áaytəntik a'étəma.

This one,
a man,
he was with his wife and here they were,
and so,
as for these (people),
they had four sons, they say.

There were four of them,
there were four of them here.

Here they were,
and so,
and he called them by name.
"You,
you will be good,
you will travel,
and you will do things.
You will hunt,"
he said.

Then,
***

another one was there,
and he said to him,
"You,
you will go along,
and at the very center of the ocean
you will live at the bottom.
There is a creature or something in there,
this one that is there.
You will watch him and take care of him,"
he said, they say.

So,
he gave (the third son a task) too, they say.

Nyiiáaytsəntim,
uuváaxayəm,
xeekónyts nyaa'íim,
family,
'ashéntts alyvák 'aláayum.
A'épəm 'a'ávənyk.
Nya'étəm 'a'áva,
Nyáany kanáavtəntik a'éta.

"Avathóxa.
Kaawémək,
'axótt tánək viithík alya'éməxa.
Alyvák matt-ta'aaláayum.
Alyvák 'atsathúts 'aláayum.
Athóxa."
A'íntik.

"Athúum,
nyáany mayúuk;
mavasháwxa,"
a'íim.
A'étəntik;
nyiikuunáavəts athúum,
nyáava ayúuk viitháwəm.

Tapáar tanəts,
'anóq tanəts,
viivák,
viivátk.
Nyáavəts amák athíi tanək,
vanyaavák.

Saathúu a'étkəm a'ávək athúum.

Iimáattənyts 'axótt-təm,
nyaathúum,
kaa'íts athúum,
vanyaathíkəm.

He gave them (their tasks),
and there they were, and all of a sudden —
when white people say it,
(in) a family,
one (family member) among them might be bad.
I've heard them mention this.
I've heard them say it.
They talk about that too, they say.

"It will happen.
Whatever he does,
it won't be very good.
He is in (the family) and he might go bad.
He is in (the family) and what he does might be bad.
It will happen."
They say (that) too.

"So,
that's what you (should) look out for;
you must be careful,"
he said.
He said it again;
that's what he told them about,
(so that) they would keep an eye on this one.

The very last one,
the very small one,
here he was,
here he was.
This one came after (the others),
and here he was.

They understood that he was like that.

His body was fine,
and then,
something happened,
and here he was.

Athúum:
vatáyk,
'améek,
viiyáanyk viiyáaptəm —
'ayúunyk —
nyáanyi avathótk,
viiyáanyk
viiyáanyk.

Mattnyiitspéetk,
alyméetanək;
nyáanyənyts,
xeykóts nyáanyts *giant* a'ím a'ítya.

Nyáanyts avathótk a'étəma.
Avathótəm.
Nyáanya,
'Anykwatsáanənyts nyáany 'ashék;
Kwayúu 'a'étəma.

Vatáyk nyiináamk,
nyaayúu tsáamk ayúuk a'íikəm a'ím,
Kwayúu a'étk,
ashét.

Təm
vuuváatk;
nya'kútsk,
'atsnyaashuupáwk vanyuuváak,
nyáava.

Ava'áak vaa'é a'étk viithíitk,
makyí av'áw 'atsayúutk,
avathótk,
ava'áak;
"Vaathóxa," a'ét,
makyí av'áwk 'atsayúutk,
avathótk;
"Vathík," a'étk,
"Vathík, a'étk,
"Vaathótk uuváat."

It happened:
he became big,
he became tall,
he went on and on (growing) —
I've seen this before —
it happened there,
he went on
and on.

He was overwhelming,
he was really tall;
those (people),
those white people call them giants, they say.

That's what happened, they say.
It happened.
That (person),
we Quechans named him;
we called him Kwayúu (The One Who Sees).

He was extraordinarily big,
and he could see everything, they say,
(so) they called him Kwayúu,
they named him (that).

And
here he was;
he got older,
and he understood things,
this one.

He came walking this way like this,
and he stood somewhere and looked around,
he did that,
he walked;
"This is how it will be," he said,
and he stopped somewhere and looked around,
he did that;
"Here," he said,
"Here," he said,
"This is how things are."

Nyuuváavəly,
pa'iipáats siitháwəm,
nyáanya,
atháwk
asóotk a'étəma!

Asóotk uuváatk,
uuváaxáyk,
nyiithíkəm,
viiyáaxáyk.
Kwanymé awét!

Avathíkəm,
viiyáaxáyk,
kwanymé awétk!
Athótk vaa'étk uuváat.

Uuváatəm,
nyáavəts awíim.
Pa'iipáavəts vanyaatháwk,
mattáar alya'émək,
nyáava,
they fight against one another,
a'íim,
athótkəm a'íiny a'étəntima.
Athúum athúuk a'étəma.

Nyaathúum,
vanyuuváak.
***
Nyáavəts,
xavík aváts,
xaasa'íly tóly kwathík,
nyáava ayúu lya'émtəm áam.
Viithíik.

Nyiinyaav'áwəntim,
nyiiv'áwk viiv'áwəm ayúut.

He was around there,
and there were people over there,
and as for that one,
(Kwayúu) caught him,
and he ate him, they say!

He went about eating him,
he was still here, when suddenly,
(someone else) was there,
and (Kwayúu) went after him.
He did it to another one!

(Someone else) was there,
and (Kwayúu) went along,
and he did it to another one!
He kept doing this.

There he was,
he was the one who was doing it.
These people were there,
they didn't like each other,
these (people),
they fought against one another,
they say,
it happened, they say.
That's how it was, they say.

Then,
he was around there.
***
This one,
this brother of his,
the one that was in the middle of the ocean,
he couldn't see this (bad brother) at all.
And (the bad one) came.

He was standing there,
and (his brother) saw him standing there.

Nyaayúuk a'ím,
"Ma'uuláayəny!
Mattmatspéetanək ammuuváantəsh!
Máany nyayúum!
Mata'aaláaytánək mayáam!

" 'Ayúuk va'athík 'athútya.
Av'athíktəsáa,
makyík mathúntik ammuuváa alyma'émaxa!"

A'étk.
Pa'iipáa tsaqwérək vuunóom,
a'ávtəsáa,
makyíts ayúu lya'émətək;
láwaláw a'ím,
vaa'íim,
vathí ayúuk,
vathí ayúuk,
uuváanyk uuváany.

Nyiinyaakwévəm,
takavéktək,
viiyémək,
aváam.

Suuváatk,
suuváatənyk,
" 'Ayáantik,
'a'ávxa," nyaaly'íim,
nyáany,
nyáavəm vanyaathíintik.

Nyaaváantik,
pa'iipáa nyaatháwtəntim,
ayúutk avathíkəny.

Ayúutk viithíknyək,
a'íim,
"Ma'uuláayənyts nyiináamtanəm!
Muuváatəsáa,
makyík ma'iipáyk ammawínti alyma'émaxa!"

When he saw him, he said,
"How bad you are!
You are going too far with it!
I see you!
You go along destroying things!

"I am here watching.
(As long as) I am here,
you'll never act this way again!"

He said it.
Someone was speaking,
and (Kwayúu) heard it, but
he never saw anyone;
he turned his head from side to side,
he went like this,
he looked here,
and he looked here,
he went on and on.

When he failed (to see anyone),
he went back,
he went away,
and he got there.

There he was,
there he was, until
"I'll go back again,
and I'll listen," he thought,
and as for that,
at that (point), he came (back) again.

He got there again,
he caught (another) person,
and (his brother) was there watching.

He was here watching,
and he said,
"How extremely bad you are!
Here you are, but
you will never do (this) again as long as you live!"

A'étk,
vuunóom,
a'ávək;
vaa'íim,
ayúuny,
nyiirísh a'ét.
'Axály athíktək,
kwa'ítsəny,
ayúulya'ém;
nyiikwévəm.

Vanyuuváak,
siiyémtək;
siithík,
siithíkxayəm,
pa'iipáa —
maawíinyts,
antáy nyakó nyáanyts siitháw.
Aváamxayk —
nyaaváamək,
awéməly ashmátk.
Apátk,
xaavíly xiipántəkəm,
iimény 'axály tsanák,
apátk viithík.

Ashmátk viithík.

Ayóovk avatháwnyək,
a'íim,
" 'Eey!
Kamánəm!
Pa'iipáats mathíik avathíi'əsh!"
a'ét.

"Kamánək!" a'étk,
shamán vuunóonyk.
"Kaawíts makyím athíikpəm,
ma'íim,"
a'ét,
takavék apátk.

He said it,
he went on,
and (Kwayúu) heard him;
he went like this,
he looked,
(but) there was nobody there.
He was in the water,
the one who had said it,
and (Kwayúu) didn't see him;
it was no use.

He was around here,
and he went away;
he was over there,
he was over there, and suddenly,
people —
his relatives,
his mother and father were over there.
He got there, and suddenly —
when he got there,
he immediately went to sleep.
He lay down,
the river was nearby,
and he put his feet in the water,
and he lay down and lay there.

He lay there sleeping.

They were watching him,
and they said,
"Hey!
Get up!
Someone is coming after you!"
they said.

"Get up!" they said,
and they went about waking him up.
"Someone is coming from somewhere,
you say,"
he said,
and he lay back down.

Ayúutk,
"Avathíim,
nya'íiva!
Kamánk!" a'étk vuunóony.
Makyík a'ávəny.

Nyáava,
antsénvəts,
nyamáam,
nyaayáak a'íim,
nyaayúu,
kaawíts,
'axá xamóoləm a'ím,
xeykóts a'étəm,
'a'ávəny.
Xányts xamóolpəm 'ayúunyk.

Nyáany iithóm tapéttk a'étəma.

Iithóm nyaatapéttk,
'axány kavkyéwk,
xaavíly avány kavkyéwk,
viiyáatk athúuk a'ét.

Viiyáatk,
viiyáat.

Viiyáatəm,
"Kaawíts avathíik!"
a'íim,
" 'Ashuupáwəsh," a'étk,
"Avathíik!
Kamánək!" a'íim.
"Kamánək!" a'íim;
shamán vuunóo,
nyiikwév.

Amánək,
ayúuk,
nyaayúuny,

They looked around.
"He's coming,
I tell you!
Get up!" they went on saying.
He didn't pay any attention at all.

This one,
his older brother,
finally,
he went along,
well,
somehow,
the water is foamy, they say,
white people say it,
and I've heard them.
I've seen how foamy the water is.

He covered his face with that, they say.

He covered his face,
and he went upstream,
he went up that river,
and he went along, they say.

He went along,
and he went along.

He went along, and
"Something is coming!"
(his brother) said;
"I know it," he said.
"It's coming!
Get up!" he said.
"Get up!" he said;
he kept trying to get him up,
but it was no use.

He got up,
and he saw it,
(this) thing,

kaly'aaxwáayəny,
'axály atápk vaawétk awét.
"Kaawíts makyém athíikpa,
ma'ím,
nyiiríish a'ím viitháwk athópəka."

"Athúum,
nya'íiva!" a'íim,
uukanáavək vuunóony,
nyiikwévəm.

Apátk alyaskyíitk.

Nyaathíkəm,
nyáanyi,
kaawémək —
makyém 'athíik 'athúm,
nyiinyatséwk,
nyiinyaapáx.

Nyáanya,
vathány,
nyáanya,
Nyi'anykwatséwənyts,
ayóov alya'éməts
kaly'aaxwáayəny.

Nyaata'úlyk,
'avíiny uushák,
vaawé nyaawíim,
vaawíim.
Xaavíly atséwk,
alytsatsénm athúuk a'étəma,
xaasa'ílya.

"Vathány,
xaavílyəny,
Kwaxwétt-ts a'íim,
maapa'iipáany nyam'axóttk,"
nyaa'ím,
nyuuváa.

his war club,
and he threw it into the water like this.
"Someone is coming from somewhere,
you say,
(but) there is nothing there."

"There is,
I am telling you!" he said,
and he kept on telling him,
but it was no use.

(Kwayúu) continued to lie there.

He lay there,
and at that (point),
somehow —
we came from somewhere, and so,
we were created,
and we were placed there.

As for that,
this one,
that one,
our Creator,
what he didn't see
(was) the war club.

He carried it,
and he stuck it into the rock,
he went like this, and then,
he went like this.
He created the river,
and he made it go down, they say,
into the ocean.

"As for this,
the river,
it's called the Colorado (River),
and it is good for you people,"
(that's what) he said,
as he was there.

"Nyiimuuváat,
'axá maa'úurək.

"A'íim,
nyiinyaauupáxts athótəm athúum.

"Kaawíts makyém athíik,
avathúwúm,"
nyaa'ét,
takavék apátk a'étəma.
"Nyáany avathúuk,
avathúu kwa'átstəsáa."

"Kaawíts kamathúum muuváam?
Nyáany athótəm,
'ayúutəm,
nyaayúunyts 'axótt alya'ém tan,"
nyaa'íim,
a'ávəx áar alya'émək;
apátk ashmátk;
nyiikwév,
atháwatanəm,
ashmát.

Ashmátk athótk,
viithíkəm.

"Avathíik,
nyaaxiipánəm,
nya'íiva!"

A'íim,
shamánək vuunóony,
nyiikwévtək,
ashmáam viithíkəm.

Nyamkwatsuumpáp,
nyamaváamək,
iimé taxpályk,
xály kavathúuntək a'étəma.

"There you are,
you are on the edge of the water.

"So,
I have placed you here.

"Someone is coming from somewhere,
and (something) might happen,"
he said,
and he lay back down, they say.
"That (might) happen,
it (might) happen, just as you said. "

"What are you doing?
It is happening,
I see it,
and things don't look very good,"
he said,
and (his brother) didn't want to listen;
he lay down and went to sleep;
it was no use;
(sleep) just took him,
and he went to sleep.

He slept,
lying here.

"He's coming,
he's nearby,
I tell you!"

He said it,
he tried to wake him up,
but it was no use;
(Kwayúu) lay there sleeping.

The fourth (time),
(his brother) got there,
and he pulled on his legs,
and he submerged them in the water, they say.

Vathúunək,
lóləl/əl awétk.
Vuuthíit.
Vuuthíixaym,
'axányts aráawəm ám,
uukavék.
Vuuthíinyk,
vuuthíiny.

Vuuthíim,
"Matsaváam mathúum.
Mawíim,
matt'atspéenypatk 'athútya,"
a'ét.

" 'Ashuumáany nyi'náam.
Nyi'anymuukáamxats athúulya'éməxa,"
a'étəm.

"Kaváarxa.
Mamánənti 'a'íim 'a'íim 'awíi aly'a'émək,
'awé'əsh,"
a'étapatk,
vuuthíit.

Vanyuuthíim,
nyáanyi,
kam'úly.
Iiwáam alynyiinyaathúutsk,
malyaxúuyk.
***
uunóok aavíirək.
Nyaayúu,
athúm,
ayérək atspámxalyk a'étk,
alynyiinyaathúuts.

Nyáavi nyaathík,
nyáavi malyxóny vaawíim,
vaa'íim.
Vaawé a'íim,
nyáanyəm.

They were submerged,
and they made (the water) bubble.
He brought him this way.
He brought him this way, and suddenly
the water ran very fast,
and it took him back again.
He brought him this way,
and he brought him this way.

He brought him this way.
"You can't do it.
You are doing it, (but)
I am powerful too,"
(Kwayúu) said.

"My dreams are powerful.
You can never defeat me,"
he said.

"It won't happen.
I am not going to let you get up again,
I am doing it,"
(his brother) said in turn,
and he brought him along.

He brought him along,
and at that (point),
(Kwayúu) struggled.
On his own, using his powers of thought,
he grew wings,
***
he went on and finished.
Well,
so,
he wanted to fly out away,
he was thinking about it.

He lay here,
he went like this with his wings,
he went like this.
He went like this,
with those (wings).

'Amáttəny,
viikwaváts vatháts,
'axáyxayíi,
amányk kaathómtəm awétk awím,
nyáanyəm —
malyxóny vaawé nyaa'íim,
nyáanyts
nyiitháawtək a'étəma.

*** *** ***

Nyáany awíim,
malyxóny vaawé nyaa'íim,
alyaskyíik nyiitháawtək a'étəma.

Alyaskyíik,
'avíinyi vaa'étk
athótəm.

Athótk,
nyiitháawtəm.
***

Viithíitəntik,
makyí atspám a'ély,
kaa'íim,
'axányts vaa'íim,
athúum,
nyiisáttk,
'axáyxayətəm,
nyáava,
mattmanyúuvtanək vanyuuváak,
amánək.

Athúum,
kaathómək vanyaayáak,
nyiinák,
nyaathúum.

The ground,
this (surface) here,
it must have been wet,
and it shriveled up somehow, and so,
at that (point) —
he went like this with his wings,
and those (imprints that he made)
are still there, they say.

*** *** ***

That's what he did,
he went like this with his wings,
and (the imprints) are still there, they say.

They are still (there),
they are in the rock, like this,
they are.

It happened,
and there they are.
***

He was coming this way again,
he wanted to get out of wherever he was,
and somehow,
the water was like this,
and so,
it had drained away there,
(but) it was still wet,
and as for this,
he was really struggling,
and he got up.

So,
somehow he went along,
and he sat down there,
he did.

Nyáanyi nyiinákəm,
awíim,
thúutt a'íim,
uunaxwílyk,
xály nyaa-áaptəntim.

Nyáanyts alyarúvk aly'avíik,
alyaskyíitəntik a'étəma.

Alyaskyíitəntim,
nyáany,
Kwayúu Iiwéy Atáp a'íim,
ashém athúuk a'étəma.
Ám,
athúum,
nyiitháawəm,
mayúuk;
pa'iipáats 'axáyəm nyiinák athúuk kwalyavíitk a'étəntima.

Athótəm,
atháwk,
vuuthíinyk,
vuuthíinyk,
viiwáamk,
viiwáamk,
viiwáam.

Viiwáamk,
xaasa'íly nyáasi nyaakamémək.

Nyamnyaapúyəm.

Malyxó nyáanyts vatátsk iináam.
Nyáavəts ashtúum,
uutsamóq vuunóok,
nyaavíirək.

Nyaayúu atséwk a'étəma —
kaathúts?
Kaawíts *teepee* a'étəntik,

He sat down there,
and so,
(his brother) tried harder,
he dragged him,
and he threw him into the water again,

That (place) was dried up and turned to stone,
and (the imprint) is still (there) too, they say.

It is still (there),
and as for that,
they call it Where Kwayúu Was Thrown Down On His Butt,
they named it, and so it is, they say.
Well,
it happened,
there it is,
and you've seen it;
it's as if a person had sat down where it was wet, they say.

So,
he caught him,
and he brought him,
and he brought him,
he kept on going,
and going,
and going.

He kept on going,
and he brought him to that distant ocean.

That's where he died.

Those wings were very big.
These (people) picked them up,
they went on pulling the feathers out,
and they finished.

They made something (out of them), they say —
what is it?
It's something called a teepee,

'a'ávənyk —
nyáany uutsáawk,
vaawíny,
tasháttk vuunóonyk aavíirək,
alyathík viithík.

Pa'iipáa Nyi'anykwatséwənyts ayúuk vanyaavák a'ím,
ayúulya'émas a'étka.

"Ma'uutsaláaytsəny!
Malyuuvév mathútya!
Máany,
muuwéxats,
'atsmatuupúyxənyts,
matapúyəm 'a'íi ly'a'ém!

"Mawétk mawítya.
Nyaamawíim,
maaxuuvíkəly,
matsláaytsək mathótk mathúum,
makyík 'amátt vathí muunóo alyma'éməxa!"

Nyaa'íim,
nyaayúuk
nyáany.
'Akwé vatháts matt-tsapéek,
nyíily tan,
nyiináaaam a'ím.

Athúm,
nyiiyúutk viithíkəm,
nyaayúu.

Uuráv aványa,
nyaayúu atséwk,
nyáanyəm aaqwéttk,
'axányily vaawíi vuunóok,
nyaayúu tsáam ta'aaláayk.
Nyáasi tapúytapatk a'étəma.

I've heard of it —
that's what they made,
they went like this,
they stood the wings upright and they finished,
and he lay there inside.

Our Creator was watching, they say,
although he didn't see it, they say.

"How bad you are!
You are both the same!
As for you,
it's what you would do,
it's your urge to kill things,
and I don't want you to kill things!

"You did it.
Whatever you did,
the two of you,
you did it because you are bad,
and you will never come to this place again!"

When he said it,
he looked
at that.
There were a lot of these clouds,
they were really black,
and they were slowly passing by.

So,
as he lay there watching them,
(those) things.

That lightning,
he made it into something,
and he struck them with it,
he was doing this in the water,
and it destroyed everything.
Over there in the distance it killed him too, they say.

Apatəm,
nyamáam,
nyáanyi íimtəm,
tək athúuk a'étəma.

Athótəm,
nyáava vaathúum,
vuuwíts nyáava.
Pa'iipáavəts —
nyiikwatháawk,
ayúuk vanyaatháwk,
nyáavi tsaamánək,
mattaashuuqwéttk,
mattnyiáar alya'ém,
matt-tapúytək awíik a'étəma.
Shiitamúuly mattáar alya'émk;
kwanyméts siivám,
mattáar alya'ém.

A'étk,
nyiixwáaytək,
nyáava athúu va'áarək athúuk a'étəma.

Athúum,
a'íim,
nyáava vaa'íim.
Kanáavtəma.
Kanáavək vuuthíitəma.

(It killed him), too,
and that's all,
it came to an end there,
it did, they say.

So,
it was like this,
this thing that he did.
The people —
the (people) that were there,
they were looking,
and starting here,
they spoke against each other,
they didn't like each other,
and they killed each other, they say.
The tribes didn't like each other;
if a different tribe was over there,
they didn't like them.

So,
they made war with them,
they used to do that, they say.

It happened,
they say,
this is what they say.
They tell about it.
They tell about it and bring it (to its conclusion).

Púk Atsé

Told by Rosita Carr

Pa'iipáats nyaváyk siivám,
makyíny,
Púk Atsé a'étəma.
Púk Atsé.

Nyáany nyaváyk siivák,
vatsíim xavíkt.
Kwalyavíita.
Vatsíim.

Viiványək,
siitháwk,
siitháwxayk,
kaa'émantik a'ím,
kaváayk a'étantik a'ím,
kaváayk,
pa'iipáa aaéevək —
kaawítsíi,
maawíi,
kaawítsk awíi a'ím.

A'ím,
siivám,
xa—
   vatsíinyts 'axá ayáak a'étəma.
'Axá ayáak.

Kwaly'ó ta'úlyk,
viiyáak;
'axáts siithíkəm,
alyváamk,
nyaasa—
nyaapó kaa'émk,
viithíi a'ím,

Someone was living there,
and whoever it was,
he was called Púk Atsé, they say.
Púk Atsé.

He was living over there,
he was with his daughter.
It was something like that.
With his daughter.

Here he was,
there they were,
they were over there, and suddenly,
for some reason,
they decided to go from house to house,
and they went from house to house,
inviting people —
perhaps they were going to do something,
for their relatives,
they were going to do something.

So,
there he was,
and water —
his daughter went to get water, they say.
She went to get water.

She carried a pottery jar,
and she went along;
the water was over there,
and she got there,
and over there,
somehow she put (water) into (the pot),
and she was about to come back,

siiv'áwxaym,
pa'iipáats katánmətək a'ím,
" 'Axá nyiinykáaym,
'asítsú."

A'étxay,
"Kaváartək."
'Atáyəm apótk athúm.
"Kaváar," a'étxayəm,
mashtaráts a'íi kaa'émtək awím,
tatapóoyvək a'étəma.

*** *** ***

Nyaatatapóoyk,
vaanayémtək,
vaanayémtək athúm,
vanyaanayém,
vathány,
nyaayúuts,
Talypóts,
'axáasíi a'ím siithíik.

Siithíixayk,
ayúutk.
Avathíkəm,
'axá kwaa'úurəny nyaatsamíim,
ka'ák ka'ák awét,
tamáar təsáa,
thomayúutəny.

***

Nyaayúutk,
vanyaavák,
viiyáak.

Viiyáak,
nyaaváamək,
kanáavk.

she was standing over there, when all of a sudden,
some people got there and said,
"Give us some water,
and we'll drink."

They said it, and immediately,
"No," (she said).
She had put a lot of water (in the pot).
"No," she said, and all of a sudden,
they must have gotten angry, and so,
they killed her, they say.

*** *** ***

When they killed her,
they left,
they left, and so,
when they left,
at this (point),
somebody,
it was Roadrunner,
he came from what they call salt water.

He was coming from over there, and suddenly,
he saw her.
She was lying there,
they had laid her at the edge of the water,
they had gone kick, kick,
and they had partially buried her, but
she was still visible.

***

He saw her,
here he was,
and he went off.

He went off,
and when he got there,
he told them.

Kanáavtəs,
iiyáa shatmatháavək a'étəntima.
iiyáa uu'áav aly'ém.

Iiyáa uu'áv aly'ém.
Shatmatháavət.

Təm
uukanáavtək,
pa'iipáa nyáanya,
kwar'ákəny ashétk.

"Púk Atsé —
vatsíits apúyk,"
a'étəs,
"Nyá nyá,
nyá nyá,
nyá nyá."
'Atsa'ítsk avák:
"Póoy!
Póoy!"
a'épətəm a'ávəny.

Nyáany ava'étk siivát.

Siivátkəm,
kaawíts a'étəs,
iiyáa uu'áavək,
shtuupáaw alya'ém.

Sanyaatháwk,
kaawíts ayáak a'étəma.
Kaawíts ayáak;
Kwash'iilá a'étk,
kwalyavíitəma.

Kwash'iilá nyáany ayáak,
kamíim.

He told them, but
they didn't know his language, they say.
They didn't understand his language.

They didn't understand his language.
They didn't know it.

And
he explained it to them,
those people,
and he mentioned the old man by name.

"Púk Atsé —
his daughter is dead,"
he tried to say, but
"Nyá nyá
nyá nyá
nyá nyá," (is what they heard).
He was saying things:
"Póoy!
Póoy!"
(that's what) they heard him say.

That's what he was saying.

There he was, and so,
he might have said something, but
they didn't understand his language,
they didn't know it.

There they were,
and they went after someone, they say.
They went after someone;
he was called Mockingbird,
(his name) was something like that.

They went after that Mockingbird,
and they brought him back.

*** *** ***

Kamíim,
a'íi viivám,
shamathíitəntík a'étəma.
Shamathíitəntík.

Shamathíitəntik.
"Kaa'émək viivák?" a'ítya.

A'étk,
vanyuunóotəm,
pa'iipáa tsuuqwér xáam uu'ítsapat.
Nyáany ayáak,
kaméxayəm,
shtuupáaw alya'ém.

Vuunóotənyk,
nyaa kwar'ák nyáava,
nyáanya,
ayáak a'étəma.

Pa'iipáany nyiikanáavəm,
"Katsawém,
kawétsk katsaváwk,
'atskamuunóotanək,
kavuuthíik katsatspátsk!"

Alyvák siivám,
nyáavəm.

Tsatspátsk,
a'íi kwa'átsk vuunóom,
shuupáwk a'étəma.

" 'Avatsíits apúyk,
a'ím.
Kanáavək viivák,
nyaa'íiva," a'ét.

*** *** ***

They brought him back,
and (Roadrunner) was saying it,
and (Mockingbird) didn't know (what he was saying).
He didn't know either.

He didn't know either.
"What is he saying?" he said.

So,
here they were,
and he said it again in a different kind of human speech.
They went after those (other people),
and when they brought them back,
they didn't know either.

Here they were,
and this old man,
he was the one,
they went and got him, they say.

He told the people,
"Take him out,
and put him down,
you guys are just hanging around,
bring him out here!"

(Roadrunner) was in there,
at this (point).

They brought him out,
and he was saying just what he had said,
and (the old man) knew what he was saying, they say.

"My daughter is dead,
he says.
He is telling about it,
that's what he's saying," (the old man) said.

A'étəm,
aayáatk,
kamétk;
uutara'úy 'ím a'ítya.
Uutara'úyk.

Nyaavíirək,
" 'Axwé,
'axwé 'aayáatapatxa,"
a'ím.

Nyáa kwawítsa.

Nyiitatapóoyapat a'ím.

'Atskanyaatháwk awím,
vaayáak a'étəm ám.
Pa'iipáanyts 'atáyk a'étk,
viitháwkəm.

Vaayáak,
nyáasi —
kaawíts?
'ats'iipáy xáam kwathútsənyts —
"Nyáasi 'ashmáxa,"
a'étxay —
Maamathíits a'éxayk,
 "Nyaayúu,
'a'íi paly'ón kwalypáa nyáasi 'aashmátsxa,"
a'étk a'étəntima.
Xáam uu'íts.

*** *** ***

Nyaa'étəntik,
vaayáatk.

Vaayáatk,
nyaayúu Maxwáa a'étəma.

So,
they went after her,
and they brought her back;
they were going to prepare her (for cremation), they say.
They prepared her.

When they finished,
"The enemy,
we will go after the enemy,"
they said.

(They meant) the ones who had done that.

They were going to kill them in turn.

(People) were around in various places, and so,
they were going to go after the enemy.
There were a lot people, they say,
here they were.

They went along,
and over there in the distance —
which one was it?
they were all different kinds of creatures —
"I'll sleep over there,"
he said, and immediately —
Owl said it, and immediately,
"Well,
we'll sleep over there in the tree stump,"
they said in turn.
(Each one) wanted something different.

*** *** ***

When they were ready to go again,
off they went.

Off they went.
and (one) creature was Badger, they say.

Maxwáa nyáanyáanyts,
nyáanyts,
kaawíts ta'úlyk a'étəntim,
áa,
'aavé a'ét kwalyavíit.
'Aavé.
Áa.

Nyáany awíim,
viiwáak,
nyáany,
nyiikw'aváy nyáasi,
'avuuyáak atápəm,
pa'iipáa tsakyíwəly a'íi kaa'émk awíim a'ítya.
Nyaawíim,
vaayáak apámk a'étəma.

Nyaapámkəm,
nyiitatapóoyk a'étəma,
kwanyváaynya,
pa'iipáa nyaakwawítsnya.
Shuupáwk wór a'ím a'ítya.

Nyaatatpóoyk,
" 'Anyáats 'atatapóoyk!"
Sanya'ákəny awí lya'émtək a'étəma.
Nyamxuuvíka.

Nyaawíi lya'émxayəm,
xuunmárəts pa'iipáyxaytəntik a'étəma.

Piinapáyxaytəm,
nyáanya,
tapúy a'étk vuunóoxayəm —
kaawítsk atápk awím,
awéxayəm —
vaan'é a'étk,
vathík avátsk,
vaa'é a'étk,
vathík avátsk,
athótəm,
makyík kaawém aly'ém.

That Badger,
he was the one,
he was carrying something,
yes,
it seemed to be what they call a snake.
A snake.
Yes.

He did that,
he brought it,
that (snake),
and over there where (the enemy) was living,
he threw it toward their door,
he did it so that it would bite people, they say.
Then,
they went along and got there, they say.

When they got there,
they killed them, they say,
the ones who lived there,
the people who had done it.
They knew for certain (that they were the ones), they say.

When they killed them,
"We killed them!" (they said).
But they didn't kill the woman, they say.
His wife.

They didn't do it, and suddenly,
(they saw that) a newborn baby was still alive, too, they say.

He was newly born,
that (baby),
and they were trying to kill him, and suddenly —
they threw something at him,
they did, and suddenly —
he went like this,
and here he was;
he moved back,
and here he was;
and so,
they never were able to do anything to him.

Kaawém aly'émək,
nyaayúu,
'a'áw taráak,
alytsaváwxayəm,
uuv'áwk,
tsúu a'étəm,
makyík apúy alya'émətək a'étəma.

Apúy alya'émtəm.

Nyaayóovək,
"Aaíiməm 'antamákəm,
viivány,
matsáam apúytəxa."

Nyaa'étk,
natuumáak a'étəma.

Nyiaantamáak,
xuumára,
nyiaantuumáak.

'Aankóoyts siivántik a'éta.
Xuumárəny namáwəts.

Nyiivántik,
nyáanyts,
nyáanyts xweyamántək avathík a'étəma.

Akyáam,
akyétstəsáa,
apúy aly'émk a'étəma.

Apúy lya'émtəm.
nyaayúuk,
xuumár aváts,
'atsshatamátstəkəm,
kaathóm,
nyamáam,
vanyaayáak,

They weren't able to do anything to him,
well,
they lit a fire,
and they put him in it, and immediately,
it (started to) rain,
(the rain) poured down,
and he never did die, they say.

He didn't die.

When they saw this,
"We'll leave him to do as he pleases,
and he (will) sit here,
and he will starve to death."

They said it,
and they left him, they say.

They left him there,
the child,
they left him there.

A little old lady was over there, they say.
She was the child's grandmother.

She was there too,
and she was the one,
she was lying there unconscious, they say.

Someone had shot her,
they had shot her, but
she wasn't dead, they say.

She wasn't dead,
and when he saw that,
this child.
he had dreams (which gave him power),
somehow,
and that's all,
he went,

'iipány uulyók atháwtək,
'aankóoyəny kwakyétsa.

***

Aa,
uulyók atháwtk.

Vuunóotk aavíirtəm,
xótt-tək a'étəma.

Nyaa'xóttkəm.

'Aakóoyənyts nyaatháwk,
xuumárəny nyaatháwk,
kaawíts kanathíitapatk,
siitháwtək athúuk a'étəma.

Siitháwtəm,
nyáava,
sanya'ákəva,
nyaatháwk,
vanyaawáak.

Nyáa vatsíi apúy nyáanyts;
nyamxavík a'étəntima.
Nyamxavík.

Tək
siitháwtək athúm,
xótt-təntim.
Iiwáa 'aláay aly'ém.

***

Siitháwtək,
təm,
'aakóoyts,
kaalwíts awétk vanyuunóok,
uunakwílytək.

and he pulled the arrow out,
(out of) the old lady who had been shot.

***

Yes,
he pulled it out.

He went on and finished,
and she was all right, they say.

She was all right.

The old lady took him,
she took the child,
and they came along doing whatever it was,
and there they were, they say.

There they were,
and as for this one,
this woman,
(Púk Atsé) took her,
he took her.

She was (taking the place of) his dead daughter;
and they were together, they say.
They were together.

And,
there they were, and so,
he was all right again.
He didn't feel bad (any more).

***

There they were over there,
and (meanwhile),
the old lady,
she was using little things,
and making a little cradle.

Aanakwílyk,
aanaxwílyk,
kaawítsk aaxwílyəm a'ítya.
Nyaaxwílyk.

Kaawíts xalykwáak kuu'éeytək,
tsuumátsxa.

Xalykwáak kuu'éeytəm,
xáyəm,
shamée kaa'émk,
amíi viithíkxáyəm
nyaayúuts atháwk a'étəntima.

Nyaayúuts aváak atháwk.
Xam'uulól.

Xam'uulól nyáanyts aváak atháwtək,
ava'étk,
nanamíilk a'íi kaa'émk,
lóləl lóləl a'étk vuunóotxayəm,
'aakóoyəny nyaaváak,
xam'uulóləny tatapóoyk a'ét.
Masharáyk.

Nyaatatpóoyk,
xuumárənyts amíim a'étəntima.
Wanyəmnyaavárəntik.
Áa-áa,
wanymaavárəntik.

Amíim siivám,
nyaayúuk,
awíi lya'émək táamək a'étəntima.

Namák 'atsknyaayém.
Suuváaxayk,
xuumárənyts,
iiwáam ayáatk —
nyaayúu 'uutíish anawéeytsəm,
kaawíts akyétk amátk,

She made a little cradle,
and she pulled it along behind her,
and she propped it against something, they say.
She propped it up.

She did her best to hunt for something,
so that they could eat.

She did her best to hunt,
and right away,
somehow the baby missed her,
he lay there crying, and suddenly
creatures were there, they say.

Creatures got there and there they were.
Crickets.

Those crickets got there and there they were,
and they said something,
they tried to comfort the child somehow,
they were going chirp chirp,
and when the old lady got there,
she killed the crickets, they say.
She was angry.

When she killed them,
the child cried, they say.
He had liked them.
Yes,
he had liked them.

He was crying,
and she saw (this),
and she didn't do it any more, they say.

She left him and went off to various places.
There he was, and all of a sudden,
the child,
he went off on his own —
she had made a little thing like a bow for him,
and he shot something and ate it,

amátk awétk,
amátstək a'étəntima.

Asóotstək.

Siitháwtək,
siitháwtənyək,
nyáanyəm,
pa'iipáa kwa'atsláytsənyts tsapéenypatk a'étəma,
nyakóra.

Pa'iipáa kaawíts a'étəm ám.
Ashiittəma.

Kwayúu a'étk,
pa'iipáats avuuváatəntik,
'atsathóshk a'étəntik,
'Aakóoy Kaa'íts avuuváak,
Mattkwashtaxathúuk,
'Aakóoy Mattkwashtaxathúuk a'étəma.

"Nyáanya,
nyaakwayúuk,
sakyínyk!" a'ím.

"Matapúyúm," a'ím,
'aankóoyənyts uukanáavək.

'Atsxalykwáak uuváamk,
iiwáam,
nyaayúu uumáxany nyaaxalykwáantik vuuváak.

A'étəm,
a'ávtəs,
avathík;
sakyíny alya'émək a'étəma.

Sakyíny alya'émək,
siiv'áwəm,
vathíi kwa'átsk a'étəma.
'Aakóoyəts,
vathíi kwa'áts.

he ate it,
they (both) ate it, they say.

They (both) ate it.

There they were,
there they were,
and at that (point),
there were a lot of bad people, they say,
long ago.

She mentioned certain people.
She listed them by name.

(One of them) was called Kwayúu (The One Who Sees),
and there was also someone (else),
she carried things on her back, they say,
Old Lady Something-or-Other was around somewhere,
Flesh-Ripper,
Old Lady Flesh-Ripper, they say.

"As for that one,
anyone who sees her,
(had better) run away!" she said.

"She will kill you," she said,
the little old lady told (the child) about her.

He was hunting for things,
by himself,
he was hunting for things to eat.

She said it,
and he heard her, but
there he was;
he didn't run away, they say.

He didn't run away,
he stood (his ground),
and she came along, just as he had been told, they say.
The Old Lady,
she came along, just as he had been told.

Vathíi kwaʹátsk,
vaawé aʹétk atháwk,
uuthóshk alytsaváwət aʹétəma.
Uuthóshkəny.

Nyaatsaváwk,
viiwáamk;
viiyáak,
"Kaʹwém tanək ʹatapúyəly" aʹíi viiyáak —
ʹatsuuthóshkəny tapómək aʹétəma.

Nyaatapómək,
atspámək.

Nyaatspám,
ʹaakóoyənyts apómtək,
apúytək aʹétəma.

***

Áa-áa,
nyáanyənyts.

Nyaapúyəm,
viiyémk aváamək,
kanáavək,
namáwnya,
uukanáav.

"Avʹawéʹəsh," aʹíim,
ʹaakóoyəny uukanáav.

"Matháwk,
nyaamatapúy aʹíim,
nyaathúuva.
Avathíkəntik,
paʹiipáa ʹatsláytsəts,"
aʹíim,
uukanáavək.

She came along, just as he had been told,
and she caught him like this,
and she put him into her bundle, they say.
(Into) her bundle.

She put him (into her bundle),
and off she went;
she went along,
she went along wondering, "How can I kill him?" —
and she burned her bundle, they say.

When she burned it,
he escaped.

He escaped,
and the Old Lady burned,
and she died, they say.

***

Yes,
she was the one.

When she died,
he went (home) and got there,
and he told her about it,
his grandmother,
he told her about it.

"I did this," he said,
and he told the old woman about it.

"She took you,
and she was going to kill you,
that's for certain.
There are (other ones) too,
bad people,"
she said,
and she told him about them.

Uukanáavəm,
a'áv alya'emək,
viiyáatəntik.
Viiyáatəntik.

Viiyáaxayəm —
kaawíts?
kaa'émək ashíit? —
'amáyɫy siivák,
nyáanyts,
Iiyáam Kwakáap a'íik a'émtəma.
Kaawíts athúm a'ítya.

Nyáanyts,
atháw a'étk,
anyíilyəqətəntík a'étəm,
tsanapéevtəm.

Anyíilyqətəxayəm,
ayúu tank,
vathíi ayúuk viiwáamək,
makyím,
matásh alya'éməm,
 nyaayúuk,
nyáanya,
kaawíts atséwəntik,
'íi!
kaa'émək awím:
uutssúlyk atspámk a'étəntima.

Nyaatspámək,
vatháts apúytəntik,
pa'iipáavəts.

***

Nyaathúum,
siiyáaxayəm,
nyaayúuts awétəntík a'étəma.
'Ashpáa.

She told him,
but he didn't listen,
and he went along again.
He went along again.

He was going along, and all of a sudden —
what was it?
what's his name? —
he was up in a high place,
he was the one,
he was called Iiyáam Kwakáap, they say.
He did something, they say.

He was the one,
he caught (the boy),
and he swallowed him, they say,
because he was so little.

He swallowed him, and immediately,
(the boy) looked around,
he went along looking;
and someplace,
(the tissue) was not thick,
and when he saw it,
that (place),
he made (a weapon),
and gee!
he did it somehow:
he ripped through it and he escaped again, they say.

He escaped,
and this one died too,
this person.

***

Then,
he was going along there, when suddenly
a creature did it again, they say.
It was an eagle.

'Ashpáa nyáanyts,
'avíily sata'ótsəts siitháwəm,
siivám,
siiyáantim;
viiyémək.
'Anyáa kwashíintəm,
athótk,
kwalyavíitəma.

Nyiitháaw a'íim,
viiyáaxayəm,
kashák!
Atháwət a'íikətama,
'ashpáanyányts.

Nyaatháwk,
sata'óts nyáanyts uusáav a'íim nyiitsamíim.

Nyiitsamíim,
a'ím,
'iipáyk,
niwaníw a'éxayəm,
mashtatháav.

Mashtatháavək,
uusáav aly'émək a'étəntima.

Uusáav aly'émək,
siitháwxaym,
kaawémtəntík:
tatpóoyk a'étəma.
Tatpóoyk.

Nyaavíirəntik,
viiyémk,
'aakóoyəny uukanáavək vuunóok a'étəma.

"Ka'wémək,
pa'iipáa 'atsláyts muu'ítsəny,
'tapóoyk va'uunóok," a'éta.

That eagle,
(she and) her babies were there on the mountain,
she was there,
and (the boy) was going along;
and (the eagle) left.
Every day,
it happened,
it was something like that.

There they were, and so,
(the boy) was going along, and all of a sudden
she grabbed him with her talons!
She caught him, they say,
that eagle (did).

She caught him,
and she put him down so those babies could eat him.

She put him down there,
and so,
he was alive,
he was wiggling, and immediately,
they were afraid of him.

They were afraid of him,
and they didn't eat him, they say.

They didn't eat him,
there they were,
and somehow he did it again:
he killed them, they say.
He killed them.

Once again, when he was finished,
he went home,
and he told the old lady about it, they say.

"Somehow,
these bad people you told me about,
I am killing them off," he said.

A'íim,
"Yaamakuupéttənyts tamatháavtək," a'íim,
wanyiiráv kuu'éeyk suunóo.

Vuunóom,
suuváanyk,
siiyáantixáyəm,
nyáanya —
kaa'émək 'ashéxa? —
ayúum.
Kwayúu a'étəma.
Pa'iipáa vatáyəts athúum a'ítya,
nyáanyts.

'Axály avátəntik uuvátk a'étəma.
'Axály —
xaatspáay,
kaawíts.

Alyvátəntík uuvát,
vanyaayáak,
alyvakaméek ayúu.

Ayúum.

"Ka'a'émək?" a'étəma.

"Ka"émək?"
"Viikayémək," a'íi.

Kaa'ém tan,
nyiiv'áwk,
uutíishəny tsa'úlytək awím,
akyáam 'ím,
ava'áwk a'étəma.

Nyaakyáam.

Vuunóoxayəly,
atháwk a'étəma.

So,
"Your craziness makes (things) difficult," she said,
and she went about scolding him as best she could, poor thing.

She went on,
and there he was,
he was still going after (bad people), and suddenly,
that one —
what do we call him? —
he saw him.
He is called Kwayúu (The One Who Sees).
He was a very big person, they say,
that (Kwayúu).

He was there in the water, they say.
In the water—
in a well,
or something.

He was sitting in it,
and (the boy) went,
and he stood at the edge (of the water) and looked.

He saw him.

"How can I do it?" he said.

"How can I do it?"
"Go away," (Kwayúu) said.

Somehow (the boy) managed to do it,
he stood there,
he held his bow in his hand, and so,
he was going to shoot him,
he was standing there, they say.

He shot him.

There they were, and suddenly,
(Kwayúu) caught him, they say.

Nyaatháwəntik,
nyáany,
kaawíts athótk athúm,
'amáy takxávək a'étəma.

Nyáanyts atsénək,
pa'iipáa atháwk,
viiwémək
nyáasily.

Sanyts'áak uutséts tsuumpápk a'étəma.

Tsuumpápk,
'amáy alythík aatsuumpáp alyatháwk,
a'étəma.

Alyatháwəm.

Nyáany nyaakamémk,
tapúyk,
tarúvək,
aax'ák.
Kanyaa'íim,
kamémxayk,
alyúlytsək,
nyáanyts,
kwatsuumpáp nyáanyənyts.

Shuuvíim,
asóo av'áarək.

Asóo av'árək suuváak awíim,
xuumár vathány atháwk,
viiwémtək a'étəma.

Vanyaawémk,
apáav a'ím a'étəma.

Apáav a'ím.
"Kawítsk," a'ítsəm,
awítsxayəly,
avathótəntik.

He caught him,
that (boy),
and he did something, and so,
he took him up into the sky, they say.

He was the one who came down,
and caught people,
and took them away
to that distant (place).

There were four women that he put there, they say.

There were four of them,
they were in the four levels of heaven,
they say.

There they were.

He brought those (people) there,
and he killed them,
and he dried (their flesh),
he hung it up.
Sometimes,
he brought them, and immediately,
they cooked them,
those (women did),
those four (women did).

They made them into gravy,
and he ate them.

He ate them, and so,
he took this child,
he took him there, they say.

He took him there,
and he was going to have him roasted, they say.

He was going to have him roasted.
"Do it," he said,
and while they were trying to do it,
it happened again.

Tsanapéevxáyəm,
awítsəm,
awíim,
tapúy a'íim,
vatsuuváarək.

Nyaalyavíitəntik a'étəma.
'A'áw taráaxáyəly,
uuv'áwtəm,
atspátstək.

Awétk a'étəntíma.

Awétəntím,
kaawémk,
tapúy a'ím vuunóonyk,
nyaavatsuuváarək.

A'ím
ayúut uuváanyək,
"Apúytəxa,"
nyaa'étk
antuumáaktək a'étəma.

Antuumáaktsəm,
nyaayúu,
xaym,
'a'íi kaawíts ayáatk,
kaawíts a'ítstəm,
suuváatk.

Suuváatnyək,
"Ka'athóm tank?
'Atakavék 'atsénəlya,"
a'étk,
alynyiithúutsk suuváak a'étəma.

Sanyuuváak.

***

Sanyuuváanyk,
nyaayúu nyáany,

(The boy) was small, and right away,
they did it,
and so,
they tried to kill him,
and they failed.

It was like that (other time), they say.
While they were trying to start the fire,
it started to rain,
and he escaped.

He did it again, they say.

He did it again,
and somehow,
they went on trying to kill him,
and they failed.

So,
they were watching him;
"He will die,"
they said,
and they let him go, they say.

They let him go,
and, well,
right away,
he went to get wood or whatever,
(he did) whatever they said,
there he was.

There he was, and eventually,
"How can I do it?
"I want to go back down,"
he said,
and he thought about it, they say.

There he was.

***

There he was, and eventually,
those creatures,

pa'iipáa tuupúy kwarúv nyáany,
sanyts'áak vatháts tawáam vuunóok,
shuuvíik a'étəma.

Shuuvíik,
nyaayúu,
bowl vatáts tan a'íts awíim,
alyaasáarək,
aasárək;
tsuumpápk a'étəma.

Tsuumpáp.

Nyáanya,
nyaayúu 'avíi athíik a'étəma.

'Avíi,
kayáaíi,
kaawémk vanyuunóok
nyáany,
alytsaváwk.

Alytsaváwk,
awíim,
kwatapáar tan vathánya,
athóoyvətant,
kwalyavíita.
Athóoyvətanəm,
alytsaváw.

Suuváam,
nyaasíim.

Atsénək,
takavék nyaaváamək,
asíi va'áarəm a'étəma.
Aava'áarəm.

Awéxáyəly —
'ashént aséxayk —

those people who had been killed and dried,
the women went about grinding them up,
and they made gravy, they say.

They made gravy,
well,
they used really big bowls,
they poured (the gravy) in,
they poured it;
there were four (portions), they say.

Four.

As for that,
(the boy) came to get rocks or something, they say.

The rocks,
maybe he sharpened them,
he went about doing something
to those (rocks),
and he put them in.

He put them in,
and so,
this very last one,
it was really sharp,
it was like that.
It was really sharp,
and he put it in.

He was there
when (Kwayúu) drank it.

He went down,
and when he got back (home),
he always drank, they say.
He always did.

He did it, and suddenly —
he drank the first (bowl), and suddenly —

'aláayəm a'ávək a'éta.
'Aláayəm a'ávtəs.
Awét.

Tsáam,
kwaxavík,
kwaxamók,
kwatsuumpáp,
vathí,
nyáavəts athóoyvətantək awím,
nyáanyats,
malyaqényi kaawém,
apúyk a'étəntima.

Nyaapúyəm,
sanyuuváak.
"Ka'thóm tanək?
Vi'ayéməly," a'íim suuváak.

Suuváam,
sanyts'áakənyts,
"Nyiinyaatuuqwíirək,
'anayémapatk,
'aaly'étka,"
a'ítsk a'étəma.

A'ítsəm.
"Kaváarək.
Ka'wémək 'awíyúm,"
a'íim,
suuváak.

Ssanyuuváam a'ím —
kaawíts? —
kaawíts mattatséwk a'étəma.

*** *** ***

Nyaayúu mattatséwk 'éta,
'Iipá.

he felt (something) go wrong, they say.
He must have felt (something) go wrong.
He did.

All of them,
the second,
the third,
the fourth,
and here,
this one was really sharp, and so,
that (sharp rock),
it did something in his throat,
and he died, they say.

He died,
and (the boy) was still over there.
"How will I do it?
I want to go away," he was saying.

There he was,
and the women (said),
"We're with you,
we'll go away too,
we think,"
they said, so they say.

They said it.
"No.
I don't know how I could do it,"
he said,
and there he was.

There he was, and so —
what was it? —
he turned himself into something, they say.

*** *** ***

He turned himself into something, they say.
An arrow.

Áa-á,
arrow.
Áa,
mattatséwk.

"Av'awétxa,"
a'íim,
uukanáavtsəm.

"Viimayáak,
maváamtəxa,"
a'ítsəm,
athúu,
viithíik athúuk a'étəma.
Viithíik.

Nyavány 'avuumák ta'axán,
shátt nyaa'íim.

"Nyaamaváamək,
makyík vaathóxa ma'íim,
'avá xán alymaxáv alyma'émətxa.

"Shamáts tsuumpáp nyiiyéməm,
mayúuxa,
'aakóoynya,"
a'ítstəm.

Siiv'áw kuu'éeytənyk,
avathúum a'étəma.

Avathúum,
aváamk mattkanáavək,
'aakóoyəny uukanáavək,
"Pa'iipáa muu'ítsəny 'atapúyəntik,"
a'íikəm.

*** *** ***

A'íim,
siitháwk a'étəma.

Yes,
an arrow.
Yes,
he turned himself into it.

"I will do it,"
he said,
and they told him (how).

"Go along,
you'll get there,"
they said,
and he did it,
he came along, they say.
He came along.

Right behind his house,
he came straight down there.

"When you get there,
she will be like this somewhere, but
you must not go into the house.

"When four nights have passed,
you will see her,
the old lady,"
they had said.

He did his best to stand there, poor thing,
he did that, they say.

He did that,
he got there and he told about himself,
he told the old lady,
"I have killed the person you told me about,"
he said.

*** *** ***

So,
there they were, they say.

Siitháwk amáam,
'akútstək,
athúm,
nyaayúu,
'aqwáaq akyáam,
kamémək,
aax'ák kuu'éeyk,
asóotstək athótk.
Siitháwtək a'étəma.

Siitháwtənyək —
siitháwtənyək,
kaawíts nyaaxalykwáantik,
suuváaxayəm,
sanya'ák nyáava —
sata'óts a'étk kwalyavíita,
suunóok,
ayóovək a'étəma.

Xayəm,
nyaayúu mattantséwk a'étəma.
Kwashkyéevək.
Kwashkyéevək asan'áw.

Shuunrémxay.

Mattatséwk,
siivám,
shuupáwk.
Shuupáwk.

" 'Aakóoy nyaa'aváaməm,
tapúytsxa 'aaly'íim."

Awím,
atháwk viiwáak kamémək.
Nyáava antáyənyts nyaváyk siivám a'étəma.
Antáyənyts.

There they were, and finally,
(the boy) got older,
and so,
well,
he shot a deer,
and he brought it back,
and he did his best to hang it up, poor thing,
and they ate it.
There they were, they say.

There they were, and eventually —
there they were, and eventually,
he was hunting for something again,
there he was, and suddenly,
this woman —
they seemed to be her children,
they were around,
and they saw him, they say.

Immediately,
he changed himself into something tiny, they say.
A dove.
A baby dove.

A newly hatched (dove).

He changed himself,
and there he was,
and they recognized him.
They recognized him.

"When we get to the old lady's house,
I think they will kill him."

So,
they picked him up and brought him there.
His mother was living over there, they say.
His mother.

Kamémxáyəm,
shuupáwtək a'ím,
"Kuuthíim 'ayúuwú,"
a'ím a'étk kwalyavíita,
kwara'ákats.

Kwara'ákats shuupáwkəm,
ayúuk,
a'ím,
awéxay,
ayérək a'étəma.
Ayérək.

Uuváak,
uuváak,
nyaayúuk,
áa,
'avá vaathúts kwa'áts,
'avá shupétt kwa'áts athótəm,
nyaayúu atséwtsəntik athúm,
'amáyəny 'avuutsúly a'étəntima.

Uunakúpk,
'amáyəly tsaváwət.

Nyaanyəm,
nyáanyəm nyaatspák,
viiyém'əsh.

***

Xuumárəvəts,
áa,
viiyém'əsh.
Viiyém'əsh.

Viiyémk,
siiyáak,
siiyáam,
tatuuvíirək,

As soon as they brought him there,
 they recognized him, and so,
"Bring him so that I can see him,"
he said something like that,
the old man (did).

The old man recognized him,
he saw him,
and so,
he did, and immediately,
(the boy) flew away, they say.
He flew away.

There he was,
there he was,
and he saw it,
well,
it was a house like this, just as they had said,
it was a winter house, just as they had said,
and they had made something,
it was a smoke hole at the top, they say.

They had made a little hole,
they had put it in the roof.

And it was through that (hole),
he went out through that,
and he went away.

***

The boy,
well,
he went away.
He went away.

He went away,
he went along,
he went along,
and they chased him,

viiwáatsənyk,
alyvatsuuváarək a'étəntima.

Atháwəts aly'ém.

Siiyáanyək,
nyáasi.

***

Nyáanya,
nyaanyamáam,
'ashuupáwtək'a.

Nyaanyamáam,
siiyáanyək vatsuuváarək
a'étəm 'a'avtək'ash.
A'étəm 'a'ávtəka.

Áa,
nyiimántək siiyáas,
'ashmátk 'a'áv aly'émk 'a'épəm ma'ám.

That's right.

Nyáanyi kanáavtəm 'a'ávtək'ash.

they went on and on,
but they couldn't do it, they say.

They couldn't catch him.

They went along there,
over there in the distance.

***

As for this story,
that's all,
(as far as) I know it.

That's all,
they went along in the distance and never did catch him,
I've heard them say so.
I've heard them say so.

Yes,
he started there and went along in the distance, but
I fell asleep and didn't hear it all, as I've told you.

That's right.

I heard them tell that story.

5. Three Stories About Old Lady Sanyuuxáv

Old Lady Sanyuuxáv

Told by an anonymous Quechan elder

*Translated by Barbara Levy,
George Bryant, and Amy Miller*

Old Lady Sanyuuxáv

Told by Josefa Hartt

*Translated by Barbara Levy,
George Bryant, and Amy Miller*

Shakwatxót

Told by John Comet

*Translated by Millie Romero, Barbara Levy, George
Bryant, and Amy Miller*

http://dx.doi.org/10.11647/OBP.0049.05

This chapter presents three narratives about Old Lady *Sanyuuxáv*. Each narrative focuses on different characters and events, with the result that the three stories are very different from one another. (A fourth version of the story, identified as "Sikwetxot," was told nearly a century ago by Felix Escalanta and is summarized by Forde 1931: 129-130.)

Notes and synopsis: an anonymous narrative about Old Lady *Sanyuuxáv*

The first narrative about Old Lady *Sanyuuxáv* was told by an elder who asked to remain anonymous. (The same elder narrated the story of *'Aréey* in Chapter 2.) It was told to Abe Halpern on April 24, 1979. Halpern later reviewed his transcript with Millie Romero.

This story focuses on the relationship of the title character to her sons and their wives. As the story opens, Old Lady *Sanyuuxáv* goes swimming, becomes pregnant, and soon gives birth to twin sons. The boys' spiritual power is evident from an early age: they turn themselves into doves and lizards and back again. They give the old woman some trouble as she raises them. Eventually they take their flutes and head east.

Eventually the boys meet twin girls and decide to get married. The old woman, thanks to her spiritual powers, intuits her sons' intentions. She is furious. She tries to prevent the marriages — but the girls are powerful too, and their powers overcome hers. At the wedding, Old Lady *Sanyuuxáv* puts a curse on one of the girls, who promptly dies. At the funeral the boy who was to have married her dies too. The old woman turns the second girl into a buzzard and sends her into the sky.

The old woman is taken to an island and abandoned there.

Notes and synopsis: Josefa Hartt's story of Old Lady *Sanyuuxáv*

Josefa Hartt told the story of Old Lady *Sanyuuxáv* to Abe Halpern on February 25, 1981. Halpern reviewed his transcript of the narrative with Eunice Miguel.

This narrative begins with a brief account of the old woman's life with her twin sons. The boys' power is evident from their personal appearance:

> *Iimáattənyts anyúurək,*
> *nyaayúu,*
> *kwal'iishée muuyúu nyáany lyavúitk a'étəma.*

> *Their bodies were multi-colored,*
> *well,*
> *they looked like the rainbow that you see, so they say.*

The story soon shifts to take the point of view of a family living near the place now known as San Xavier, Arizona, whose people — Papagos — are said to be at war with the Quechan. The family in this story consists of an old man, his wife, their two daughters, and their grown son. The old man is blind. The daughters live separately from their parents, in a house not far away, but they are still under their parents' care and authority.

The sons of Old Lady *Sanyuuxáv* find the girls and move in with them. The girls' parents become suspicious and send first their grown son and then an orphan boy to check up on the daughters. These emissaries see nothing more than the shimmering colors of the twin boys. Eventually the younger girl gives birth to a son. As the child grows, members of the girls' family catch glimpses of him playing outdoors. The old man (the child's maternal grandfather) declares that if the child is a girl everything will be all right, but if the child is a boy he must be killed in order to prevent a future disaster.

Confronted by their brother, the two girls claim that the child is female. Eventually the truth is discovered, however, and the old man sends his son and a gang of men to kill the child. The child's mother (the younger of the twin girls) uses her powers to hide the child inside a housepost, and he escapes unharmed. The sons of Old Lady *Sanyuuxáv* flee. They are chased and killed by Gila Monster. When they die, they go into the ground, and a cloud of steam comes out; that is said to be the origin of the measles.

The old man and his followers rejoice at the boys' death, thinking that disaster has been averted — but they are mistaken. After four days, a wind and a blazing fire come from the distance and engulf everything. The old man's son escapes by turning himself into an ibis, and the child and his aunt (who is the elder of the twin girls) escape by running ahead of the flames. The child turns his aunt into a meadowlark. He goes to the home of his paternal grandmother, Old Lady *Sanyuuxáv*. Together he and his grandmother go west to the ocean. The Old Lady throws the child towards the middle of the ocean and says,

Avnyaathúum,
mataxáyk,
'akwíik,
uuv'áwk,
nyaathúum —
uuqásk ava'íim,
vanyuuváam,
Kwayaaxuumárəts àra'óoyk uuváam a'íyum.

When it happens,
it's windy,
and it's cloudy,
and it rains,
and then —
it thunders like this,
and when it does,
they might say Kwayaaxuumár is playing.

She returns home. The child, *Kwayaaxuumár*, is said to be responsible for thunder and lightning.

Notes and synopsis: John Comet's story *Shakwatxót*

John Comet told the story *Shakwatxót* to Abe Halpern on May 5, 1979.

Shakwatxót is concerned with the twin sons of Old Lady *Sanyuuxáv* and their relationship with each other. Like the others in this chapter, this story begins with the birth of twin boys to the old woman. The boys are named *Paar'áak* and *Paaraxáan*. We find out later that they shimmer like rainbows — a sign of spiritual power — but even in infancy the younger twin is more powerful than his brother. While their mother is out, the younger brother leaves his cradle and goes hunting, catching butterflies to hang from the hoop of his cradleboard. As a youth, his powers help him to succeed where the older brother fails: he is able to gather cattails from an area inhabited by snakes, and to get eagles from a high and dangerous mountain.

The twins travel. They meet twin sisters and move in with them. Returning to the girls' house after a brief absence, they hear an owl call their names. This is an omen of death. The following day they are seen by their own father, Yellow Gopher. Yellow Gopher digs a trap, intending to capture and kill them. When the boys fall into the trap, they survive the fall, but they are killed anyway when Gila Monster hits them on the head with his war club.

When the boys are dead, the people rejoice. They use the boys' skulls for kickballs and their hands for eating utensils.

Shortly afterwards, the younger of the two girls bears a child, fathered by the younger of the twin boys. The people decide to kill the child. Like his father, however, the child has great powers, and these powers enable him to escape. He goes to his four uncles, Shifting Wind, Storm Wind, Strongest Wind, and Blazing Fire, and he enlists their help in avenging his father's death. The four uncles pass over the land, leaving everyone dead except for the child's aunt (the older of the twin girls), who has been protected by the child. The child takes his aunt south and transforms her first into a dove and then into a red wren.

Travelling on, the child finds two *tiimáa xuutsé*. The term *tiimáa xuutsé* is not in current usage, but it seems to refer to tied bundles which stand upright. *Par'áak* and *Parxáan* had noticed (or perhaps had constructed) these two *tiimáa xuutsé* on the morning of their death and evidently had placed their souls inside them for safekeeping. When the child finds the *tiimáa xuutsé*, he burns them, understanding that in doing so he is cremating his father and his uncle.

The child continues traveling and eventually reaches the home of his paternal grandmother, Old Lady *Sanyuuxáv*. She is old and evidently disabled, and her house is full of unwelcome carousing guests. The child takes her to an island in the middle of the ocean and leaves her there. He himself goes up into the sky and becomes *Kwayaaxuumár*, 'The One Who Acts Like a Child,' who is said to be responsible for thunder and lightning.

Comparative note

Stories involving some of the same characters and events are told in other Yuman tribes, under names such as "The Satukhota Story" (Kroeber 1972: 99-116) or "Flute Lure" (Spier 1933: 367-396). Similar stories are found throughout the western half of the Southwest, according to Bierhorst (2002: 94). Exactly how much the stories share across tribes is an open question, however. Bierhorst summarizes the Southwestern "Flute Lure" myth as "the story of dangerous females and how a hero finally gets rid of them," but this summary fits at best one of the three Quechan stories in this chapter, and does not capture the essence of any of them.

'Aakóoy Sanyuuxáv

Told by an anonymous Quechan elder

'Aakóoy aváts nyaváyk siiványk,
kaawíts kanáavəm athútya,
nyaayáak xaly'úp.
"Xaly'a'úpk 'ayáawu."

A'ím,
"Kanúp,
katsuumpáp,
katkavék kaváak.

" 'Axtá mashtúum matsíkxa."

Kaawíts uukanáavəm a'ítya.

Nyaayáakəm —
'aakóoyənyts xaly'úp —
nyaayáak anúpk,
viiyáaaak,
aalyuuvéevəm takavék.

Nyaanúpəntik,
nyaayáaaak,
'anóqəm,
kúur a'ím,
takavékəntik.

Nyaayáanyk,
kwaxamókəny,
nyaayáa nyaanúpəntik,
vanyaayáaak,
xáyk —
" 'Awa'áw!" a'ím,
takavék atspákt.

That old lady was living over there,
and something told her
to go swimming.
"I'll go swimming," she said.

And so,
"Duck down (under the water),
do it four times,
and come back up.

"You'll gather willow (roots)."

Something told her this, they say.

She went —
the old lady went swimming —
she went along and ducked down (under the water),
and she went along,
and halfway (there) she came back up.

She ducked down under the water again,
and she went along,
a little (way),
and in a little while
she came back (up) again.

She went along, until
the third (time),
she went along and ducked (under the water) again,
and as she went along,
all of a sudden —
"Oh!" she said,
and she came back out.

Takavék atspák,
siivák —
kaawítsəts xá maxák uuváak uuváata!

A'ím,
siivám,
a'áv alya'ém,
thúutt 'im,
nyaayáantixayəm,
xtány uukyítt.

Nyuukyíttk,
xavíkəm,
nyaashtúum,
nyaatspák,
viithíik,
nyavá aváamk siivá.

Aváak,
wilawíil atsóowk uuváam.
Xavíkəm aavíirək,
atsáam.

Siiváxáyk —
'aakóoy ta'axáns athótk —
xuumáar xaaváak ayúut.

Ayúuk siiváa,
'aakóoyənyts.

Nyaatspámək viiyáak,
atspámək viiyáaxaym,
'aványik amánk.
Kwashkyéevkanyts.
Uuyáarək uutspák,
'anyáa kwatspáatsəny nathómək viiwétsəm,
ayúuk viiv'áw.

"Kaathómk 'asta'óts athótk kwalyvíit,"
a'ím,
ayúuk siiv'áw.

She came back out,
and there she was —
there had been something there under the water!

So,
it was there,
(but) she didn't pay it any attention,
she went farther,
she went down again, and immediately,
she cut the willow (roots).

She cut them,
two of them,
and she picked them up,
and she came out,
and she came back;
she got home and there she was.

She got there,
and she went about making flutes.
She finished (making) two,
and she put them away.

There she was, and suddenly —
(even though) she was a really old lady —
she gave birth to twins.

She gave birth and there she was,
the old lady.

She went out and went along,
she went out and went along, and suddenly,
they came from the house.
Doves.
They came flying out,
and they headed off towards the rising sun,
and she stood there watching.

"Somehow they seem to be my children,"
she said,
and she stood there watching.

Xayəm,
takavék,
nyavály axávxayəm,
nyáanyts athútsəm nyaayúuk.

" 'Awa'áw,
'aláayk nyiikwév."

Nyuuváak,
viiyém.

Nyaatspámantik,
siiv'áwxaym,
nakavék uupúuv.

Matsats'íim vuunóot.

Nyaayúuk,
takavék nyaaváak,
'atsnyiiáayk vuunóom,
'atsamátsxa viitháwk.

Vuunóonyk,
nyuuv'óontik xayk,
kwaasáany mattiitsóowtəntik,
uutspámək viinayém!

"Kaathóm
muuthámək vuunóok athúm?" a'ét.
'Aakóoyənyts ayúuk uuváak.

Uuváak
nyamáam nyaakúutsk,
vanyuunóom.

"Nyaayúu mathúts,
matsaanyíik ammuunóot mathúm.
Ka'ávtan nyaayúu kathúum!
'Ashéntəts 'aláayk ma'ávxa."

All of a sudden,
they came back,
they went back into the house, and immediately,
she saw that it was them.

"Oh, no,
this is terribly bad," (she said).

They were there,
and off they went.

When they came back out again,
she was standing there, and immediately,
they went back inside.

They were crying.

She saw them,
and she went back (inside),
and she gave them things,
and they were about to eat.

There they were,
and they stood up again, and suddenly,
they turned themselves into lizards,
and they went out, and away they went!

"Why is it
that they are making such trouble?" she said.
The old lady was watching them.

There she was,
and finally they grew up,
and there they were.

"The things you do,
you go too far with them.
Be careful when you do things!
One of you will have a bad time."

A'íim,
a'áv alya'ém.

A'áv alya'émək,
nyaayúu,
kwaasáany mattiitsóowk,
nyaawéeeetskəm,
nyaayúu maxák atháw.

Xayəm,
'atsnyaayúuts —
'aavé kaawíts athúukəm,
nyáanyts nyiinyíilyq a'íi vuunóom,
nyaayúuk,
astuukyáanyk viinathíik,
nyavály uupúuvkəm,
pa'iipáats athótk vuunóot.

Uunóony,
nyaanymáam nya'uukúutsəm;
'aakóoyənyts wanyiirávək vuunóom,
nyaa'ávək anáak viitháwk.

Anáak,
xayəm,
wilawíiləny nyaashtúum;
nya'kúutstək athúum,
nyaashtúum.

'Anyáaxáap,
'anyáaxáapəm uupúuvk viiwétsk,
'avíi 'amáy alytháwk siitháw.
Wilawíil atsáam vuunóo.

A'ávək,
'aakóoyənyts a'ávək viiv'áw.

"Wilawíil 'uutsóowəny ashtútsk athúm,
'atsnyaayúu aashtuuváarək vuunóom,
'uuxúuttəny,"
siiv'áw.

She said it,
(but) they didn't pay attention.

They didn't pay attention,
well,
they turned themselves into lizards,
and off they went,
and they lay underneath something.

Suddenly,
a creature —
it was some kind of snake,
and it was going to swallow them,
and they saw it,
and they ran away and came (home),
and they went into the house,
and they became people again.

There they were,
and finally they grew up;
the old lady kept scolding them,
and they paid attention to her and settled down.

They settled down,
and suddenly,
they picked up the flutes;
they were grown up now, and so,
they picked them up.

The west,
they went into the west,
and they sat on the top of a mountain over there.
They were playing their flutes.

She heard them,
the old lady heard them, standing here.

"They've picked up the flutes I made,
and they are singing things,
the good (songs),"
and she stood there in the distance.

Siiv'áwxay,
'amatt 'nyáaly,
'amátt 'nyáak atháwapatk.
Mashtxáats,
xaavákt.

Xaavákəntik,
siitháwapatk,
a'áv.

"Ka'áv!

"Maxáa xaaváakanyts!
Maxáa xaaváakanyts wilawíil atsáam vuunóom,
'uuxúutt!
Ma'ávək viimavák?"

Sanya'ákəny a'íim.

"Áa,
'a'ávək 'avák."

Uunáw matt-tsapéem,
a'ávk.
'Avíi 'amáyəly atháwk,
awítsk uunóotəm a'íim,
anáwk matt-tsapéetk a'ítya.

" 'Awétsk 'ayóovúum?"
nyaa'íim,
xaaváakapatənyts viiwéts.

Nyavány katán aly'ém nyiikwévtəm;
'aakóoyəny kwashuuthíiny matt-tsapéek uuváak.

Xayəm,
nyiishtriiqəm,
makyík katánəm takavék viiwéts!

There she was, and suddenly,
in a place in the east,
(other people) were in a place in the east.
They were young women,
and they were twins.

They were twins too,
they were over there in the distance,
and they were listening.

"Listen!

"It's twin young men!
Twin young men are playing flutes,
the good (songs)!
Do you hear it?"

She said it to the (other young) woman.

"Yes,
I hear it."

The sound was overwhelming,
and they heard it.
(The young men) were on top of the mountain,
and they were doing something,
and the sound was overwhelming, they say.

"Shall we go see?"
she said,
and (those) twins went off too.

They didn't get anywhere near the house;
the old lady's powers were overwhelming.

Suddenly,
she took control (of their actions),
and they got just so far and then went back!

Nakavék viiwétsəm,
ayóovkəm,
ayóovk vanyaatháwkəm —
'aakóoy mashuuráyəny matt-tsapéetk avuuváat.

Nyaatkavék nyaakatánmək athúm.

Nyiitháawkəm;
" 'Anyáats 'uuv'áa 'awétsúm 'atháwk,"
nyaa'íim,
maxáanyənyts,
viiwétst.

'Anyáam uupúuvk viiwétsxayəm,
nyáasily nyiitsxakyéek uukavékapatəm!
Nyáasi nyiiáar alya'émapatk,
awítsəm.

Nyaanakavék katán,
viitháwəm.

'Aakóoyənyts masharáytək uuváatəs a'étk,
uuváatk;
iiwáanyts 'axótt-təm uuváa.

Awím,
wilawíil nyáany nyaatsétsəntik,
siitháwxayəm,
mashtxáany
mashtxáanyənyts,
sanyaawétsk,
kaathóm naxkyíik katán!

Katánmək,
maxáanyənyts,
wilawíil atsétk siitháwəm,
nyaakatánəm.

Aatsíirək vuunóom,
a'ávək,

They went back,
and (the young men) watched,
they were watching —
and the old lady's anger was overwhelming.

(The young women) had gone back home.

There they were;
"We might take a walk,"
they said,
the young men (did),
and off they went.

They went off into the east, and immediately,
(something) over there made them go back across!
(The old lady) didn't want them over there,
and she did it.

They came back and got here,
and here they were.

The old lady was angry, but
there she was;
she went around (pretending to be) happy.

So,
they played their flutes again,
there they were, and suddenly,
the young women,
it was the young women,
they went after them,
and somehow they went across and got there!

They got there,
and the young men
were playing their flutes,
when (the young women) got there.

They were laughing flirtatiously,
and she heard them,

'aakóoyənyts a'ávək,
av'áwtəm;
" 'Amáy alytháwk" a'étəma.

"Nyaakatánək!
Saathóxa lyavíim!
'A'íim va'uuváam!
Nyiis'íirək 'uunóom!

"Kaathómk nyiinykáamək,
naxkyíi'ənkáa?"
a'étəma.

A'íim,
nyiithúutsk siiv'áwt.

Nyiithúutsk siiv'áwk;
"Vatháts uutsóoy a'íim katánək vuunóok athútya."
a'éta.

"A'ím,
'axóttk,
aaíimək mattatsúytəxa.

"Mattuutsóoyts 'uuxúutt alya'éməxa,"
a'ím,
'aakóoyənyts a'ím.

Nyaa'ávkəm,
'aakóoyəny.
"Mattmatsúy ma'ím muunóokəm,
mathúum?"
maxáany tsakakwétəm.
"Áa."

"Xóttk.
Matt'aaéevxa."

Mattaaéevək,
pa'iipáa aqáask vuunóok vuunóok.

the old lady heard them,
and she stood up;
"They're on top of the mountain," she said.

"They got here!
This was bound to happen!
I kept saying so!
I forbade them to do it!

"(But) somehow they overpowered me,
and they went across, didn't they?"
she said.

And so,
she stood there thinking.

She stood there thinking;
"These young women got there intending to get married,"
she said.

"So,
all right,
they'll get married, no matter what.

"Their marriages won't be good ones,"
she said,
the old lady said it.

They heard her,
the old lady.
"You are going to get married,
are you?"
she asked the young men.
"Yes," (they said).

"All right.
We'll have a gathering."

They had a gathering,
they went on and on inviting people.

Awíim,
" 'Ats'iimák va'uunóom.
Ammuunóok,
màra'óoyk,
màra'óoyk muuváanyk muuvák.
Ma'ávək,
nyáanyi mathútsxa,"
a'éta.

A'ítsəm,
nyaa'ávək,
pa'iipáanyts
'aváats kaváay kanáavək viiwáam,
pa'iipáanya aqáas.
"Tsuumáavək vuunóo!
Tsuumáav a'íim vuunóo!"

Tsuumáav vuunóom,
pa'iipáanyənyts aashtuuvárək vuunóom,
'atsiimák uuváa.

Mashaxáyənyts aatsíirək a'ét-tək,
aatsíirtək a'ét-tək.

Vuunóom,
'aakóoy vaashuuqwétsənyts iináamk uuváat.

Nyuuváakəm,
nyaamaatsíirəntik siiv'áwxayəm,
kuu'íirək,
'aakóoyənyts mashaxáyəny mattatháwəm.

Mattatháwəm!

Kúur 'ím nyaa'áampət!
Mashaxáyənyts apúyt
'atsiimáts atóly!

Nyaapúyəm,
nyaapúyəm,

So,
"We're (going to) dance.
You'll be there,
and you'll have a good time,
you'll be there having a good time.
You'll experience it,
and you'll (go on from) there,"
she said.

She said it,
and when they heard her,
someone
went from house to house telling about it,
and inviting the people.
"They're having a feast!
They're going to have a feast!"

They had a feast,
and the people were singing,
and they were dancing.

The young woman was laughing flirtatiously,
she was laughing flirtatiously.

There they were,
and the old lady's hatred was extraordinary.

There she was,
and one of them was laughing flirtatiously again,
and all of a sudden,
the old lady put a curse on the young woman.

She put a curse on her!

And in a little while she fell face down!
The young woman died
in the middle of the dancing!

When she died,
when she died,

viitíivəkəm,
nyamáam,
uutara'úy a'íi vuunóo.
Qwalayéwəm,
uutara'úy a'íi vuunóo.

Xáyəm,
maxáyəny iiwáanyts 'aláay a'ím,
uuváak.

Nyaaqwalayéwəm,
mashaxáyəny uutara'úyk aavíirtst.

Uutara'úyk nyaavíirtsəm,
maxáyənyts
uuváatapat.

Avuuváanypatk,
nyáany nyáalyvíitəntik.
Kúur a'ím apúytapatk,
xuumár xaaváká.

Nyáam 'ashéntəm,
'ashéntts áampək,
mattaaly'ák vuunóok
'aakóoyəny.

Nyuunóom.

'Aakóoyənyts takavék a'ím.
"Mashxáyəny 'uutara'úyk 'aavíirək,"
aaly'éxay.

Nyaayúu,
katél a'étəntima,
nyáany.
Nyáany atháwk awím,
xama'úlyny ashtúum vuunóok,
aavíirxáyəm,
maa'íilykəts tama'órət!

they all sat here,
and finally,
they were going to prepare her (for cremation).
The next morning,
they were going to prepare her (for cremation).

Right away,
the young man's heart was about to break,
there he was.

The next morning,
they finished preparing the young woman (for cremation).

They finished preparing her (for cremation),
and the young man
was there too.

He was there too,
and he did just what she had done.
In a little while he died too,
the twin (young man).

Now there was one,
one (from each pair of twins) was left,
and they stayed together
(with) the old lady.

There they were.

The old lady was going to go back home.
"I'll get that young woman taken care of,"
she thought.

Well,
it's called a parching tray,
that (thing).
She took that (tray), and so,
she went on gathering ashes,
and she finished, and suddenly,
(the tray) was full of maggots!

Maa'íilykəts tama'órəm,
nyaayúuk.

Nyáavəm,
nyaatama'órəm nyaayúuk,
mashaxáy,
mashaxáy 'ashént,

"Máanyts,
vathányəm,
vathányi,
matspáq!
mathótk ammuuváatxa!"

"A'ím,
'Ashéets 'a'íim nyashém,
'atskamuuváak,
nyáava mamáatsk ammayáatxa!"

A'ím,
mashxáyəny alyaats'átk,
'ashée atsóowəm,
'amáyvi uuváak,
uuváak athúuk a'éta.

'Aakóoyənyts awíim.
'Aakóoy Sanyuuxáványts.

A'ím,
nyuunóok.

Vanyuunóokəm,
nyaayúu tsáam,
máam,
nyiiríish a'ím viitháwk.

Nyuunóok,
vanyuunóok awím,
"Ka'thúum 'uunóok 'athútya?

It was full of maggots,
and she saw this.

At this (point),
when she saw that it was full of maggots,
(she said to) the young woman,
the one young woman (who was left),

"You,
right now,
right here,
you'll pop these in your mouth like grapes!
That's what you'll do from now on!

"So,
I name you Buzzard,
and wherever you might be,
this is what you will eat from now on!

And so,
she shoved the young woman,
she turned her into a buzzard,
and there she is up in the sky,
there she is, they say.

The old lady did it.
Old Lady Sanyuuxáv.

And so,
there they were.

There they were, and so,
(out of) everything,
finally,
there was nothing (left).

There they were,
there they were, and so,
"How can we put up with this?

"Kamawíi ma'ím
matatapóoyk muunóok nyammaavíirək?

"Maaíimək viimayáak!

" 'Amátt mashmuuthíi makayáam,
nyáasi muuváak nyiimakwévtəxa!

"Aanyóntik vathí muuváa alyma'ém!"

A'ítsəm,
viiwétsk,
'anyáavi nathómək viiwéts.

Viiwétsk,
xaasa'íly atóly nyáanyi,
'avíits uuvám,
nyáanyi tsuunóoyts,
nyáanyi uuváak uuváak.
Athúuk a'étəma.

A'ím,
mayúuwúm,
a'ítstəma.
Nyáany a'ím.
Nyáanyi avák uuvá.

"What did you think you were doing
 when you went about killing them off?

"Just go!

"Go away to a place you don't know,
 and come to your end over there!

"Don't ever come here again!"

They said it,
and off they went,
they headed east and off they went.

Off they went,
and in the middle of the ocean
there was an island,
and they abandoned her there,
and that's where she stayed.
It happened, they say.

So,
you can see her,
they say.
They say that.
She is (still) there.

'Aakóoy Sanyuuxáv

Told by Josefa Hartt

Pa'iipáats,
sany'ákəts siivák,
nyaváyk siiványk,
saathúum,
pa'iipáanyəny 'atáyk,
vaa'íim,
vathík vathík a'íim,
athúuny.

Nyáava,
siiványk,
nyaváyk siivány.

Xuumáar ayúuxáyəm;
xaavák a'étəma.

Xaavákəm,
nyaxáyk,
matháavtək:
anyúurtək a'étəma.

Iimáattənyts anyúurək,
nyaayúu,
kwal'iishée muuyúu nyáany lyavíitk a'étəma.

Athúum,
anyúurtək.
Suuméevək vuunóom,
uutsétk uuváanyk uuvány.

Uuváany,
nyáany ava'ítstəma.
'Avíinyts,
vaa'ée a'íim,
nyiikúpk va'íik a'ém a'ítya.

A person,
a woman was over there,
she was living over there,
that's how things were,
there were a lot of people there,
like this,
they were here and there,
they were.

This one,
she was over there,
she was living over there.

She gave birth to children;
they were twins, they say.

They were twins,
and immediately,
there was something peculiar about them:
they were multi-colored, they say.

Their bodies were multi-colored,
well,
they looked like those rainbows that you see, they say.

So,
they were multi-colored.
They depended on her,
and she looked after them, on and on.

There she was,
and (people) talked about that.
The mountain,
it was like this,
and there might have been a cave in it, like this, they say.

Athúuk a'émək,
xaavíly viikwathíi nyáava,
kwashathúk nyáavəm,
makyí athúum a'ítya.

Athúum,
 nyáanya,
sanya'ákənya,
'Aakóoy Sanyuuxáv a'ím,
amúlyk athúuk a'étəma,
nyamáam,
nya'aakóoyəm.

Nyáany nyaváyəm,
nyáany nyaváytk siivám,
sata'óts nyáanyts avathótk anyúurtəm.

Sata'ótsk siivá,
uutsáa va'árk viiványk viiványk,
nyamáam,
nya'uukúutsk;
vanyaatháwk,
saathúum:
pa'iipáavats
mattmaawíik,
pa'iipáa kwanymé shiitamúuly mattashék,
makyík a'íim,
makyík kwa'ítsányts.

Saathúum:
mattnyiitsúyk,
mattnyiimaawíik,
mattnyaashuupáwk.

Nyaathúu,
nyaa'íim,
nyáanyts xiipúk athúum athúuk a'étəma.

Maxáanyənyts vanyaatháwk,
Xatpáa Nyavátan alynayém.

Maybe
this river that comes along here
and heads this way,
maybe it's somewhere around there, they say.

So,
that one,
the woman,
they called her Old Lady Sanyuuxáv,
(that) was her name, they say,
that's all,
now that she was old.

She lived there,
she was living over there,
and those children of hers were multi-colored like that.

She gave birth to them,
and she looked after them, on and on,
and finally,
they grew up;
here they were,
and it was like that:
these people
were related to each other,
(but) they belonged to a different tribe,
wherever it was,
the one that was wherever it was.

It was like that:
(in order to) get married,
(they needed to know how) they were related to one another,
they needed to know about themselves.

(That) was (the situation),
and so,
they were the first ones to be (in this situation), they say.

The boys were there,
and they went off into real Papago territory.

A'étk,
vanyaatháwk,
matt-tsakuunávǝk a'íim,
" 'Uuv'áak,
'avíi kavée 'anyáak 'anayém 'a'ím 'atháw'ǝsh,"
a'ét.

Sany'ákǝny antáytsǝny uukanáavxáyǝly —
"Kaawíts mawéts ma'ím ma'ítya?
Mapóoytǝxa!

"Pa'iipáanyts mayúuk athúuly'ǝm!
'Axwáaytank avatháw alyaskyíixáyǝm,"
a'étkǝm a'ítya.

A'étk vuunóotǝs,
makyík a'áv alya'émǝk.
Kaathúts a'étk a'íim,
nyiikwévtǝk,
nyáany.

Xuumáar muuxamíik,
'atsnyaamuukanáavǝm,
a'áv alya'émǝk.
Nyaathúwúm.
Nyaatsiinyúuvúm a'étǝma.

Nyaathúu nyaa'íim,
nyáanya athúum athúuk a'ét.
A'étǝma.

Nyáany athúu a'íi vanyaatháwk;
mattsaa'étk suunóok,
a'étǝma.

*** *** ***

Nyáanya avathúuk a'étǝma.
Nyaa'íim,
viinayémtǝk a'étǝma.
Viiwétstǝk.

So,
here they were,
and they talked among themselves, and so,
"Let's travel,
let's go to the southeastern mountains,"
(one of them) said.

They told the woman, their mother, and immediately —
"What are you about to do?
They will kill you!

"People don't want to see you!
There is still a real war going on there,"
she said, they say.

She went on saying it, but
they didn't listen to her at all.
She said something,
but it was no use,
that (which she said).

You have children,
and you explain things to them,
but they don't listen to you.
That might happen.
They might follow that example, they say.

When they intend to do (something),
that's what they are going to do.
So they say.

That's what they were intending to do;
they had made up their minds,
they say.

*** *** ***

That's what happened, they say.
And so,
they left, they say.
They went along.

Nyamathúts kwa'átsk:
viiwétsəm,
pa'iipáats Xatpáa 'amáy 'aványi athúm —
mapísa 'atsvéek vanyaavám.

Xama'úlyk nyiivák,
San Xarvíir a'épəm 'a'ávənyk.

Nyáanyi athúum,
Xatpáanyts 'amátt mattnyiitsamíim uuváanyk,
uuváak athúuk a'étəma.

Uuváam,
pa'iipáats viitháwəm,
kwara'ákts,
alykwatanák ta'axánənyts,
nyáanyts,
kwara'ák tánək viithík,
tasínymətk a'étəma.

'Atsayúulya'ém.

Vatstsáats xavík,
mashatxáaxáyk viitháwəm.

'Ashéntts 'akútsk,
'ashéntts alyaaéevək athúum,
nyáany,
'avá awíim shapéttk a'étəma.
Nyakór nyaawíim awíim.
Shapéttəm,
nyáany alyatháwət av'ártək,
iiwáam alyatháwtək avatháwət av'árt.

A'étəma.

Alyatháwk,
siitháwəm.

It happened just as she had said it would:
they went,
and there were people there in Papago territory —
nowadays whoever-it-is is there.

Priests are there,
I've heard it called San Xavier.

That's where it was,
the Papago settled the land and stayed there,
they stayed there, they say.

They stayed there,
and there was someone there,
an old man,
he was their real leader,
he was the one,
he was very old,
and he was blind, they say.

He couldn't see.

He had two daughters,
and they were young women.

One was older,
and one was younger,
and those (young women)
were kept isolated in a separate house.
They did that, long ago.
They isolated them,
and (the young women) would stay in that (house),
they would stay in there by themselves.

So they say.

There they were in there,
they were over there.

Nyáava ayúutkəly,
nyáasi nayém a'étk vuunóotk,
a'étkəm.

Vanyaawétsk,
vanyaawétsk,
nyáasily katánmət.
Makyíts uuyóov alya'éməxayəm,
alykatánətəm.

'Atskuunáavək aatsxwáar a'étk vuunóot av'ártum.

Xiipán atháwkəm,
"Ka'ávək!
Siitháwənyk!" a'íim.

"Ava'íily'əmk,
náq a'íi va'árək avatháwəm,"
a'ávxayəm —
"Kaawíts kaathómk,
avatháwk!" a'ím,
"Tsakavárək anáaw tánək avuunóotəm.
'A'ávək va'avák 'athó'əsh!" a'étk,
kwara'ákənyts a'étk.
" 'A'ávəsh!"

A'íim,
nyaa'ávək,
'aakóoyənyts a'íim,
"A'étk a'ítya,
'aaly'étk.
Iiwáam tsakuunáavək avatháwk,"
a'ím.

A'éxayəm,
"Kaváarəm!
'A'ávək 'a'ítya!"
a'étk;
kwara'ákənyts aníimtək vuunóom nyaa'áv.

(The two young men) wanted to see them,
and they were planning to go over there,
they say.

They went,
and they went,
and they got to that (place) over there.
Nobody saw them, and all of a sudden,
they got there.

They were always talking and laughing.

It was near (the girls' parents' house), and so,
"Listen!
There's someone over there!" (the old man) said.

"They never (used to) say anything!
They've always been quiet," (he said),
and he listened, and suddenly —
"There's something going on,
(someone) is there!" he said,
"They are laughing really loudly.
I can hear them right here!" he said,
the old man said it.
"I can hear them!"

And so,
when she heard him,
the old woman said,
"It's nothing,
I think.
They're by themselves, talking (to each other),"
she said.

As soon as she said it,
"That's not (what is happening)!
I can hear them!"
he said;
the old man could hear them doing as they pleased.

Xuumáyəts suuváam,
aqásk a'ím.

"Kaawíts kaathúum.
Vatháwk waashtuuqwíivək vuunóota.
Mayáak alymarpéem mayúuly 'aaly'ét,"
a'íik a'étəma.

A'íim,
nyaa'ávək,
"Ée'é" a'étk,
viiyáatk.

Nya'avuuyáany av'áwtk,
ayúutk,
aváts nyakór a'ávək athúm,
aashtuuthúuly.

Athúm,
nyiiv'áwk,
ayúutk nyaakwén a'étk,
nyiirísh a'ésh.
Nyaaváamk —
"Nyiirísh.
Kaawíts makyí uuváaly'eməsh,"
a'ét.

A'ím,
a'ávtəka.
Náq a'étk siithík.
Nyaa'íim,
viiyémtəm ayúutka.

'Aakóoyənyts siiványk.
"Kaváarək a'ítsəm;
ma'ámək,"
a'éxaym,
"Kaváarək,
ayúulya'éməs,"
a'étk kwalyavíita.

His son was there,
and he called him.

"Something is going on.
They are making noise over here.
I think you should go and peek inside and see,"
he said, they say.

So,
when he heard him,
"Oh, all right," he said,
and he went along.

He stood outside their door,
and he looked,
(but) those (young women) had heard him coming, and so,
they had hidden (the young men).

So,
he stood there,
he went around looking,
and there was nothing there.
When he got back home —
"Nothing.
There isn't anybody there,"
he said.

So,
(the old man) heard him.
He lay there without saying anything.
Then,
he saw (the young man) go away.

The old lady was still there.
"He said it wasn't (like that);
you heard him,"
she said, and immediately,
"He's wrong.
He probably didn't look,"
(the old man) said something like that.

A'étk,
aníimtək vuunóom.

Xuumár xatáləts.
Kaa'íim 'atskuuváatəm 'ayúunyk;
maatsawíts nyiirísh a'ím.

Nyáany lyavíik,
xuumár 'iikyínyts suuváatk.

Aaíimək,
'aváats kaváayk,
'atssavíily kuu'éeyk,
athúm.

Kaawíts áaytsəm,
amátk athót;
suuváat av'ártəny.

Siithíim —
siithíim,
'aakóoyənyts ayúuk siiványstk.

*** *** ***

Ayúuk siiványstk,
uuváaxaym,
kwara'ákənyts a'ím,
"Kaawíts av'áak?" a'ím,
a'étəm,
"Nyáanyts athótəva," a'í.

A'éxayəm,
kwara'ákənyts a'ím,
"Ée'é,
nyáany,
nyaayúu,
tathíts kamaxúulyk avkuunóok,
káayəm;
nyaayúu tsapóxəm,

So,
they went on doing as they pleased.

There was an orphan.
I've seen them at different places;
they have no relatives.

There was one like that,
there was a little boy over there.

He did what he could,
he went from house to house,
and he begged for things, poor thing,
he did.

They gave him something,
and he ate it;
he was always there.

He was coming from over there —
he was coming from over there,
and the old lady was watching him.

*** *** ***

She was watching him,
there she was, and suddenly,
the old man said,
"Who's that walking by?" he said,
and so,
"It must be that (little boy)," (the old woman) said.

As soon as she said it,
the old man said,
"Okay,
as for that,
well,
(go ahead and) parch some corn,
and give it to him;
he'll munch on something,

nyáany 'a'íim,
ayáak
ayúuwú,"
a'íik a'étəma.

"Alyarpéemək ayúuxa,"
a'étəm,
nyaa'ávək.

"Xóttk," a'ím.
'Aakóoyənyts awíi kwa'átsk,
"Éey,
nyayúu!
Nyáayú!" a'étəm,
nyaa'ávək,
av'áwxayəm,
tathíts nyáany maxúuly kwa'átsk vuunóok,
nyaavíirək,
iisháaly uutama'órək
áaytk a'étəma.

Áayəm,
iisháalyk atsétəm,
nyaashtúum,
"Viimayáak.
Mashtaxáa nyaváts aví avák,
siikwavátsnya.
Alymarpéem
mayúu," a'íim,
a'étka.

"Áam,
pa'iipáa alyatháwəm,
a'íi kaathómək a'ím.
Tsaqáavtək,
tsakavárətsk a'íim vuunóom;
'a'ávək va'thík 'a'étka,"
a'étk vuunóom,
nyaa'áv.

and I'll say that to him,
and he'll go
and take a look,"
he said, they say.

"He'll peek in and see,"
he said,
and she heard him.

"All right," she said.
The old woman did as she had been told,
"Hey,
I see you!
I'm going to give you (something)!" she said,
and the boy heard her,
and he stopped, and immediately,
she went about parching corn, just as she had been told,
and when she finished,
she filled her hand (with parched corn),
and she gave it to him, they say.

She gave it to him,
she put it into his hand,
and when he took it,
"You go along.
The girls' house is there,
it's the one over there.
Peek inside
and see," she said,
they say.

"Well,
there are people in there,
there might be.
They are talking,
they keep laughing;
we've been hearing them,"
she went on saying it,
and he heard her.

"Xóttk," a'étk,
áam a'étk,
tathítsəny nyaatsa'úlyk;
nyaatsapóxk viiyáam.
Nóq a'ím,
iisháalyəm nyatama'órək áaytəm athúm,
makyík aváam alya'éməxáyk,
atsáavək a'étəma.

Nyaatsáavək,
nyáasik athíik,
takavék nyaaváak,
"Nyiirísh a'ésh," a'íik a'étəma.

Kwara'ákənyts siithík.
"Ayúu lya'émətək uu'áv lyavíita.
Kamathúm,
'atáyəm káayk.
'Anóq ta'axánəm máay kama'émtəm,
atsáavtək a'ítya,
matsáampúytək awím,"
a'íik 'etəma.

A'étəm,
nyaa'ávək,
'aakóoyənyts "Xóttk," a'íim,
nyaawíntik vuunóok vuunóok,
kwaskyíily atsáam,
áayk a'étəma.
Uutama'órək,
áayəm,
nyaayúuk.

Nyaatháwk.
"Muká!
Vathány mayúu alyma'émək?" a'íim,
"Mayáatanək,
alymapám,
mayúu a'ítsəm ma'ámək,"
a'ét.

"All right," he said,
and he went a little way,
holding the corn in his hand;
he munched on it as he went along.
It was just a little bit,
she had given him (just) a handful, and so,
he hadn't gone anywhere, by the time
he had eaten it up, they say.

When he had eaten it up,
he came back from over there,
and when he got back,
"There's nothing there," he said, they say.

The old man was lying there.
"It sounds like he didn't (even) look.
Whatever you do,
give him a lot.
You must have given him just a little bit,
and he ate it all up,
because he's so hungry,"
he said, they say.

So,
when she heard him,
the old woman said, "All right,"
and she did it again, going on and on,
and she put it in a dish,
and she gave it to him, they say.
She filled it up,
and she gave it to him,
and he saw it.

He took it.
"Now!
Didn't you see this?" she said.
"Really go,
and when you get there,
take a look, as you heard him say,"
she said.

Vuunóom;
" 'Axótt," nyaa'étəntik,
kwaskyíi nyaatháwk.

Nyaatspóxəntik,
viiyáanyk viiyáanyk;
'atáytəm,
atsáav alya'émxayk,
aváamtək a'étəma.

Nyaaváamək,
'avány alyaa'áshk,
ayúuxayəm,
'aványts avathúum,
kwal'iishíik anyórək.

Tama'órtanəm,
ayúuk aaly'éxáyk,
axweshxwéshk apámk!
Apúytək siithík 'etəma.

Athúm,
athúum,
iiwáanyts ép a'íik a'ím athútya.

Siithíkəny,
'akóortanəm,
nyaamánək,
nyáany viithíik,
nyaaváam,
"Kaathótíi?" a'éxayəm —
"Ée'é,
kaawíts anyúurək mattapéek,
'avány alytama'órəm!

" 'Ayúuk,
'ayúuxayk 'apámək.
Si'athíkənyk,
si'athíkənyk,
'amánək vi'athíik 'athópək athó,"
a'íik 'etəma.

There they were;
"All right," he said again,
and he took the dish.

He was munching (corn) again,
he went on and on;
there was a lot of it,
and he still hadn't eaten it up, by the time
he got there, they say.

He got there,
and he peeked into the house,
he looked, and immediately,
the house was like that,
it was multi-colored and shining like a rainbow.

It was full (of color),
and as soon as he saw it,
he spun around and fell down!
He fainted dead away, they say.

So,
it happened,
he just blacked out.

He lay there,
for a really long time,
and he got up,
and he came back,
and when he got there,
"What happened?" they said, and immediately —
"Well,
there are all kinds of colors
and they're filling up the house!

"I looked,
and as soon as I saw it, I fell down.
I lay there,
and I lay there,
and I got up and came back and here I am,"
he said, they say.

Nyaakanáavəm,
nyaa'ávək,
kwara'ákənyts,
"Móo,
ma'ávk!
Saathúum!
Kaawíts uuvátk kwalyavíita, "
a'éxayəm,
"Mamuuvílytək ammuuváanyk!
Kaawíts athúum athútya!"
nyaa'étk.

Xuumáy nyáanyts nyiishamathíik,
nyuuváam.
Kaawíts kaawíim,
pa'iipáa uutsáam,
ara'óytək suuváam,
nyaayúuk aqásək vuunóom.

Nyaayáak uukanáavətsəm,
nyaa'ávək viithíitk,
aváatk a'étəma.

Nyaaváak,
nyaaváam,
a'ím,
"Vaathóm!
Vaathúwúm 'a'épək 'a'ávənyk!
'A'éxayəm,
mayúu alyma'éməs,
ma'étəm!
Nyaatháwəm!

"Nyaathúum,
avány 'a'íim,
ayáaxayk,
vaathúum ayúuk!" a'éta.
"Pa'iipáa mashtúum mayáak,
alymaxávək mayúuxá!"
a'ét.

He told them about it,
and they listened,
and the old man (said),
"Okay,
you heard him!
It's true!
There seems to be something there,"
he said, and immediately,
"You (had better) hurry!
There is something there!"
he said.

That son of his didn't know about it,
there he was.
He was doing something or other,
he was in charge of (a group of) people,
he was having a good time over there,
and (someone) saw him and called him.

(That person) went and told him about it,
and when (the son) heard about it he came,
and he got there, they say.

He got there,
he got there,
and (the old man) said,
"This is how it is!
I said it would be this way!
I said so,
but you didn't really look, even though
you said you did!
And they were there (all along)!

"Then,
I said that (to the orphan boy),
and he went there, and immediately,
he saw that this is how it is!" he said.
"Get some people together and go,
go in there and see!"
he said.

Vuunóotəm,
nyaa'ávək,
"Xóttk," a'ím,
pa'iipáa —
'iipáts 'atáytanəm nyaaqáask,
nyaashtúum.

Vaayáak apámək,
a'éxayəm,
nyiirísh a'étəm;
alyarpéemtək uuyóovək,
xayəm,
mashtaxáany a'ím,
"Kaawíts kamathúum viimatháwəm?"
a'ím.

A'étk,
a'ávək a'ét,
suunóom,
náq a'étk,
uuyóovtək siitháwk.
Kaa'ém alya'émək siitháwəm.

A'ím,
uuyóovtk,
nyaayúu,
aaíimək,
kaly'aaxwáay awíim —
nyaayúu tsuuxáy uutséw,
nyáava atávək a'ávək,
kaawémək a'ávək,
awétk suunóonyk,
nyiuutspák.

Viinathíik,
nyaakatán,
"Nyiiríish a'ím nyiikwévəsh."

"Kaawíts makyí uuváalya'ém."

Here they were,
and (his son) heard him;
"All right," he said,
and people —
he called a whole lot of men,
he gathered them together.

They went along and got there,
and by the time they did,
there was nothing there;
they peeked in and looked,
and immediately,
he said to the girls,
"What are you up to?"
he said.

So,
they heard him, and so,
there they were,
they kept silent,
and they sat there watching.
They sat there not saying anything.

So,
the men looked around,
well,
they did as they pleased,
they used war clubs —
(the walls) were made of adobe or something,
and they hit them, all over the place,
they did whatever it was, all over the place,
they went about doing it,
and they came out.

They came back,
and when they got there,
"There's nothing there at all," (they told the old man).

"There isn't anything there anywhere."

A'étk,
suunóom,
a'ávətk aványk.
"Ée'é,
kaathóm ma'íim ma'ítya."
" 'Aakxávtanək 'uuyóovtəs,
kaváarəsh,"
a'étk vuunóom.

Nyaa'ávək.
" 'Axóttk," a'íim,
kaa'ém alya'émətək.

Siithíkəm.
Nyáavəm,
nyiipúuttk vaayémtəm,
nyiiríish a'étəm,
siitháwtək,
kwara'ákənyts iiwáa xakwatháw va'árəm,
siithík.

Nyáanyəm,
tsaqwértək a'étk vuunóom.
"Kamawíim ma'ím?"
'aakóoyəny.
"Kaváarək," a'ím,
"Nyaamuukanáavtsəm,
nyaamayúuk,
thúutt ma'étk ammuunóotəm."

A'étk vuunóom,
nyaa'ávək,
náq a'étk siithíkt av'áartək vuunóony.

Viitháwnyək,
viitháwəm,
nyáasəts alyatháw av'árkəm,
siitíivnyək.
'Anóqəts viivákəm,
mattshakyévətk a'étəma.

So,
there they were,
and he heard them.
"Well,
that's what you say," he said.
"We really did go in and look, but
(the situation) is not (what you feared it would be),"
they kept saying.

(The old man) heard them.
"All right," he said,
and he didn't say anything.

He lay there.
At this (point),
(the men) scattered and left,
and they were gone,
but (the young women) were over there,
and the old man was just as worried as ever,
lying there.

From that (point),
he went on talking about it.
"Why are you doing this?" (she asked),
the old woman (did).
"It is not (what you feared it would be)," she said,
"They told you,
and you saw (that they were right),
and (yet) you keep on (pursuing it) more and more."

She went on saying it,
and he heard her,
and he lay there, silent, as usual.

Here they were,
here they were,
and those (young people) were still in there,
they were over there.
The younger ones were there,
and they got married, they say.

Mattshakyév,
a'ís,
kwakútsənyts kaváarək a'étəma.
A'íim,
nyáam,
mattshakyév va'árək,
siitháawnyək,
siitháawnyək,
siitháw.

Siitháw va'árənyk,
siitháwxayəm,
nyiitíiv va'árətsk,
nyam nyiiríish a'ím,
a'étkəm,
nyáany —
kwa'kútsənyts atspák,
'axá athíitk,
axávək athót av'árək,
suuvám,
ayúut.

'Akóoyənyts siivátk.
"Avatháwtəkəm athúum.

"Atspák,
suuváanyk,
axávəm;
'ayúuk 'avá'əsh," a'ét av'ár.

Vuunóom,
viitháwnyək,
viitháwk,
viitháw.

'Akór alynyaayém ta'axánəm.

Nyáavəts,
'aakóoy nyáava,
kwasta'ótsənyts alynyiithúutsk uuváatk,

They got married,
but
the older ones didn't, they say.
So,
at that (point),
the (younger people) were married,
and there they were,
there they were,
there they were.

They were there, as usual,
they were there, when all of a sudden,
they were sitting there as usual,
and there was nobody (else) there,
and so,
as for that —
the older one came out,
she came for water,
and she went back in as usual,
and there she was,
and (the old woman) watched her.

The old woman was over there.
"They are there.

"She came out,
and there she was,
and she went back inside;
I saw her," she always said.

She was around here,
and here they were,
here they were,
here they were.

A really long time passed.

This (other one),
this old lady,
the one who had given birth to them was thinking about them,

"Kaawíts,
apóoyíi.
Kaathómk viitháawtǝk a'ím,
makyík nakavékǝly'em,
Nyiikwévǝm.

" 'A'ávtǝk va'uuváak 'athó'ash,"
a'étk.
Alynyiithúutst av'ártǝk,
amétk uuváat av'árt.

" 'Akór alynayémǝk,"
a'íim.

A'íi va'árǝk uuváanyk,
kaváartǝkǝm a'ávǝk athúm,
"Vathám,
nyaanakavékǝlys,
nyiiríish a'ím vanyaatháw.

"Kaawíts kaathómk a'émǝk athútya,"
a'étk aav'ártǝk.
Uuváanyk,
uuváany.

'Akór alynyaayém.
Mattnyaatspée ta'axánǝm.

Nyáava,
xuumárǝnyts —
xuumárǝts nya'iikyínyts nyiivák,
nya'kútskǝm athúm.

Xuumár 'atsma'ím,
a'áv alya'émǝk vanyaathíkǝm,
nyáany lyavíik awétk awím,
"Katspám alyka'émǝk,"
a'ítsxayǝm —
'avály uuváak uuváxayk,
ayúuts alya'émxayǝm,

"Whatever they did,
 they're probably dead.
Whatever they were up to,
 they are never coming back.
They have come to their end.

"This is how I feel about it,"
 she said.
She was always thinking about it,
 and she was always weeping.

"It's been such a long time,"
 she said.

She was always saying it;
 she sensed that (something) was wrong, and so,
"At this (point),
 they should be back, but
 there has been nothing.

"Something must have happened to them,"
 she was always saying.
There she was,
 there she was.

A long time passed.
It really was overwhelming.

This one,
 the child —
 the little boy was there,
 and he had gotten older.

You say something to a child,
 and he doesn't listen,
 that's what he was like, and so,
"Don't go out,"
 they said, and immediately —
 he stayed in the house,
 (but) as soon as they weren't looking,

atspám,
mat'ár uuváak,
kúur axávtək uuvám.

Uuyóovək vuunóonyk,
" 'Éey!
Xuumárəts alyuuváak!
Atspák uuváanyk,
axávtək kwalyavíit," a'ím,
'aakóoyənyts a'ét.

" 'Ayúutanək 'aváxayəm,
xuumárəts atspámək,
aví uuváak,
kúur a'éxayəm,
alyaxávək athótk kwalyvíim.
'Ayúutk 'avák'ash,"
a'íim.

Suunóom,
a'ávək uuvány k.
" 'Éey!

"Avathúum 'a'épək 'a'ávənyk!
Avathótk kwalyvíita 'a'íim!
Nya'uunóom,
kaváarkəm ma'étk ammuunóonyk,
athúum!
Athúum a'ítya!"
a'íim.

Siitháwk,
siitháwəm,
nyáava mattnyaakatsuunávək vanyaatháwk.

Nyaa'ávək,
***
xuumáy nyaaqástəntim,
nyaaváam a'ím,
"Vaathúum,

he went out,
and he stayed outside,
and in a little while he came in and there he was.

They were watching,
"Hey!
There's a child there!
He came out for a while,
and (then) he seems to have gone (back) in," she said,
the old woman said it.

"I was watching, and all of a sudden,
a child came out,
and he stayed there,
and after a little while,
he seems to have gone (back) inside.
I was watching him,"
she said.

There they were over there,
and the old man was listening.
"Hey!

"I said it would happen!
I said it seemed to be happening!
There we were,
and you kept saying no,
but it's happening!
It's happening!"
he said.

There they were,
there they were,
and they discussed this among themselves.

He heard them,
***
and he called his son again,
and when (the son) got there, he said,
"This is what's happening,

mayúuk," a'éta.
'Aakóoyavats ayúuk vanyaavák,
kanáavtək a'ítya.

Nyuunóom;
"Mayáatan mayúuly 'aaly'étka,"
a'íim.

A'íim,
nyaa'ávək,
"Xóttk," a'ím,
pa'iipáa nyaaqáasəntik mattnyaashtúum,
vaayáak alyapám.

Uuyóovək.
Vuunóoxayəm,
xuumár tsanpéevəts alyuuváatk uuváam,
uuyóovət.

Suunóo,
nyakórtanəm,
vatháts aashtuuthúulyk.
Nyiirísh a'ét.

Nyaayúuk,
nyaatakavék,
nyaaváamək,
"Athúu kwa'átsəsh," a'ím.

"Xuumárəts alyvák uuváatəməsh.
Uuvám 'ayúu'əsh," a'íik 'etəma.
A'íim,
a'íim,
kanáavəm,
kwara'ákənyts a'ávək siithíkənyk,
a'íim,
"Ée'é.

"Xuumár xatsíny nyaathúum,
'axótt-təxa.

you see," he said.
The old woman had been watching,
and she told him about it.

There they were;
"I think you really should go and take a look,"
she said.

And so,
when he heard her,
"All right," he said,
and he summoned people again and they got together,
and they went along and got there.

They looked.
There they were, and suddenly
there was a little child in there,
and they saw him.

There they were,
(but) already,
these (people) had hidden him.
He was gone.

They looked,
and they went back,
when they got there,
"It's just as you said," he said.

"There's a child in there.
We saw him there," they said it, they say.
They said it,
and so,
they told him about it,
and the old man lay there listening,
and he said,
"Yes.

"If it's a girl,
it will be all right.

"A'íis,
xuumár 'iikyíny nyaathúum,
'aláaytəxa.

"Nyáanyts,
nyaayúu 'aláay athóxa.
Athóxa lyavíim,
nyáany 'áar aly'a'émk,
vany'avám.

"Nyáanya vanyaathúum,
mattapóoyvətxa,"
a'íik 'et.

"A'íis,
xuumár nyaathúum,
uuváanyk,
nya'akútsk sanya'áktiya.

"Athúum,
nyáany,
kaawíts kaathóm alya'éməxa.
A'íis,
xuumár 'iikyíny nyáanyts,
uuváavəly,
avathúum,
'ats'aláay athúum,
nyiinyta'aaláayxa lyavíim.

"A'íim,
nyáanyəm,
nyáany xuumár 'iikyíny nyaathúum,
mattapóoyətxa,"
a'ét.

"Ée'ée" a'étk,
" 'Atskakwék 'a'áv aly'éməsh,"
nyaa'étk,
takavéktək,
nyaayáantik.

"But,
 if it's a boy,
 it will be bad.

"That
 will be a bad thing.
 It's likely to be bad,
 and I don't want that,
 as I am here.

"If that's what it is,
 you will have to kill him,"
 he said, they say.

"But,
 if it's a (female) child,
 she will be there,
 and when she grows up she will be a woman.

"So,
 (in) that (case),
 she won't be any (trouble).
 But,
 that boy,
 in being there,
 he'll do something,
 and there will be trouble,
 he will probably destroy us.

"So,
 in that (case),
 if it is a boy,
 you will have to kill him,"
 he said.

"Oh," they said,
"We didn't ask (whether it was a boy or a girl),"
 they said,
 and they went back,
 they went along again.

Aváamək,
a'íim,
nyáanyts,
nyáavəts 'iipáavəts nyaaváamək a'ím,
"Xuumár kaathúts athúm?"
a'íik 'etəma.

'Akútsk uuváas,
awétk avathúum:
avathóxa lyavíik nyaa'íim,
vaathíim,
nyaayúuk,
uukavék,
akwílyk aavíirtək a'étəma.
A'étkəm,
siithiktəm a'íim.

Nyáanyi,
kwa'kúts nyáanyts a'íim,
"Máany manyuuwítsk mathúm?"

"Makaváark.
Avány athó'əsh," a'étk,
anyáqəny a'étəm.

Nyaa'ávək.
"Xuumár kaathúts athúm?
Xuumár xatsínyts,
xó
xuumár 'iikyínyts?"
a'íik 'et.

A'éxayəm,
"Xuumár xatsínyts," a'íik 'et.
Xuumár 'iikyínyts athúus a'ét,
tatapóoyəv a'étəm a'ávək a'ím.

Vaa'étk a'étəma.
A'étəm,
nyaa'ávək.

They got there,
and so,
they were the ones,
these men got there and said,
"What kind of a child is it?"
they said, they say.

He was (too) old (for it), but
this is what they did:
when it was about to happen,
(when) they were coming,
and (the young women) saw this,
they put (the boy) back,
they wrapped him in his cradle and finished, they say.
So,
he was lying there, they say.

At that (point),
the older (boy) said,
"Is (this child) yours?"

"You're mistaken.
It's hers," she said,
and he said it to the younger sister.

She heard him.
"What kind of a child is it?
Is it a girl,
or
is it a boy?"
he said, they say.

He said so, and immediately,
"It's a girl," she said.
She said so, even though it was a boy,
(because) she had heard that they would kill (a boy).

This is what she said.
She said it,
and he heard her.

"Ée'é,"
a'étk,
siiv'áwnyk atspámtək,
vanyaayém,
nyaaváam,
kwara'ákəny uukanáavək.
"Vaathúum.
Vaathúts athúuk 'eta,"
a'íim,
uukanáavəm,
"Ée'é.
Nya'xóttəntim."
Nyaanymáam,
nyáany a'étk a'étká.

"Xuumár 'iikyíny nyaathúum,
'áar aly'a'émk,
'a'épəm ma'ámək,"
a'ét.
Suunóom,
nyaa'ávək.

Nyaapúuttəntik,
vaayémək,
nyiirísh a'ítstəm.

Siitháawtək,
siitháawxayəm,
"Nyaa'iiwáam.
'Anymawáam.
'Ayáatanək
'atskakwék 'a'ávxa."
Nyaa'étəntik,
sanyuuváam,
nyaa'ávək.

'Aakóoyənyts uunaxwílyk,
vanyaawáaak,
alykamémk 'etəma.

"Okay,"
he said,
and he stood up and went out,
he left,
and when he got (home),
he told the old man about it.
"It's like this.
This is how they are,"
he said,
and he told him about it.
"Okay.
It's all right again."
That's all,
that's what he said, they say.

"If it had been a boy,
I wouldn't have wanted that,
as you heard me say,"
he said.
There they were,
and they heard him.

They scattered again,
they went away,
and they were gone.

(The young people) were over there,
they were still over there, and all of a sudden,
"I'll do it myself," (said the old man).
"Take me to them.
I will go
and ask them and hear (the answer)."
He said it again,
there he was,
and she heard him.

The old woman dragged him,
she took him along,
and she brought him there, they say.

Alykamémǝm,
nyaatskakwém,
kanáavǝk ava'íntik:
"Xuumár xatsínyts athúu kwa'átsk athúm,"
a'éxaym,
"Áa-áa," a'étǝm,
nyaa'áv.

"Ée'é,
'axótt-tǝxa."

"Uuváany,
nya'kútsk,
pa'iipáa atsúyk,
nyaváytiya."

Nyaa'étk,
nakavéktǝk viinayémtǝm.
Siitháwnyǝk,
siitháwǝny.

Siitháw,
nyaamáam,
atspámǝk,
avathótk uuváat av'ártǝk,
'ara'óyk uuváak,
kúur axávtǝk,
athótk uuváam.

'Aakóoynyǝnyts ayúutk uuváat av'ártǝk,
uuváatǝnyk,
uuváatǝny.

Uuváanyk,
kaawémǝk vanyuuváak,
makyípǝts ayúukǝm.

"Éey!
Xuumár 'iikyínyts athúus," a'étk a'épǝka,
a'íim,
nyaakanáavtsǝm.

She brought him there,
and he asked them,
and they told (the same story) again:
"The child is a girl, just as we said,"
she said, and immediately
(the other one) said "Yes,"
and he heard them.

"Okay.
It will be all right," (he said).

"She (will) stay here,
and when she gets older,
she (will) get married,
and settle down."

He said it,
and they went back (home).
There they were,
there they were.

There they were,
and finally,
(the child) went out,
and he did things as usual,
he played,
and in a little while he went back in,
that's what was happening.

The old lady was watching him, as usual,
there she was,
there she was.

There she was,
and somehow,
someone (else) saw him.

"Hey!
It might be a boy after all," they said,
and so,
they told (the old man) about it.

Nyaa'ávək,
kwara'ákənyts
xuumáyəny nyaaqásəntik a'íim.

"Vaathúum!
'A'íim 'a'épək 'a'ávənyk,
mayúu ta'axánək ma'íilyəm!
Maaíimtanək ma'íim,
muuváatəny!

"Vaathúum athúukəta!
Athúum.
Nyamathútsk.

"Nyamathútsk.
Xuumár 'iikyínyts athúum!
Atspák,
nyáasi uuváak!
'Akútstanək,
aar'óoy uuváanyk,
axávtək,
athúu uuváam,
'Aakóoyvəts ayúutanək uuváa va'árk,
awím,
mapís uuyóovək vuunóotsk a'ítsta,"
a'ím.

"Nyuunóom,
mamuuvílytanək,
'anyáa vathám mayáak,
matapúytəxa!"
a'íi.

A'étk,
suunóotk,
xuumáyəny a'ím.

Athúum,
nyaa'ávək,
" 'Axóttk," a'étk,

When he heard them,
the old man
called his son again, they say.

"It has happened!
I said it would,
but you didn't really look into it!
You were careless,
when you were there!

"It has happened!
It did.
It happened because of that.

"It happened because of that.
It was a boy!
He came out,
and there he was, over there!
He had grown,
and he was playing,
and he went in,
he was doing (that),
and the old lady has seen him all along,
and so,
now they have seen him too,"
he said.

"There they are,
and you really (must) hurry,
you (must) go this very day,
and kill him!"
he said.

He said it,
he went on,
he said it to his son.

And so,
when (his son) heard him,
"All right," he said,

viiyáatk,
pa'iipáava nyaashtúntik viiyáatk aváam.

A'ím,
a'éxayəm,
xuumár 'iikyínyənya —
sanya'ákənyts 'atsshamáatk iináamk athúuk awím,
nyaayúu —
'avuulypóts a'íim,
atók av'áwk,
'a'íi awítstəm 'ayúuny.
Nyáanya,
uuthápk,
nyaalyaakxávək aashuuthúlyk a'étəm;
alyaxávək,
alyaatséqtək.

Aashuuthúlykəm.

Alyaakxávək,
"Makyí uuváam?" a'ím,
a'étk.

Nyáasily xalykwáak,
nyaayúu nyatamán aaly'íim uunóony.

Nyiiríish a'étəm ayúutk.
'Avuushxwíirəny kastútsk a'ávək,
kaawémək a'áv kwa'áts,
nyiiríiish a'étəm ayóovək vuunóony.

Nyuutspámək viinayém.
"Nyiiríish a'épəka.
Makyík kaawéts makyí uuváalyəm nyiikwév.

"Kaawéts mayúupk ammatháwk ma'ítya,"
a'étk,
vuunóom.

and he went along,
and he gathered people together again and went along
    and got there.

So,
immediately,
that little boy —
the (young) woman was very powerful, and so,
well —
it's called a housepost,
it's in the middle of the house,
I've seen them use trees.
That (housepost),
she split it,
and she said (the boy) should go in and hide inside it,
and he went in,
and he was wedged in there.

She had hidden him.

They went in (the house).
"Where is he?" they said.
They said it.

They looked for him, over there,
they lifted things up everywhere (to look underneath).

They saw that there was nothing there.
They hit all the corners of the house,
they did whatever they could, just as they had been told,
and they saw that there was nothing there.

They went out and left.
"There is certainly nothing there.
There is nobody there at all.

"I don't know what you saw,"
they said.
and there they were.

" 'Ayóovtanəs,
nyiiríish a'ésh,"
a'étk,
vuunóom.

A'ávtək,
"Tó.
Avathúwúm 'a'épk 'a'ávəny.

"Nyikamánək katánək.
Nya'láayk vanyaatháwəm,"
a'étk.
Kwara'ákənyts siithík.

Nyaapúutt-təntik,
nyiiriish a'ítstəm,
suuváanyk.
" 'A'ávənyk.
Thomayúuvəm nyaa'a'ávək nyaqástəntixa,"
a'étk,
vuunóom;
"Ée'é,"
nyaa'étk,
viiyémtəm.

Nyáavəm,
siitháwtəny,
siitháwəm,
nyaa'ávək —
aváts a'ávətsk viitháwənyk —
"Éey!
Vi'nayémxa.
'Anakavékt.

"Vi'nayémúm,"
a'étk,
'iipátsavəts.
"Nyamáam,
'ankavékxa,"
a'ét.

"We looked closely, but
there was nothing there,"
they said,
and there they were.

(The old man) heard them.
"Okay.
I said this would happen.

"It started there and it reached (this point).
It is bad,"
he said.
The old man was lying there.

They scattered again,
and they were gone,
and there he was.
"I will listen.
When I hear (something) clear, I will call you again,"
he had said,
(while) they were there;
"Okay,"
they had said,
and they had left.

At this (point),
they were over there,
they were over there,
and they heard about it —
those (twin young men) heard about it —
"Hey!
We'd better go.
We're going back (home).

"We'd better go,"
they said,
those men.
"That's all,
we will go back (home),"
they said.

Nyaa'étk,
nyauutspá a'étk,
viiwétstək 'etəma.

Viiwétstəm.
"Pa'iipáats viiwétstək uulyavíi'əsh,"
a'étk,
katsuunáavəm,
nyaa'ávək,
matt-tsáam vaathíi kaa'íim.

'Avány alyaakxávək,
uuyóovək a'ávək,
kaathómək a'ávək,
athúu vuunóony,
nyiirísh nyaa'íim.

Tatuuvíirək a'étəntik,
'amáttva kaváayk,
avkwuunóony,
nyiiríish a'étk nyiikwévtəm.

Nyaakavéktək.
"Nyiirísh a'ím nyiikwévtək viitháwk.
Pa'iipáa makyí uuváaly'eməsh,"
a'étəntik,
nyuukanáavtsəm.

Kwara'ákənyts nyaa'ávk a'ím,
"Saathúwúm 'a'íim 'a'épk!
'A'ávənyk!
Alynyi'thúutstənyk!
Nyakór 'a'íim,
'aavíir.

"Máany 'atsmuuyúutsəny nyiimakwévtantəm athótk athútya!"
a'étk;
xuumáyəny wanyiirávətk vuunóony.

They said it,
and they came out, and so,
they went along, they say.

They went along.
"Some people seem to be going this way,"
(someone) said,
he told them about it,
and when they heard him,
somehow they all came.

They went into the house,
and they looked all around,
they did whatever it was, all over the place,
they were doing it,
(but) there was no-one there.

They chased after them, and so,
they went from house to house,
(but) the (people) who had been there
were long gone.

They went back.
"They're long gone.
There is no-one there at all,"
they it said again,
they told him about it.

The old man heard them and said,
"I said it would happen like that!
I sensed it!
I thought about it!
I said so a long time ago,
and I finished.

"You have been completely useless at looking (into the situation)!"
he said;
he went on scolding his son.

" 'Anyáats nyi'anáamapatk 'a'íim,
nyaayúu 'ayúuk va'uunóos,
kaváarəm,
nya'étk 'a'ítya!"
a'étk,
suunóony,
nyaaníimək.

Nyaa mattuutsqáavək nyiixúuu a'étk,
"Pa'iipáats katánək —
'axwéts katánək!
Vuunóo ta'axán!

" 'Uuyóovalyem nyiikwéevəm!
Vuunóonyk,
vuunóonyk,
uutspámək vanyaawétsəm,
uuyóovək!" a'íim.

"Taxalyuukwáatsk vuunóony,
nyiiríish a'étk!
Viitháwkət," nyaa'étk,
mattuukanáavək aaíimxayəm,

nyiiváam aváam a'étk,
vuunóom.

'Aayúu —
Xantas'ílyts a'étəma.

Nyáanyts,
nyaayúu,
lizardts vatátskəm,
'ayúu,
kwathíkəny.
Nyáanyənyts.

Makyíly uuváak,
suuváanyk,
viithíik,

"I have powers too,
I see (certain) things, but
there wasn't anything happening,
I tell you!"
(the son) said,
and they went on (arguing),
and they got through it.

They were talking noisily to each other:
"People came —
the enemy came!
They really were here!

"We didn't see them at all!
They stayed here,
and they stayed here,
and (only when) they came out and left
did (anybody) see them!" they said.

"People went searching for them,
but they were gone!
That's what happened," they said,
and they were discussing it carelessly among themselves,
    when suddenly,
he got there, they say,
(while) they were there.

Something —
it was Gila Monster, they say.

Those (things),
well,
they're big lizards,
I've seen them,
the ones that are there.
That's what he was.

He was there somewhere,
there he was,
and he came this way,

aváatk xáyəm,
vaa'étk:
mattuutsqáavək,
nyiixúuu a'étk vuunóom nyaa'áv.

"Kaawíts kamathópk muunóokəm?" a'íim.

*** *** ***

Ava'íim,
ava'étk,
uukanáavtsəm,
a'ávəts
avány.

"Amma'íim ma'íim,
nyiiməkwévəts tánək ma'ítya!
Nyaathúum!

" 'Anyép nyama'íim,
nyamaatsxwáar ma'ím:
' 'Atsmattxalykwáayk,
kaawíts makyíly avák,
'aakóoy lyavíik,
kwaskyíi atséwpəm'ashk athútya,'
ma'ím.

"Maatsxwáar muu'ítsk ammuunóony!

"Nyiiməkwévts tánək mathúum!
Mathúus ma'étk ma'ítsəm,
vanyaatháwəm.
Kaawíts axwíivəm avmavárək ammuunóok ma'ítya!"
nyaa'étk.

" 'Anyáats nyi'attavíirək 'ayúuxá,"
nyaa'étk.
Nyiittavíirək,
vuuthíinyk,
vuuthíinyk,
vuuthíinyk.

and by the time he got here,
it was like this:
they were talking among themselves,
and he heard the noise they were making.

"What are you up to?" he said.

*** *** ***

He said that,
he said that,
he told them about it,
and they heard him,
that one.

"You say whatever you want to,
(but) you're no good (yourselves)!
So be it!

"You talk about me,
and you laugh at me:
'He hunts for things for himself,
he sits somewhere,
he's like an old lady,
making pottery as usual,'
you say.

"You are laughing (at me)!

"You really are no good!
You say you will do something (about the enemy), but
there they are.
And you are too weak to do anything about it!"
he said.

"I'll chase them and see (what happens),"
he said.
He chased them,
he brought them this way,
and he brought them this way,
and he brought them this way.

Nyamáam,
'akór alynyaanayémək,
a'ím,
athúm:
'amáayi náamək athúunyk,
natséntək.

Uuv'áak siinathíi,
siiwétstək.

A'ét,
viinathíik;
tatavíirək,
viiwáanyk,
viiwáanyk,
viiwáanyk.

'Amátt alythíktək —
vaathópəm 'ayúuny,
'amáttk av'áak,
nyaayúunyənyts —
avathótəm,
nyamayóov alya'émək;
nyiishtamatháav.

Siiwétstəm,
viiyáanyk,
viiyáany,
nyiinyuutsakxávək,
nyáanyts nyiitsatapóoytək a'étəma.

Xantas'ilyənyts.

Nyiinyaatsatapóoytəm,
nyáanyts,
nyiinyaatsatapóoyəm,
nyaapóoyk,
'amátt uupúuvtək a'étəma.
Iiwáam.

Finally,
a long time passed,
and so,
it happened:
they passed by overhead,
and they came down.

They went walking in that direction,
and they went along.

And so,
they came this way;
(Gila Monster) chased them,
he went,
and he went,
and he went.

He lay down on the ground —
I've seen them like that,
they walk on the ground,
those things —
he did that,
and they couldn't see him;
they didn't know (that he was there).

They went along,
and he went after them,
he went after them,
and he caught up with them,
and he is the one who killed them, they say.

Gila Monster (did it).

He killed them,
he is the one,
he killed them,
and when they died,
they went into the earth, they say.
By themselves.

'Amáttəm uupúuvtəm,
nyuupúuvəm,
'amáttənyts ava'é a'ím.

Muuxóoyk atspáktək.

Muuxóoyk atspáktək,
'axwáak 'úts a'étk,
nyáanyts,
xamiilyúusk athúuk a'étəma.

Nyáanya,
it's a disease that they left,
a'étəma.

Athúum athúuk a'étəma.

Nyáava,
nyáanya,
xamalyús palytéerəts a'étəma.
Nyaayúu,
measles a'íim a'ítya.

Nyáany palytéerəts a'étəma.
A'íim,
nyáany,
nyáanyaxan avathúum.
Nyáany,
nyiinamákəm athúuk a'étəma.

Namákəm,
nyaayúuk,
nyaatakavék,
viiyáak nyaaváam,
mattkanáavək uuváam.
" 'Atatapóoyəm nyiikwévək!"

"Athúum,
iiwáam,
'mátt uupúuvək;
mattaanáartək athútya!"

They went into the earth,
they went in,
and the earth went like this.

Steam came out.

Steam came out,
and it rose up like smoke,
and that (smoke),
and that was the measles, they say.

As for that,
it's a disease that they left,
they say.

It happened, they say.

As for this,
that (disease),
it's the measles, they say.
Well,
they call it measles, they say.

That's the measles, they say.
So,
as for that,
that's how it came about.
That (disease),
they left it behind, they say.

They left it behind,
and he saw (this),
and he went back,
he went along and got there,
and he went about telling them (what he had done).
"I killed them off! " (he said).

"And so,
all by themselves,
they went into the earth;
they buried themselves!"

A'étk,
kanáavtəm,
nyaa'ávək siithíkənyk.
"Nyamáam.
'Axóttəntim.

" 'Ats'iimák,
'ara'óoyk 'athúum,
'uuváaxá.

" 'Axalakúyk!
'Anykwa'ítsəny!
Nyamáam,
'axwéts apúytəm 'athúm!"
nyaa'étk,
nyamathútsk.
Ara'óoy tsavóowk,
'atsiimák a'ávək,
kaawíts awíim,
mattamáarək a'ávək,
awíim,
aatsxwáaar a'étk,
suunóo va'ár.

Suunóoxáyly,
kaawíts a'íim:

"Ma'uutsláytsənyts!
Mattmatspéek!
Ma'xóttk manyváyk ammuuváalyma'émtək mathútya!

"Muuváa alynyaama'émək!
Mathúum,
nyaamuuváak,
ammathótk ammathótk viimanathíik,
nyaayúu 'axótt mathúum makaa'áaməts vanyaamanathíim.

" 'Anyáa makyípəm,
nyaayúuts,
'a'áw aráats avathík,

He said it,
he told them about it,
and (the old man) listened.
"That's all.
It (will) be all right again.

"We (will) dance,
and enjoy ourselves, and so,
we will be here.

"Let's rejoice!
We've done it!
Finally,
the enemy is dead!"
he said,
and that's what they did.
They put on a fiesta,
there was dancing everywhere,
and they did whatever,
they (gambled and) won,
and so,
they were laughing,
there they were.

There they were, and all of a sudden
he said something:

"How bad you are!
You go too far with it!
You don't live in a good way!

"You don't!
And so,
here you are,
you come along doing whatever you do,
you come along never doing anything good.

"Some day,
well,
there (will) be a blazing fire,

viithiik,
viithíik,
nyiinyaamáttəm nyiikwévəm!

" 'Uupóoytíi va'tháwk 'athútya!"
a'étk.

Mattkatsuunávək vuunóotstəm.
Vaa'ítst a'éxayəm,
pa'iipáanyts xalypámək.
"Kaawíts a'épk 'aaly'íim."

" 'A'étk,
'atsalynyiithúutstək a'ítya.
Kaawémək athúwum,"
a'étk.

Vuunóok,
viitháwxayəm,
shamáts tsuumpáp nyiinyaayáam.

Asháamxayəly,
avathúu kwa'átsk!
Kanyaa'íntim,
matxá siithíik athúuk,
uuyúu lyavíik.

Siithíitk,
kwaráam takyévtək siithíitk,
siithíim,
nyuuyóov.

"Nyaathúu kwa'átsk!
Makyík 'uuthúutsxəlyá!"
a'étk,
aaíim.

Nyaavəm áam a'étk,
vuunóonyk,
vuunóoxayəly,
nyamaváa kwa'átstək avathótk,
nyaayúu kwaráanyanyts.

it (will) come,
and come,
it (will) sweep over us and that (will) be the end!

"We will probably die!"
he said.

They were all talking about it.
He said this, and immediately,
the people didn't believe it.
"I think he's just saying it."

"I say
that he's just making things up.
It will never happen,"
they said.

Here they were,
here they were, and suddenly,
four nights had passed.

They saw something in the distance, and suddenly
it was happening, just as he had said it would!
Somehow,
a wind was coming,
(that's) what it looked like.

It was coming from the distance,
and a blazing fire was coming with it,
it was coming from the distance,
and they saw it.

"It's happening, just as he said it would!
We have to do something!"
they said,
and they did what they could.

It was about to pass by,
and here they were,
here they were, and suddenly,
it got there, just as he had said it would,
that flaming thing (did).

Athótk,
siithíitk,
mataxám kuuéevək.

Siithíik,
nyaamáttk.

Nyáavəts,
kwara'ák alykwatanáktan xuumáyvəts,
nyáavəts a'étk,
"Ka'wémək 'apúyum!
'Anyáats,
'ats'ashuumáany nyiináamapatəm,
nyáaytsəm 'avátk 'athúm.

" 'Atspámxá!"
a'étk.

A'étk,
'atsayér nyáany mattatséwtək,
xamáalyk nyiipáq a'étk.
Ayérək 'amáy axáavək aaly'étəsáa,
kwapómənyts aváamtəm athúm.

Kamúly takavék a'ím,
pa'iipáany athúntixalyk a'ím —
a'étənyk,
alyaskyíitk,
alyaskyíitk siiyáat.

Vatháts,
xuumár nyáavəts nyaayúuk;
"Nyáanyts viithíik," a'íim vuunóom,
nyaa'ávək.

" 'Astuukyáanyú!"
a'ét.

"Móo,
'astuukyáanyú!" a'éxayəm,
sanya'ák kwa'nóqənyts as'ílyt.

It happened,
it came from the distance,
and it was mixed with wind.

It came from the distance,
and it swept over them.

This one,
this son of the old man who was their leader,
this one said,
"We might die!
As for me,
my dreams are powerful too,
I have been given (power).

"I will get out!"
he said.

He said it,
and he made himself into a bird,
and he was pure white.
He thought he could fly high enough in the sky, but
the fire reached him.

He tried to go back (to the way he used to be),
he wanted to be human again —
he wanted to,
(but) he remained the same,
he went along still the same.

This one,
this little boy saw it;
"That thing is coming!" he said,
and they heard him.

"Let's get out of here!"
he said.

"Okay,
let's get out of here!," he said, and immediately,
the younger woman refused.

Nyaas'ílyəm,
aváts,
"Máanyts kama'étk?
'Astuukyáanyú!

"Aváts viithíiny!
Nyaamáttəm,
'uupóoy 'a'étk 'athótkitya!"
a'étk vuunóom.

Nyaa'ávək,
sanya'ákənyts a'ím,
" 'Axóttk," nyaa'íim,
kwa'kútsənyts,
nyaaly'ák.
"Máanyts,
kathíik!" nyaa'ítsəm a'éxayəm;
"Kaváarək,
kaawíts 'ayáak va'ayémum va'avátxa,"
a'étk,
nyiikwévtək siivám nyaayúuk.

Nyaaxiipánək.
"Nya'awétsú!"

Nyaa'étk,
iisháaly nyaataxpályk,
nyiitsavakyévək,
nyiistuukyáanyk.

Alynanáktək viiwétstək,
a'étəma.

Alynanáktək viiwétsənyk,
viiwétstəm,
vatháts viivány,
nyaamatt-təm,
nyuupóoyíi kanyaa'ím.

Nyiíimtək.
Nyáany aavíir a'étk awétəny,
nyíimtəm.

She refused,
and he said,
"What are you saying?
Let's run away!

"It's coming!
It's going to sweep over (everything),
and we are going to die!"
he went on saying.

When she heard him,
the woman said,
"All right," she said,
the older one (did),
and she took (the boy) with her.
"You,
come on!" they said, and immediately,
"No.
I suppose I could go, but I will stay here,"
(the younger woman) said,
and she saw that it was no use (arguing with her).

(The fire) was getting closer.
"Let's go!"

She said it,
and she pulled (the boy) by the hand,
and they ran,
they ran away.

They ran just ahead of (the flames),
they say.

They were just ahead of (the flames),
and they went,
and this (younger woman) stayed here,
and (the fire) swept over (everything),
and it probably killed her somehow.

That was the end of her.
It finished her off, and so,
that was the end of her.

Vatháts,
siiwétsənyk,
alyuutspámtək.
Viinathíitk,
viinathíitk,
viinathíitk,
mattaaly'áktək,
viinathíim,
viinathíim.

Xáyəm,
'atsayér nyáanyts —
xanymasháv a'ím ashétəma.

Nyaayúu shuuvíi kwalyvíis,
xamáalytan páq a'étum.

A'íim,
ava'ítstəm 'a'áv,
'ayúuny;
nyáany avathúum.

Ayérək,
yáash a'étk,
siiyáam.

Xuumár 'iikyínyənyts láw a'ím,
nyaayúuk
a'ím,
"Kayúuk!
Avány 'anakwíits athúum,
'ashuupáawtəsáa,
kamúly takavékəly kaa'íim athúunyk,
nyiikwévək.
Nyamáam,
saathúum,
siiyáanyk alykwévtəxa."

Avathúum.
Xanymashávəts avuuváak a'ítstəm,
nyaanymáamtiya.

As for these (other two),
they kept going,
and they escaped.
They came,
and they came,
and they came;
they stayed together,
and they came,
and they came.

Suddenly,
there was a bird —
it's called an ibis, they say.

It was something like (the color of) porridge,
it might have been pure white.

So,
I've heard them say that.
I've seen it;
that's what it was.

It flew,
it soared through the air,
(as) it went along.

The little boy turned his head,
he saw him,
and he said,
"Look!
That's my uncle,
I recognize him, but
he is trying to go back (to his original form) somehow,
(but) it's no use.
That's all,
that is how he is,
and he will go along like that until he comes to his end."

It happened like that.
He was an ibis, they say,
that's all.

Athúum,
siiyáak athópəka,
a'ét.
Xuumár 'iikyíinyənyts kanáavtək viiwáatəm
a'ávəm.

Viinathíitk,
viinathíitk,
viinathíitk,
makyí nyaanathíik,
nyáany xiipáníi,
kanyaa'émək a'íim.

"Ka'wémk viinyawáak nyakamémúum?
Muuwáarts alya'émtapatxa."

Tapátiim,
nyaa'ávək.
"Kaawíts nyatséwəm,
nyiimuuváatapatxa,"
a'étk.

*** *** ***

Kwalytéshq atséwk
'uu'ítsa.
Áa.

Nyáany avawíim:
aaíimək,
'atsayér awétk,
kaawéxayəm,
nyamayáalya'émək a'étk.

Namáktək.

"Kwanymé 'awíntixa,"
nyaa'ét.
***

So,
he went along like that,
they say.
The little boy told her about it as he went along,
and she listened.

They came,
and they came,
and they came,
they came to someplace,
perhaps they were getting near it,
and at some (point) he said it.

"How can I take you there?
They won't want you either."

(They wouldn't want her) either,
and he understood (this fact).
"I'll turn you into something,
and that's how you'll be too,"
he said.

*** *** ***

He made her into a meadowlark,
that's what I was saying.
Yes.

That's what he did:
he did as he pleased;
he (tried) birds,
he did it somehow, and immediately
he didn't like (what he made), they say.

And he quit.

"I'll do another one,"
he said.
***

Kwanymé awétəntixayəm,
ayúutk viiv'awəny;
"Nyiikwévtəsh."

"Nyáanyts mathúulyma'émexa,"
a'étk,
vuunóony.

Viiwáamtək,
nyaata'aatáyk,
kwalytéshq nyáanya.

A'étk,
nyiitséwtək vuunóok,
namáktəm,
'amátt nyuuváak,
mattavék kaathómək athúm,
uuváam,
ayúutk av'áw.

"Nyáavəts 'axóttəsh.
Nyáava mathótxa.
'Nyáava Kwalytéshqəts,'
a'ítstəm,
mathótk ammuuváata,
ammuuváam 'axótt-təm muuváatxa.

"Nyaanymáam,
'anyáats nyi'mánək vi'yémtəxa."

A'étk,
viiyémtək,
ayáatk aváamtək athúuk a'étəma.

*** *** ***

Xuumárvəts vanyaayáak,
aváamtək a'étəma.

He made another one, and immediately,
he stood here looking at it;
"It's no good," (he said).

"That's not what you will be,"
he said,
and he kept on (trying).

He went along,
he made more and more of them,
those meadowlarks.

So,
he kept turning her into (things),
and he quit,
and there she was in the dirt,
she was scratching in the dirt somehow, and so,
there she was,
and he stood looking at her.

"This is good.
This is what you will be.
'This is Meadowlark,'
they will say,
and wherever you are,
wherever you are, you will get along fine.

"That's all,
I will leave now."

He said it,
and he went away,
he went along and got there, they say.

*** *** ***

The boy went along,
and he got there, they say.

Nyaaváamək,
shamánək,
mattnyaakanáavəm a'ávək.
"Ée'é. "

"Kamathómək.
Makyí muuváak,
maxótt ma'ím mathúum,
nyaa'aaíimək va'athúu va'thíkənyk.

" 'Apúytəxa,
nya'étk,
'athúu va'thíktək 'athútya."

A'étəm,
a'ávtək,
"Ma'íilyma'émək!
Mamánək!
Kaawéts alynyiimathúutsxa."

A'étəm,
nyaa'ávək,
nyaamán kwa'átsk siivátk,
siivátyk.

" 'Anyaaxáapəm 'uupúuvək 'awétsk,
vany'awétsk,
vanya'awétsk —
'axá sa'ílyts a'íim,
'axá mattkwatspéets siithíkəm.

"Nyáasi 'katánək,
nyi'uuv'óok,
nyaayúu 'a'íim ma'ávxa,"
a'étka,
'aakóoyəny.

Nyaa'étəm,
" 'Axóttk," a'étk,
iisháaly mattnyaataxpályk,

When he got there,
he woke her up,
and he explained (his idea) and she listened.
"Okay," (she said).

"You (will) do it somehow.
Wherever you are,
you (will) do all right,
(but) I would just as soon stay here.

"I am going to die,
I tell you,
that's how I am."

She said it,
and he heard it,
(and he said,) "Don't say that!
Get up!
You will think of something."

He said it,
and she heard him,
and she got up, just as he had said,
and there she was, over there.

"We will go into the west,
and as we go,
as we go —
it's called the ocean,
there's a great body of water over there.

"We will get there,
and stand there,
and I will say something for you to hear,"
she said,
the old lady (did).

Then,
"All right," he said,
and they held hands,

viiwétsənyk,
viiwétsk,
viiwétsk,
xaasa'íly nyáany —
katán kwa'átstək a'étəma.

Nyaakatánəm,
"Vathí muuváa alyma'émtəxa."

Athúm,
" 'Anyáa 'aaíim 'atakavék si'thikənyk,
 nyamáam.
'Athótkəm,
'apúyəm 'axótt-təxa.

" 'Íis,
 máany,
 maxuumárxayk mathúm.

"Kaawíts mathóxa,
'a'íim.

" 'A'íim,
 nyáavi nyuuthíik 'a'íim,
'a'étkəm 'awíim,
awíim,
miisháaly 'ataxpály,
nyataxwéshk vanya'wáaaaaak,
xaasa'íly tóly 'a'ím,
nyaayúu 'amátt-ts siivám,
nyáasi nyatápxa,"
a'ét.

"Nyáanyi muuváatapatxa,"
a'ét.

'Aakóoyvəts a'étk vuunóom,
a'ávət.

and they went,
and they went,
and they went,
and that ocean —
they reached it, just as she had said, they say.

They reached it.
"You won't stay here."

So,
"I would just as soon go back over there,
that's all.
The way I am,
it's all right for me to die.

"But,
as for you,
you are still young.

"You will do something else,
I say.

"I say so,
and (that's why) I have brought you here,
I say so,
and so,
I'll take you by the hand,
and as I go along I'll fling you,
and in the middle of the ocean,
there is an island,
and I will set you down in over there,"
she said.

"You will stay there,"
she said.

The old lady went on saying this,
and he heard her.

Awíim,
uuváam,
nyáany,
'axá vatháts athúum,
'akwíik íiip a'ím;
'akwíik vanyuuváam.

"Nyaayúunyts,
athúm,
nyuuv'áwəm,
uuqásk anáwk nyaa'íim —
nyáany máanyts mathóxa.
Mathúum.

"Mathúum.
Nyayúu,
nyáasi muuváak,
siimuuváanyk.
Avnyaathúum,
máany mattmakwiishány
'amáy nyaaxáv.

"Saathúum.
'A'áwtan nyiikwakwévənyts.
Nyaayúu nyaaspérək,
saathúum,
aráak,
alkyémp alkyémp a'íim vanyuuváam.

"Nyáany máany mathúum.
Muuváak ma'ítya.

"A'íim,
nyashéxa.
Kwayaaxuumár 'a'íim nyaashéxa."

Nyáany ashém,
nyáany.

So,
there he was,
and as for that,
because of that water,
clouds were gathering;
as it was getting cloudy.

"Well,
so,
when it rains,
when it thunders loudly —
that will be you.
It is you.

"It is you.
Well,
you will stay over there,
you (will) stay there.
It (will) happen,
your shadow
(will) go up into the sky.

"It happens like that.
My own grandson is the one who comes to an end there.
It's a powerful thing,
that's what happens,
it blazes up,
it goes flash! flash!

"That (will) be you.
You will stay there.

"So,
I will name you.
I will name you Kwayaaxuumár (The One Who Acts Like
    a Child)."

That's what she named him,
that (name).

"Avnyaathúum,
 mataxáyk,
 'akwíik,
 uuv'áwk,
 nyaathúum —
 uuqásk ava'íim,
 vanyuuváam,
 Kwayaaxuumárəts ara'óyk uuváam a'íyum.

"A'ítstəxa."

A'étk,
 uukanáavək vuunóok,
 nyaanamák,
 avawíi kwa'átsk.
"Nyaanymáamtəxa" nyaa'íim.

Nyaataxwésh kwa'átsk,
 makyí,
 kaawíts siivám.

'Amátt xaasa'íly tóly avám;
 nyáasi atápk,
 alynyaatápk nyaakwíinək,
 'aakóoyənyts viithíitk a'étəma.

Viiyémək,
 nyavá nyaaváamək,
 siithíkənyk,
 nyiipúytək a'étəma.

Nyiinyaapúyəm,
 aváts avathúu kwa'átsk.
Suuványk,
 saathótk.
Nyáanyts uuqásk.

Uurávək a'ávk;
 athúum athúuk a'étəma.
Uu'ítsənyts athúum.
Athúum athúuk a'étəma.

"When it happens,
it's windy,
and it's cloudy,
and it rains,
and then —
it thunders like this,
and when it does,
they might say Kwayaaxuumár is playing.

"They will say so."

So,
she went about explaining it,
and she left him,
she did that, just as she had said.
"That will be all," she said.

She flung him, just as she had said,
and somewhere,
there is something over there.

There is a place in the middle of the ocean;
she put him down over there,
she put him down and turned around,
and the old lady came this way, they say.

She went (home),
and when she got to her house,
she lay there,
and she died there, they say.

She died there,
this is what happened, just as she said it would.
He stayed over there,
and that's how he was.
He is the one that thunders.

One can hear him when there is lightning;
that's him, they say.
That's what they say.
That's him, they say.

A'étk,
nyáava kanáavtǝma.
Kwa'ítsǝnyts,
kanáavǝk vaa'íim.

Nyáavǝm aawáamtǝk.

So,
they tell about this.
The ones who say it,
they tell about it like this.

They go through this.

Shakwatxót

Told by John Comet

'Aakóoy,
'aakóoyəny amúly,
'Aakóoy Sanyuuxáv a'éta.
Amúlya,
'aakóoy amúlya
'Aakóoy Sanyuuxáva.

A'ím,
'Aakóoy Sanyuuxávənyts nyuuváak,
xaly'úp ayáatk suuváak a'ét.
'Axáts siithíkəm,
xaly'úp ayáat.

'Ashént nyaváyk suuváak,
'Aakóoy Sanyuuxávány.

Xaly'úp ayáak uuvát.
Suuváany,
uuváatkitya.

Viithíi takavék aváat.

Nyaa'íim,
viithíkəm,
athótk athót.
Ayáak xaly'úpt.

Aváak,
vanyuuváam —
Takashé 'Aqwáas a'éta.

Takashé 'Aqwáasəts,
nyáasi 'axá —
nyaváytapat suuvát.

(There was) an old woman,
and the old woman's name
was Old Lady Sanyuuxáv, they say.
Her name,
the old woman's name
was Old Lady Sanyuuxáv.

So,
Old Lady Sanyuuxáv was there,
and she was going to bathe, they say.
There was water over there,
and she went to bathe.

She was living alone,
Old Lady Sanyuuxáv (was).

She went to bathe and there she was.
There she was, over there,
she stayed there, they say.

And she came back (home).

Then,
here she was,
and it happened (from time to time).
She went and bathed.

She got there,
and while she was there —
it was Yellow Gopher, they say.

It was Yellow Gopher,
over there (in) the water —
he was living there too.

Suuvám,
alyayémk sanyuuváak,
kaathómək athúm:
uuváavi,
kaathómək nyuuváak,
máam,
atúyvətkitya.
'Aakóoyəny.

Atúyvək vanyuuváak.

Vanyuuváak,
kór nyaayémk,
nyuuváak,
amáam,
xuumáar ayúutkitya,
xuumáar xavík vathány.

Pa'iipáy.
Siitháw,
xuumáar 'iikyáarəts a'ét.

Atháwəm,
saa'íim ashékitya.
Amúlya,
Paar'áak Paaraxáan a'ím ashék.

Kwa'nóqəny amúly Paar'áaka,
kwakútsa Paaraxáan a'ét.

Siitháwk,
matsuuts'ítsəts siitháwət,
xuumáarəny.

Matsats'íim,
akwév aly'émək viitháwk.
  "Kaawíts tan kaathómək viitháwk?"
a'ém a'étk,
'aakóoyənyts.

There he was,
and as she was about to leave,
something happened:
at (the place) where he was,
he was able to do it somehow,
and finally,
she got pregnant, they say.
The old woman.

Here she was, pregnant.

Here she was,
and a long time passed,
and there she was,
and finally,
she gave birth to children, they say,
(to) these two children.

They were alive.
There they were,
they were little boys, they say.

There they were,
and she named them like that, they say.
Their names,
she named them Paar'áak and Paaraxáan.

The younger one's name was Paar'áak,
and the older one was Paaraxáan, they say.

There they were,
and they were crying,
the children (were).

They cried,
and they didn't stop.
"What exactly are they up to?"
she managed to say,
the old woman (did).

'Aakóoyənyts awíim,
awíim,
aa'én siiványk,
akwév alya'ém.
Xuumáar matsats'étk viitháw.
Akwév aly'ém.

"Kaawíts tan kaathómək viitháwkitya?"
a'ét.
'Aakóoyənyts siivát.

Siivám,
'aayúuts —
xam'uulól a'éta.
Xam'uulóləts amíim,
"xrrr xrrr xrrr xrrr xrrr," a'im.

Nyáanyts aváak viivák amét.
"Xrrr xrrr," a'im,
xuumáarənyts nyamáam matsats'íim ashnyítsq awítsta.

Xuumáar nyiinamíilək a'ét,
xam'uulóləts.

A'ét,
amáam,
'aakóoyənyts avathíim,
nyaayúu xamuulólənyts sakyínyəv viiyémt.

Nyaayúuk amáam,
xuumáarənyts,
***
uu'íts nyáava,
wanymuuyétstəkəm viitháwk,
vanyaayém,
nyaamtsats'ínyəmasht.

" 'Uy!
Kaawíts kaathómtanək viitháwk?
Kaa'ém matsats'ét,
nyaa nyaváatan matsats'étk.

The old woman did (what she could to comfort them),
she did (what she could to comfort them),
she sat there rocking them,
(but) they didn't stop.
The children kept crying.
They didn't stop.

"What exactly are they up to?"
she said.
The old woman was sitting there.

She was sitting there,
and a creature —
it was a cricket, they say.
A cricket was chirping,
he was going "xrrr xrrr xrrr xrrr xrrr."

He came and chirped.
He went "xrrr xrrr,"
and finally the children stopped crying.

He comforted the children, they say,
the cricket (did).

So,
finally,
the old woman came along,
and the cricket ran away and left.

They had seen him,
the children (had),
***
and this sound that he made,
they liked it,
and when he left,
they cried again.

"What now!
What are they up to?
Whatever I do, they cry,
the moment I get here, they cry.

"Matsats'íilya'émk viitháwxayəm,
'atkavék,
nya'aváatan matsats'étk,"
a'ét.
"Kaawíts tan kaathómək?"
a'ém a'ét,
'aakóoyəny.

'Aakóoy amák vanyaayém,
amáam,
xam'uulólənyts nyaaváak nyaa'ínymashk,
"xrrr xrrr xrrr xrrr," a'étəm,
xuumáarəts amáam uushmátk athúum.

Xam'uulóləts nyavály aváak,
"xrrr xrrr,"
atók avák.
***
Xuumáar uushmáam siitháw.

Siitháwəm,
'aakóoy nyaaváam,
'uulól vanyaayém,
nyaamáam,
xuumáarənyts matsts'ínymash,
"Áaaa!
Áaaa!"

Suunóok,
kaawíts tan kaathómək viitháwk ayétsk.

Viiyémxayəm,
'aakóoy,
makyí amák,
nyamáam,
'uulólənyts aváatk,
nyamáam nyiinamíilək awét.

Nyamáam,
"xrrr xrrr," a'ím,
xuumáar nyamáam uushmátk.
***

"They weren't crying, and then suddenly
I came back,
and when I got here they cried,"
she said.
"What exactly are they up to?"
she managed to say,
the old woman (did).

The old woman went out behind (the house),
and finally,
the cricket got there and did it again,
he went "xrrr xrrr xrrr xrrr,"
and the children finally went to sleep.

The cricket got to her house,
(he went) "xrrr xrrr,"
and he sat in the middle.
***
The children lay there sleeping.

They lay there,
and the old woman got there,
and the cricket left,
and that's all,
the children started crying again,
"Waaaah!
Waaaah!"

There they were,
they went on doing it for some reason.

As soon as she left,
the old woman,
(she was) somewhere behind (the house),
and finally,
the cricket got there,
and finally he calmed them down.

Finally,
he went "xrrr xrrr,"
and the children finally went to sleep.
***

A'ím,
'aakóoy vanyaathíinyəm,
xam'uulólənyts iiwáa nyiipéttəm,
uuvákitya.
Alyavák,
"xrrr xrrr xrrr," uuvákitya.

Iiwáa nyiipéttəm,
skyíny aly'émt áam,
alyvák,
"xrrr xrrr," alyvám.

'Aakóoy nyaaváak,
masharáyt!

" 'Uy!
Máanyts ammathútan muuváam,
xuumáar matsats'íim!" a'íika.
Nyaa'ím —
iimény katsalyéshk a'éta.

Xam'uulóla.

Nyáanyi amánk,
xam'uulóləts 'órsh 'órsh 'órsh lyavéek.

Athúum,
uuváak;
mapís uuváam,
xam'uulól mayúum,
iiméts váy awétk,
katsuulyésh alyaskyíik,
'aakóoy.

Ayúukəm ám,
'akúutstsək,
ayúuta.
Xuumáar nyamáam nyaakúutstsəm,
xam'uulól iiménts alyésh amáam.

So,
(once) when the old woman was coming (home),
the cricket forgot,
and there he was, they say.
He was in there,
he was there (going) "xrrr xrrr xrr," they say.

He forgot,
he didn't run away (this time),
he was in there,
he was in there (going) "xrrr xrrr."

The old woman got there,
and she was angry!

"What now!
You are the one who has been doing it,
(making) the children cry!" she said, they say.
She said it —
and she broke its legs, they say.

The cricket's.

From then on,
crickets have gone hop-hop-hop like that.

And so,
there he was;
nowadays he is around,
you see a cricket,
and its legs are mangled,
they are still broken,
(because of) the old woman.

She watched, and finally,
they grew older,
and she watched them.
The children were finally growing up,
and the cricket's legs had been broken.

Xuumáar matsts'ínyəmashk viitháwəny,
'aakóoyənyts namák viiyém.

Xuumár kwanóqány kwasuuthíinyts tsaanyíik a'éta.
A'íis kwakútsənyts kaváarəsh,
kwa'nóqənyts kwas'iithíik.

Nyaamánək ayáak.
Xuumáarəny aatéerək akwílyk 'éta.
Akwílyk viitháwk,
nyamáam,
uushóxk!

Atspámək,
viiyáak áam.
'Atsanyér kaathú,
xanaavlyép kaawíts tatpóoy nyaakamíim,
aví —
ashpúur a'éta —
nyáavily stawíinək vuunóom,
nyiixánt.
Avá sawénapátkəm,
nyáany nyaayóovək,
uushmátk avatháwət.

'Aakóoy nyaaváak,
" 'Úy!
Kaawíts nyuuváakəm,
aaíim,
xanaavalyép kaawíts ashtúum,
nyiistwíinək vuunóokitya!"
'et,
'Aakóoyənyts ashtúum,
tsaxwéshxwésh alyaapáx.

A'im,
xuumáarənyts matsats'íik a'ét.
"Áaaa!
Áaaa!"

The children were crying again,
and the old woman left them and went away.

The younger child's powers were too much for her, they say.
Although the older one did not (have any),
the younger one had powers.

She got up and went.
She had wrapped the children in their cradles, they say.
They lay here wrapped in their cradles —
and finally,
(the younger one) took off (the wrapping)!

He came out,
and he went along.
(There were) little flying creatures of some kind,
he killed butterflies of some kind and brought them (home).
and here —
it's called ashpúur (a hoop over the cradle) —
he went about hanging them up here,
and they were pretty.
He hung them up (on his brother's cradle) too,
and they watched them,
and they slept.

When the old woman got there,
"What now!
Something has been here,
they have done as they pleased,
they've gathered butterflies and things,
and they've gone about hanging them up!"
she said.
The old woman gathered (the butterflies),
and she flung them down.

And so,
the children cried, they say.
"Waaaah!
Waaaah!"

'Aakóoy,
"Kaawíts tants uuváatk awíim vuunóom athúm?"
a'ét.

Uuváany,
'aakóoy vanyaayém,
a'ím,
viiyáak,
'aayúunya xanaavlyép awétk,
kaawíts 'atskatsó,
xamér nyiistawíin ava'étk,
nyáany ayóovək viitháwk,
amáam uushmát.

Ashtótk vuunóok athúuk 'eta.

Vuunóonyk,
amáam,
'akúutsk.

Nya'kúutsk viitháw amáam,
" 'Áy!
'Aayúu,
'axtáts siitháwət.
'Axtáts siitháwk,
kamathótk mathúuk 'íisaa —
mawétk mashtútsk,
sáa
matsuuváamxats athúu lya'éməs" a'étk 'íi.
Nyuukanáavətək,
a'íik 'eta.

'Axtáts alytháwk,
'axály atháwk siitháw,
sáa
nyaayúu kamashtarátsəts,
'axá maxákəly tama'órtantəm,
muuváamxats athúu lya'ém."

Athúum,
siitháwət.

The old woman,
"What exactly is here doing (this)?"
she said.

He stayed (where he was),
and the old woman left,
and so,
he went along,
he (worked on) the butterflies and things,
he pounded them lightly with something,
and he just hung them up like that,
and (the children) lay there watching them,
and finally they went to sleep.

He went on gathering them, they say.

(This) went on, until
finally,
they grew up.

They grew up and here they were, and finally,
"Hey!
Well,
there are cattails over there.
There are cattails over there,
and you might do it somehow —
you (might) do (something) and gather them,
but
you might not succeed," she said.
She told him about it,
she said it, they say.

"There are cattails in there,
they are in the water there,
but
(there are) angry creatures,
the water is full of them,
and you won't be able to get there."

And so,
there they were.

"Áa,
'awétsk 'ayóovxa," a'ét;
siitháwət.

Siitháwnyək,
viiwétsk
'axtány ayóov 'í.

Vanyaawétsk,
'axtá nyuuv'óo kwa'áts.
'Axály uuv'óokəm,
katánək ayóovəm;
'axá kamatháavətəm,
tsúu,
vathá lyavíim.

'Axtányts alyuuv'óok vathá lyavíik.
Avuuv'óo kwa'áts a'ét.
'Axtány nyuuv'óo kwa'áts.

"Ka'athútsxá.
'Ashtúu ka'athúu,
ka'athómxa,"
a'ím,
nyiitháwk,
ayóovək siitháwəta.

Nyáanya shaavárk,
nyáanya,
xtánya.

Nyáany aashváarək 'im:

"Minyixáata,
áamkwayáa áamkwayúuulya,
minyixáata,
áamkwayáa áamkwayúuulya a'íit."

'Axtányts suuv'óom ayúuk,
'eta.

"Okay,
we'll go and see," he said;
there they were.

There they were,
and they went along
to look at the cattails.

They went along,
and the cattails were standing there, just as she had said.
They were standing in the water,
and (the boys) got there and saw them;
the water was very difficult,
it poured down,
like this.

The cattails were standing there like this.
They were standing there, just as she had said, they say.
Cattails were standing there, just as she had said.

"We'll do it somehow.
We might gather them,
we'll do it somehow,"
he said,
and they stood there,
they stood there looking, they say.

That (song) is sung,
that one,
(about) the cattails.

They sing about that:

> "You cattails,
> (I am) the one who would like to go and see you,
> You cattails,
> (I am) the one who would like to go and see you."

He saw the cattails growing over there,
(the song) says.

'Im,
ayóova.
Ayóovək 'im,
nyáany aashváarək 'íik 'et,
nyáava.
Nyuuv'óok nyaayóov.

"Nyuuv'óom;
máanyts mayáak mayúuxa," 'íik 'et,
nyaanatsénək,
avány,
nyakútsnya.
"Máany mayáak mayúu," 'ét.

"Áa,
'athóxa,"
'íik 'et.

Kwa'kútsənyts
siiyáak nyiixávək 'eta.
'Axányi.

Nyaaxávək,
viiyáak aváamək,
ayúunyk;
" 'Úy!"
'Aayúu kamshtaráts,
'aavéts uuvátk,
kaawíts uuvá tsanpéet.
Makyík ayáak,
'axtány aauukyíttxats athúulya'ém.

Siiv'áwk ayúuk athúunyk,
nyaakwévəm,
takavék atspák a'ét.

Takavék atspák,
nyaathíik nyaav'áak,
ashúts uukanáavət.
Ashúts,
"Matsuuváamxa alyathómǝta," a'íik 'et.

So,
they saw them.
They saw them, and so,
this is what they sang about, they say,
(about) these (cattails).
They saw them standing there.

"They are standing there;
you will go and see," he said, they say,
and he called him his older brother,
this one,
the older one.
"You go and see," he said.

"Okay,
I'll do it,"
he said, they say.

The older one
went along and went in there, they say.
Into the water.

He went in there,
he went along and got there,
and he looked;
"What now!"
(There were) angry creatures,
a snake was there,
and something (else) was there, and it was small.
Wherever he went,
he could not cut the cattails.

He stood there looking,
(but) it was no use,
and he came back out, they say.

He came back out,
and he came walking along,
and he told his younger brother about it.
His younger brother (said),
"You weren't able to do it," he said, they say.

" 'Ayáak,
'anyáats 'a'kútsk 'iináam,
vanyaa'aváam,
saváts nyaaváam nyaa'ayúukəm,
mashtaráts matt-tsáaməly 'axtány aakakyáavtanək,
'atkavék.
'Uuwéxats athúulya'ém.
'Ashuutóxa alya'ém.

"Shuutóxa muuthómxa alyathóməsh," 'ét.

"Áa-aa,
'athúunypatk 'ayúuxa."

Nyaa'íim,
siiv
ányk,
kwa'nóqənyts.
Kwas'iithíitk,
mattnamíilək avák,
'axányi axáv awéta.

'Axá nyaaxávək,
siiyáam,
saathúuk,
'atsaayúu kamashtarátsəts.
'Atsaakakyáav kwa'áts avatháwəm,
nyaayúunya.

Ayúuk suuváany,
mattnamíil,
'aayúu,
'aayúu shaly'áy ashtúum,
vaawíim:
nyuuwíits.
Aváts ayúuk,
mashtarátsəts —
éee! —
mátt talàpaláap.

Aváam,
'axtány ashtúuk 'eta.

"I went,
(because) I am the one who is older and more important,
and while I was there,
I saw those (creatures) get there,
all those angry (creatures) were surrounding the cattails,
and I came back.
I couldn't do it.
I couldn't get them.

"You won't be able to get them either," he said.

"Well,
I'll see if I can do it."

He said it,
and there he was,
the younger (brother).
He had powers,
and he used his powers,
and he went into the water.

He went into the water,
and he went along,
and they did that,
the angry creatures (did).
They were surrounding (the cattails), just as he had said,
(those) creatures (were).

He was watching them,
and he used his powers,
well,
well he gathered sand and things,
and he did this:
he poured it on them.
That (younger brother) was watching,
and the angry (creatures) —
gee! —
they flattened themselves out.

He got there,
and he got the cattails, they say.

Ashtúum;
'ashént tsapéev,
'axtá kwavatáyány,
kwatspéevənyəny ashtót.

Nyaashtúum,
nyuutspák,
nyáanyi,
kwakútsənyts
'axtá kwavatáyəny atháwət.

A'ím,
nyáanyəm manyúuvək viinthíik 'eta.

" 'Anyáats 'a'akútstəm,
kwavatáyəly 'awéxa."

"Kaváar!
'Anyáats 'ayáak 'ashtótəm,
kwavatáyəny.
Máanyts kwa'anóqəly mawétxa,"
a'ét.
Nyáaly manyúuv vinthíik 'eta.

Vinayém.
'Aakóoyənyts ayúuk siivát.
"Manyúuv kaathúu,
manyúuv vinathíik,"
nyakóra ayúut siivát.

Nyaathíik,
nyaakatánək.
Iiwáanyts 'aláayt
kwa'kútsənyts kwavatáyəny atháwət.

Nyáavi,
iiwáanyts 'aláayk nyuuváak,
kwa'nóqənyts.
Viiyáakitya.
Iiwáa nyaa'aláayəm,
'avíi akúlyk viiyáat.

He got them;
one was small,
and (he got) the big one,
and he got the small one.

When he got them,
they were protruding (from his hands),
and at that (point),
the older (brother)
took the big cattail.

So,
they came (home) fighting about that, they say.

"I am the oldest,
(so) I will use the big one."

"No!
I am the one who went and got it,
the big one.
You can use the small one,"
he said.
They came (home) fighting about that, they say.

They went along.
The old woman sat and watched them.
"They might be fighting,
they are coming (home) fighting,"
and for a long time she sat and watched them.

They were coming (home),
and they got there.
(The younger brother) felt bad
(because) the older one had taken the big one.

At this (point),
he was feeling bad,
the younger one (was).
He went along, they say.
He felt bad,
and he went climbing on the rocks.

Vanyaayáak,
nyáasi,
'avíits suuváa vaa'étk,
uuvám,
nyáany maxák axávətək,
'avíinyts arík a'íkəta.

Arík a'im,
xuumár kwa'nóqənya,
aanáməm,
apúyk.
Apúy siithík 'eta.

Apúy siithíkəm,
shtaméev,
kaathómk viitháwətk,
xamnyéwəts awét.

Viitháwəm,
siithík.

Nyáanya shaavárəntik.

Ée,
shaavársáa,
'iiwáa nyapétt-ta.

   "Mayáaxáa mayáaxáa,
   'amayáaxáa, yáaxáam,
   nyáaykúum asúlyúum,"

a'éta.

Iimáatt-ts asúulyk 'ím;
'avíinyts tanám,
iimáattənyts asúulyk 'ím,
a'éta.

Siivány,
'aakóoyənyts ayúuk siiványk,

He went along,
and over there,
there was a rock like this,
there it was,
and (the younger brother) went in under it,
and the rock fell, they say.

It fell,
(on) the younger child,
it landed on him,
and he died.
He lay there dead, they say.

He lay there dead,
and they couldn't find him,
whatever they did;
his footprints (misled them).

(The footprints) were here,
and he lay over there.

That (song) is sung.

Ah,
it is sung, but
I've forgotten it.

> "You will go, you will go
> you will go, will go
> it might be daytime, he might be crushed,"

(the song) says.

It is going to crush his body;
the rock falls on him,
and it is going to crush his body,
it says.

She sat there,
the old woman sat there watching,

"Ée'é,
'ayáak 'atháwxa.
Siithíksáa,
iiwáany ta'láayətəm siithík.
Athótəs,
'axóttxa,"
nyaa'étk,
viiyáak.

'Aakóoyənyts mattnamíil nyuunóok,
uukavék 'ét,
xuumára.

Uukavék,
viitháwk,
uutara'úyk awítsk 'ét,
'axtánya.
Uutara'úyk.

"Mattkáayk!"

" 'Axóttk," nya'étk,
amáam,
vaashkwéem,
'akútsənyts kwa'nóq atháwk.

Kwa'nóqənyts kwavatáyəny atháw 'ét.

Wilawíil uutara'úyk vuunóo,
maxák takwalaasháw,
vathály aatskyétt,
vathá lyavéet.

Nyam uukúpənyts,
vathí tsuumpápk viitháw viitháwetəm.

Nyiitháwəm;
" 'Awím,
'atsétsk 'a'ávnyək,
mattkwiisháaytant,
uunáwa."

"Well,
I will go and get him.
He is lying there,
he is lying there because (something) is making him feel bad.
He is, but
he will be fine,"
she said,
and she went along.

The old woman went about using her powers,
and she brought him back, they say,
the child.

She brought him back,
and there they were;
and they worked things out, they say,
about the cattails.
They worked things out.

"Trade with each other!" (she said).

"All right," they said,
and finally,
he hated to do it,
(but) the older one took the small (cattail).

The younger one took the big (cattail), they say.

They went about preparing flutes,
they cleaned out the insides,
and they cut them in several places,
(so that they were) like this.

The holes that they made,
there were four of them, here and here.

There they were;
"So,
(when) we play them and listen,
it is wonderful,
the sound."

Siitháwət.

Athúum,
'amátt vathík,
'anyáak uunóok,
pa'iipáats siitháwk.

Aashalyám Kwanáwəts,
amúlya.
Kwara'ákəts,
Aashalyám Kwanáw.

Siivám,
nyáaly vatstsáats siitháwapat.
Xavík siitháwapatk,
'ashént 'anóq,
'ashént 'akútstan.

Siitháwəm.
Nyáanyi wilawíil atsétsəm,
a'áv a'étk avatsétsk a'éta.

Atsáam viitháwəm,
mashxáy nyáanyts 'ashént,
kwa'nóq,
nyáanyts kwas'iithíi nyáany lyavíitapat,
maxáy kwanóq kwasiithíiny nyáany lyavíinypat,
kwas'iithíitkəm.

Wilawíil uutséts kwanáwəny
nyáasi aváam,
'a'ávək siitháawk 'eta.

Siitháawəta.

Maxáanyanyts,
wilawíil atsét siitháwət.

Siitháwk.
" 'Anyáa kaathútsəm,

There they were.

So,
in this place here,
they were in the east,
people were over there.

Aashalyám Kwanáw,
(that was) his name.
He was an old man,
Aashalyám Kwanáw (was).

There he was,
and his daughters were there too.
There were two of them over there,
one was younger,
and one was older.

There they were.
When (the boys) played their flutes there,
they played so that (the girls) would hear them, they say.

They were playing,
and one of those girls,
that younger one,
she was just like that powerful one,
she was just like that powerful younger boy,
they (both) had power.

The sound of them playing their flutes
reached (the girls) over there,
and they sat there listening to it, they say.

They sat there, they say.

Those boys,
they sat there playing their flutes, they say.

They sat there.
"Some day,

matt'ayúuxa,"
a'ím,
siitháawk 'eta,
mashtxáanyənyts.

Nyaa'ím,
kwara'ákənyts áaralyemk,
maxáa avány áaralyem.

"Nyáar," a'ítsəm,
mashtxáanyənyts.
"Matt'amayáatkəm,
aauutsétsənyts mattkwiisháaytanəm 'a'ávət."

Siitháwk 'éta.

Nyam maxáa nyaalyavíinypat.
" 'Anyáa kaathúts,
'awétsk 'ayóovxa."
Siitháw.
***

Awétəm,
" 'Atskuunáavxa,"
a'íim viitháwət.

Nyam atsétstsək,
atsétk avatháwət.

"Xaly'áw 'akyáawu 'awétsxa," 'et,
xaly'áw akyáaw awéts.
'Uutíish awíim.

Atséw vuunóok awét,
xaly'áw awétk,
akyáam.
Viitháwənyk,
'atsakyétk.

Kamétk
asóot awét.

we will see each other,"
they said,
and they sat there, they say,
those girls (did).

Then,
the old man didn't want them,
he didn't want the boys.

"They want us," they said,
the girls (did).
"We like each other,
and their playing is wonderful to hear," (they said).

There they were, they say.

The boys did the same (thing).
"Some day,
we will do (what it takes) to see them," they said.
There they were.
***

So,
"We will talk to them,"
they were saying.

So they played (their flutes),
there they were, playing (their flutes).

"Let's go shoot cottontails," they said,
and they went to shoot cottontails.
They used bows.

They went about making them,
and they did cottontails,
they shot them.
Here they were,
and they shot (things).

They brought them (home)
and ate them.

Awétk suunóot.

Sanyuunóom áam,
'aakóoyənyts nyaakanáavkəm,
"Nyaayúuts,
'ashpáa manyxátt-ts avatháwk,"
a'íikəta.

" 'Ashpáa manyxátt-ts avatháwsáa,
'avíi 'amíits,
'avíi alyuuméeny apéetan,
nyáany 'amáy tan alyatháwk viitháwət.

"Kamathóm mashuutóxa alyathómtək.
Avatháwət.

" 'Ashént nyíilyk,
'ashént xamáalyət.

"Avatháwət.

"Kamawétk kamathótk mathúukəs,
kamathómtəxalyáa,"
nyaa'íik 'et.

Nyaa'áv vuunóony.
"Nyáa kaathútsəm,
'awétsk 'ayóovxá.
'Ashpáa 'anyxátt-ts avatháwk,"
a'éta.
A'íik 'et.

*** *** ***

Nyáava siitháwnyək.

" 'Awétsk 'ayóovxa," 'étk,
awéts.

They went about doing this.

There they were,
and the old woman told them,
"(There are) creatures,
your pet eagles are there,"
she said, they say.

"Your pet eagles are there, but
it's a very high mountain,
the height of the mountain is just too much,
and those (eagles) are in that really high (place).

"There is no way you will be able to get them.
There they are.

"One is black,
and one is white.

"There they are.

"Whatever you might do,
I hope you will be able do it somehow,"
she said, they say.

They were listening to her.
"Some day,
we will go and see them.
Our pet eagles are there,"
they said.
They said it, they say.

*** *** ***

There they were.

"We'll go and see them," they said,
and they went.

Nyaawétsk katán.
Suuv'óok ayóov.
Saathúukəs,
'avíi 'alyméeny —
éeee,
'amáy tan axávət!

Nyáasi kwapár nyiipíiltan,
nyáasi nyaváy.
'Avíi kyelakyéltan,
nyáasi atháw,
avatháwəm 'ét.

Vinthíiktan.
Nakavék vinthíik 'eta.
'Avíi savány a'íi kwa'átsəm,
matt-tsapéek,
uuv'óowtək athómək.

'Atkavék nyiikatántək 'ayóov," nya'étk,
vinthíik a'éta.
Viinthíik.

Nyaakatántək,
katsuunávək.
"Áa,
'akatánək 'ayóovtəsáa,
'avák,
'avíi 'alyuuméeny apéek 'etk,
'uuvák sáa,
'anyáa kaathúts aly'awétsəntik 'athútsk 'a'ávxa,"
a'ét.

"Áa,
nyuukanáapk.
Mawíi matsuuváamxats athúu lya'émək.
'Avíiny 'aluuméeny mattapéet.

"Nyaayúu kwamshtarátsənyts aaíimt,
'avuuyáa tama'órək athúm,
avatháwəta.

They went and got there.
They stood there and looked.
They were like that, but
the height of the mountain —
gee,
(the eagles) went into a really high (place)!

Over there, at the farthest (high point),
they lived over there.
(There was) a cave in the rock,
and they were over there,
there they were, they say.

(The boys) came (home).
They came back (home), they say.
That mountain was just as she had said it was,
it was overwhelming,
and they stopped.

"We'll come back and look," they said,
and they came (home), they say.
They came (home).

When they got there,
they told her about it.
"Yes,
we got there and looked, but
there it was,
the mountain was terribly high,
there it was, but
some day we will go and try again,"
they said.

"Yes,
I told you so.
You wouldn't be able to do it.
The mountain is terribly high.

"There are angry creatures all over the place,
they fill up the entrance, and so,
there they are.

"Vaathúu," a'ét.

Siitháwk,
siitháw.
Kaawíts awétkitya.
'Atsqwáaq vanyaawétskitya.
A'étəs awét.

'Atsuukyéts tsémaly'émətək.
Tapúytək,
asóot.

Nyaatháwk,
amáam,
siiwétskitya.
Máam,
nyiiwéts.
" 'Ayóovxa," nyaa'ét,
siiwéts.

Nyaawétsk,
nyáasi,
'avíi kwalymeenyi katán,
suuv'óok 'eta.

"Máany,
kwa'kúts,"
nyaa'ínymashkəm,
" 'Antsén," a'ím,
"Máanyts maxiipúk mayáak mayúuxá,"
a'et.

"Áa-á.
Matt-tsapéet.
'Ayúusaa,
'athótxá," a'et.

" 'Anyáats nyaav'áwk 'av'áwəm,
mayáak mayúutxa."

"This is how it is," she said.

There they were,
there they were.
They did something, they say.
They went after deer, they say.
They might have done it.

They didn't miss a shot.
They killed them,
and they ate them.

There they were,
and finally,
they went after (the eagles), they say.
Finally,
they went after them.
"We will see," they said,
and they went after them.

They went after them,
and way over there,
they reached the high mountain,
and they stood there, they say.

"You,
(you are) are the elder (brother),"
he said it again,
"Older brother," he said,
"You'll go first and see,"
he said.

"Okay.
It will be difficult.
I see (that), but
I will do it," (the older one) said.

"I (will) stand (here),
and you will go and see," (the younger one said).

Nyáam kwakútsənyts viiyáak 'eta.
'Avíiny akúlyk,
'avíi kwalyaméenyá.

Akúlyk vanyaayáanyk,
viiyáanyk viiyáanyk viiyáanyk viiyáanyk viiyáanyk,
'améeeeetan atspámk awítya,
nyáany.

Avatháw kwa'áts,
'ashpáany;
'avíi kyelakyél kwaaxwíir alytháwk avatháwkəs.

Ayúukəs,
avathúu kwa'áts:
'aavéts athótk,
kaawíts athótk,
a'ávəm;
'avuuyáanyts apétt,
nyiixítsk a'étəm,
kaathómək alyuuxávxats athúu lya'ém.

" 'Úy!
Ka'wém 'ashuutóxəts athúulya'émət kwa'áts'ənkáa?"
aaly'étk,
ayúuk siiv'áw 'eta.

Nyaayúu kamshtarátsənyts apétt,
'ashpáany amák alyatháw.

Siiv'áwnyək,
viithíik 'eta.
Takavék atsén.
Tsuuváamxa alyathóm.

Ayúut.
Siiv'áw nyiitkwíinək atsénək,
viithíinyk viithíinyk viithíinyk viithíinyk,
'amátt alytsén.

So the older one went, they say.
He climbed the mountain,
the high mountain.

He went climbing up,
he went and went and went and went and went,
and he came out very high up,
that one.

There they were, just as she had said,
the eagles;
they might have been in a corner of a cave in the mountain.

He looked,
and it was just as she had said:
there were snakes,
and there were (other) creatures,
and he sensed them;
the entrance was blocked,
(the creatures) were lined up there,
and there was no way he could get in.

"What now!
There is no way I could ever get them, just as she said, right?"
he thought,
and he stood there looking, they say.

The angry creatures were blocking (the entrance),
and the eagles were behind them.

He stood there,
and (then) he came (home), they say.
He came back down.
He wasn't able to do it.

(His brother) watched him.
He stood and turned around and came down,
he came and came and came and came,
he came down to the ground.

Aváts shuutháaw siiv'áwət,
kwa'nóqənyts.

Nyaaváak a'ím,
"Nyiikwévək awétk.
Tsuuváamxats athúu lya'ém kwa'átsk.
'Aavé kaawíts avathúuk," a'ét.
Nyamtsapéttk,
matt-tsapéetan nyaakwa'átstəm,
'ayúut si'av'áwət.

"A'ét,
'atkavék vi'thíik 'athósh," 'íik 'et,
Uukanáav,
kwanóqənya.

"Ée'é.
'Athúunypatk 'a'ávxa."

"Kaawíts axwíivək athúulyək avatháws athóts,
'aavé viikwatháw aváts," a'ét.
" 'Anyáats 'ayáak,
'awéxa," a'íik 'eta.

"Áa,
ammathóxá.
'Ashúts,
viimayáanyək ammathóxa," a'ét.

"Áa,
'athúum,
mayúuxa," nyaa'étk,
vanyaayáanypatk 'eta.

Vanyaayáak,
vanyaayáak,
vanyaayáak,
méeeenyi atspám awét.

This one stood there waiting for him,
the younger (brother).

He got there and said,
"It's no use.
I couldn't do it, just as she said.
There were snakes and things," he said.
"They were blocking the way,
and they really were too much, just as she said,
and I stood there looking.

"So,
I have come back," he said, they say.
He told him about it,
(he told) the younger (brother).

"Okay.
(Now) it is my turn to try.

"They are probably not strong enough (to defeat me),
those snakes that are there," he said.
"I (will) go,
and I will do it," he said, they say.

"Yes,
you will do it.
Little brother,
you will go and do it," he said.

"Yes,
I (will) do it,
you will see," he said,
and (now) it was his turn to go, they say.

He went along,
and he went along,
and he went along,
and he came out in a very high (place).

Nyaatspám,
avathúuk 'et:
'aayúu mashtaráts nyamatspétt siitháw,
siitháwəm,
ayúuk siiv'áwət.

Ayúuk siiv'áwnyək,
avathúum,
vaawée 'et;
'amátt ashly'áy ashtúum,
vaawíim:
'aayúu kamshtaráts 'amáyk uuwíits.

Nyaayúu kamshtaráts vaa'ée 'étk,
làpaláapk,
'amáttəly atháwkitya.

A'ét,
nyamayém,
aaxkyéevətka.

Nyaaxkyéevək,
amáam,
'ashpáany ashtúuk 'eta.
Xuuvík.
Kwaxmáalya,
kwanyíilya nyaashtúum.
Viithíik,
tsaatsénk.

Atsénək viinthíiny,
'amátti alytsén.

Nyaatsénk amáam,
kwakútsənyts siiv'áwəm.
Nyaakamíim,
kwakútsənyts kwaxmáalyəny awíi 'etk,
nyaamanyúuvəm'ashk vinthíitkitya.

When he came out,
it was like that, they say:
the angry creatures were blocking the way,
there they were,
and he stood there watching them.

He stood there watching them, and then,
he did that,
he went like this, they say;
he picked up sand,
and he went like this:
he poured it on top of the angry creatures.

The angry creatures went like this,
they flattened out,
and they lay on the ground, they say.

So,
he went through,
he went across.

He went across,
and finally,
he got the eagles, they say.
A pair of them.
(He got) the white one,
and he got the black one,
He came,
and he brought them down.

He came down (with them),
they came down to the ground.

He came down, and finally,
the older (brother) stood there.
(The younger brother) brought them,
and the older (brother) wanted to have the white one,
and once again they came (home) fighting.

"Máanyts,
ma'anóqts athúm.
Kwanyíilyəny mawéxa," a'ét.

'Anóq,
"Xamáaly avanyts
taaxán lyavíits athótəm,
nyáany,
'anyáats 'awétəny."
'Akúts,
" 'Anyáats 'a'kútstək,
kwaxmáaly avány 'atháw," a'ét.

"Kaváar.
'Anyáats 'ayáak 'ashtótk awim,
xamáaly 'awéxa," a'étk,
nyamáam,
manyúuv avuuthíik 'eta.

Vinthíitk amáam,
kwatsnyúuv awínyəm;
"Vathány 'atháw," 'ét.
"Vathány 'atháw," a'étapatk,
kwaxmáalyəny manyúuvək vinthíik 'eta.

Vinthíim.
'Aakóoyənyts
kwas'iithíit.
'Akór ayúuk siithík 'eta.
Manyúuvk suuthíit.

Ayúuk siithíkitya.
"Áa-áa,
nyaayúuts.
Manyúuv vuuthíit.
Kaathúu vuuthíikitya,"
a'étk,
ayúuk siithík.

"You,
 you are the younger (brother).
You will have the black one," he said.

The younger one (said),
"That white one
 seems to be the best one,
 that one,
 and I will have it."
The older one (said),
"I am older,
I am taking that white one," he said.

"No.
I am the one who went and got them, and so,
I will have the white one," he said,
and finally,
 they came (home) fighting about it, they say.

They came (home),
 the fighting (brothers) did;
"I am taking this one," (one of them) said,
"I am taking it," (the other one) said in his turn,
 and they came (home) fighting over the white one, they say.

They came (home).
The old woman
had power.
She had already seen them, they say.
They brought them (home) fighting.

 She lay there watching them, they say.
"Well,
it is something.
They are bringing them (home) fighting.
They are bringing them (home) somehow,"
she said,
and she lay there watching.

Siithíkəny,
nyamáam,
'amátt nyaavéevk athíi,
amáam,
'aakóoyts uuv'ów a'érək 'eta.

Uuv'ów a'ér,
máamk,
uuv'ów.
Tsúu.

Nyamáam,
'ashpáanyts apóoyk 'eta,
xatsúurəm.

'Ashpáa nyaapóoyəm,
ashtúum,
uuxúly 'éta.
Nyaayúu,
nyaayúu uuxúly 'étsaa,
nyaayúuts avathík,
'aavée lyavíik,
'anaqólək avathíkxa.

Nyáany nyaváts,
avám,
nyáaly aapáxəta.
Uuxúlyəva alyaapáxt.

" 'Anyáap 'ashpáanyts apóoya!"

Alyaapáxk,
nyaawíim,
nyuutíish 'iipány tsáam ashtúum,
alyaapáxk awíik 'eta.

Nyaawíim,
matsats'íim vinthíiketa.

Matsats'íim vinthíik.

She lay there, and then,
finally,
they came to the halfway point,
and finally,
the old woman used her powers to make it rain, they say.

She used her powers to make it rain,
and that's all,
it rained.
It poured.

That's all,
the eagles died, they say,
from the cold.

The eagles died,
and they gathered them up,
and they dug (a hole), they say.
Well,
they intended to dig something, but
there were creatures there,
they were like mice,
they would have been very tiny.

That was their house,
there it was,
and (the boys) put (the eagles) inside.
They put them in the hole.

"Our eagles are dead!" (they said).

They put them in there,
and then,
they gathered up all their bows and arrows,
and they put them in there too, they say.

Then,
they came (home) crying, they say.

They came (home) crying.

Vinthíik katán.
'Aakóoyənyts ayúuk siithík,
uuxúly avály alyaapáx aalyuupóoy.

***

Xuumáarənyts matsats'íim,
vathí katánək;
"Kamathúu mamíim?" a'ét.

"Áa-á,
'anytsxáatt 'ashtúum,
va'thíinyk.

"Amáam,
uuv'óowk,
vathám áam apóoyəm,
uuxúlyəva aly'aapáx.
'Antamáak vi'nathíik,
vathány 'iiwáany 'aláayəm,
matsats'étk vi'nathíik 'athósh,"
a'íik 'eta.

Nyamáam,
'aakóoyənyts 'aválya kuuv'óowəny sharéqt.

Nyáanyts awétk,
avuuv'óow sharéqəm,
akwévətk.

Siitháw,
amáam,
amáam,
'ashpáanyts siitháwnyək,
amáam tatuukwáatsk 'eta.

Uuxúly atháw.

A'ét,
nyáanyəm shaavárəntiyum.

They came (home) and got there.
The old lady lay there watching them from the distance,
as they put them into that hole and covered them.

***

The children were crying,
and they got here;
"Why are you crying?" she said.

"Yes,
we got our pets,
and we were coming (home).

"Finally,
it started to rain,
and because of that they died,
and we put them in this hole.
We left them behind and came (home),
and we feel bad about this,
and we came (home) crying,"
they said, they say.

Finally,
the old woman, in her house, took control of the rain.

She is the one who did it,
she took control of the rain,
and it stopped.

There they were,
and finally,
finally,
the eagles were over there,
and finally they regained consciousness, they say.

They were in the hole.

So,
(this song) is sung about that.

Máam,
amáanək,
siitháwk 'eta.

Avatháwk,
a'éta.
Shaaváravats:

"Iinyáaxáats,
amán wengee,
mán wengee,
iimán wengee,
iimán wengee,
mán wengeem."

Amánək,
viitháw 'eta.

Nyaa'íim,
shaavár amáka,
shaavár amák athík,
nyáanyts:

"Inyaaxáats,
amán wengee,
pam kwiitháav,
amán wengém."

Atspámək viitháw,
awítsxa.

"Pám kwiitháavts,
amán wengee,
mán wingii,
amán wingii,
amán wingii,
amán wingii,
iimán wengéem,"

a'ét.

Finally,
they recovered,
and there they were, they say.

There they were,
they say.
This is the song:

    "Their pets,
     they got up,
     they got up,
     they got up,
     they got up,
     they got up."

They recovered,
and here they were, they say.

Then,
the song after that,
the song that takes place after that,
this is it:

    "Their pets,
     they got up,
     they got there and there they were,
     they got up."

They came out and here they were,
and they were going to do it.

    "They came out and there they were,
     they got up,
     they got up,
     they got up,
     they got up,
     they got up,
     they got up,"

(the song) says.

Uutspámək viitháwk 'et.
Mat'ár atháw.

Nyaatháwk,
xuumáara nyiipá nyáany,
ashtúum,
xalyuuqítsk avatháwk 'eta.
Náak.

'Iipánya,
ashtúuvash,
iisáalyi.

***

'Iipá tsuu'úlyá,
ashtúum,
iisháaly,
atsáam,
nyáany.

Mariikáan nyumpées 'ashént alytháwk,
mayúmək,
vaawíim,
'iipány tsa'úly.
Nyáalyavíik;
avatháwk a'éta.

A'étk,
siitháwm,
aashváarək 'eta.

'Iipánya,
'iipá tsa'úlyá.

*** *** ***

Nyaathúum ám;
nyaamám uutspám siitháwətka.
Athúum,

They went out and here they were, they say.
They were outside.

There they were,
and as for the children's arrows,
(the eagles) gathered them up,
and they clutched them (with their talons), they say.
And they sat down.

The arrows,
they gathered them up,
in their talons.

***

The arrows that (the boys) had carried,
they gathered them up,
in their talons,
and they put them down,
those (arrows).

There's a certain American coin,
you've seen it,
they go like this,
they clutch arrows (in their talons).
It was like that;
there they were, they say.

So,
there they were,
and they sing about it, they say.

About the arrows.
about the arrows that they carried.

*** *** ***

It happened;
finally they went out and there they were.
And so,

nyamáam ashtót.
"Póoy aly'ém!
Póoy aly'ém!"
Máam amáank atháwk,
ashtót.

Ashtúum,
sanyaathúuk amám.
Iiwáanyts 'axóttəm siitháawətka.
Atháw.

Nyaavəm,
viitháwk,
amám,
mashtxáa nyavály nyáasik nayém;
ayóov a'íim avatháwitya.
A'étk,
siitháwət.

Wilawíil uutséts nyáany a'ávapat siitháwtk
    a'ím,
" 'Ayóovək,
katánəm 'ayóovxa,"
a'ínypatk siitháwk,
mashtxáanyanyts.

A'ím,
nyáasi,
"Ka'thómək 'ayóovxa," a'ím,
siitháawət.

"Áa,
mathúum,
mayúuxa.
Páa 'ats'atsláyts aathúuva.
Pa'iipáa siimawétsk
ma'ávəxa.
Mayúuk siimawétsxa,"
a'ét,
'aakóoyənya.

finally the boys got them.
"They're not dead!
They're not dead!"
Finally (the eagles) recovered and there they were,
and (the boys) gathered them up.

They gathered them up,
that (is what) happened.
They were happy, over there.
There they were.

At this (point),
here they were,
and finally,
they went over there to the girls' house;
they wanted to see them, they say.
So,
there they were.

The girls were there wanting to hear the flute-playing,
    and they said,
"We'll see them,
they will get here and we will see them,"
they were saying it in turn,
those girls (were).

So,
over there,
"We will see them somehow," (the boys) said,
and there they were.

"Yes,
you (will) do it,
you will see them.
They certainly are bad people.
You will go to those people
and experience it.
You will go and see (for yourselves),"
she said,
the old woman (did).

"Mhm,"
siiwéts.

Nyaa'ím,
siitháwəm,
nyuutíishəny,
antamákalyem,
'uutíish tsa'úlyət,
nyaanymáam,
siitháwətkəm.
Nyaatsa'úly siiwéts.

Viiwéts,
'anyáak nathómək viiwétsk,
aaíimək xaly'áw akyét.
Kaawíts akyétk siiwéts.

Siiwéts.

Siiwéts siiwéts siiwéts siiwéts siiwéts,
siiwétsəly nyaaxiipáan.
Siiwéts.

Tsakavár apóoytk,
kaawíts uunyáq,
siiwéts.

Sanyaawétsk,
alykatánək 'eta,
'avá nyáasi.
Viiwéts,
nyakuuyáamsi.

Mashtxáa nyavási katánəm.

Athúm,
Paar'áak Paarxáan uu'íts,
aaíim kwanyúur tíi tíi tíi tíi tíi tíi 'ét,
a'ím,
'avá alyuupúuv,

"Mhm," they said,
and they went.

Then,
there they were,
and as for their bows,
they didn't leave them behind,
they carried the bows in their hands,
and finally,
there they were.
They were carrying them along.

They went along,
they went along heading east,
and they shot cottontails as they pleased.
They went along shooting things.

They went along.

They went and went and went and went and went along,
they went along and got closer.
They went along.

They were laughing fit to die,
they were making fun of something,
as they went along.

They went along,
and they got there, they say,
(they got to) a house way over there.
They went along
to their destination.

They got to the girls' house, over there.

So,
the ones called Paar'áak and Paarxáan,
their colors just shimmered like a rainbow,
and so,
they went into the house,

sanyaatháaw,
'avá tsáaməly anyúur;
tíi tíi tíi.

" 'Úy!"
Mashxáayəts aváak ayúuk,
" 'Úy!
Kaawíts kanyaathómantik!
'Avány tsáamək anyúurak,
tíi tíi tíi tíi tíi 'ét!"

Nyaa— kwara'ákəts,
"Áa-á,
pa'iipáa nyáanyts athúwúm,"
a'ét.

"Paar'áak Paarxáan katanək athúwúm.
Kayóovək
pa'iipáanya."

Siitháwəm,
kór aly'ém,
qwalayéwəts a'ím,
uutspám awítsa.

Uutspáməs amáam,
a'ím,
mattxa'áaw namák.
Aváam,
'aványts anyóorək xalyavíit.

Pa'iipáanyts uuyóov avuunóot.
Vinthíik a'ét,
uutspák.

Viitháw,
nyaaqwalayáawk,
vinthíit.
Nakavék vindíi.

and there they were,
and the whole house was colorful;
it shimmered like a rainbow.

"What now!"
(One) girl came and looked;
"What now!
Something is happening again!
The whole house is colorful
and shimmering like a rainbow!"

The old man said,
"Well,
it must be those people,"
he said.

"Paar'áak and Paarxáan must have gotten there.
Take a look
at those people."

There they were,
not far away,
and (when) it was morning,
they went (back) out.

They went out, but,
they say,
they left their spirits behind.
(The people) got there,
and the house seemed to have horizontal stripes.

The people were watching them.
(The boys) wanted to come (home),
(and so) they came out.

There they were,
and when it was morning,
they came (home).
They came back (home).

Vinthíik vinthíik vinthíik vinthíik vinthíik.
'Amátt aalyuuvéev vinthíit,
vinathíim,
'anyáaxáv awét.

Siiwétsk,
xaly'áwəny akyáam,
apáavək,
asóotsk,
kaathómək vinthíit.

Máam,
nyaaxávək viiyémt.

Nyaanthíik,
"Nyáavi 'uushmáxa," nya'ét.

Taráak,
vuunóok,
vaawím,
'uutsény péem,
nyiitháw siitháw 'eta.
Atskuunáav siitháwət.

Siitháwnyək,
avík apáam,
avík apáam 'étapatk,
siitháawət.
Nyamáam,
uushmátk.
Tiinyáamtəkitya.

Nyuushmáam,
siitháwm,
amáam,
nyakór apóoy.
Nyakór viitháawətəm,
awítya,
xuumáarənyts nyaathúum.

They came and came and came and came and came.
They came to the halfway point,
and as they came,
the sun was going down.

They went along,
they shot a cottontail,
and they roasted it,
and they ate it,
and somehow they came along.

Finally,
the sun went down.

As they came,
"We'll sleep here," they said.

They lit a fire,
and here they were,
they did it like this,
they moved the coals around,
and there they were, they say.
They were talking about things.

There they were, and then,
(one of them) lay down here,
and (the other one) lay down here, they say,
and there they were.
Finally,
they slept.
It was dark, they say.

They slept,
there they were,
and finally,
they were already unconscious.
They had been there before,
they had been,
when they were children.

Nyaayúuts —
maamathíits aváak 'eta.

Maamathíits aváak;
uushmáam atháw,
nyuutháw 'amáyvi anáktək,
amétk vuunóot.

Amétk vuunóony,
nyakór a'im;
amúly ashék 'éta,
maamathíinyanyts.
Xuumáarəny.

"Áaa áaa," nyaa'íim,
"Paar'áak!
Paarxáan!
Paar'áak!
Paarxáan!"
a'íik 'eta.

A'íim,
kwa'kútsəts amánək,
a'ávəs athík,
"Áay!
Kamánk,
'ashútsá!
Kaawíts kaathúum!
'Atháwətəm,
'atsayérəts aváa!
'Amáy anák,
'amúly nyiishétk vuunóotá!"
a'íik 'eta.

"Kaawíts kaathóm a'étk,
'atháwəm," a'ét.
" 'Amúly ashétk vuunóot!
Kamánk ka'áv!"
Uu'íts.

A creature —
an owl got there, they say.

An owl got there;
they were sleeping,
and it sat above (the place) where they were,
and it went on crying.

It went on crying,
for a long time;
it called their names, they say,
that owl (did).
The children's (names).

"Aaah, aaah," it said,
"Paar'áak!
Paarxáan!
Paar'áak!
Paarxáan!"
it said, they say.

Then,
the older one got up,
and although he heard him, (the younger brother) lay there.
"Hey!
Get up,
younger brother!
Something is happening!
While we were here,
a bird got here!
It's sitting up high,
and it's calling us by name!"
he said, they say.

"Something is going to happen,
(while) we are (here)," he said.
"It's calling our names!
Get up and listen!"
(That's) what he said.

'Amáy alyaváts,
nyáany amétk vuunóot.
Paar'áak!
Paarxáan!
Áaaa!
Áaaa!
Paar'áak!
Paarxáan!

"Éey," a'étk,
amánk 'eta.
Kwa'nóqəny nyaamánk,
a'áva.
"Nyama'íts a'étəm
pa'iipáa ta'axán 'atskáamk áamsh.
A'íim nyaa'íiva," a'íik a'eta.

"Pa'iipáa ta'axán 'atskáamək áam,
nyam'íts.
Nyaayúuts nyuuváak,
'iipáys a'étəm ma'ávət."
Nyáaly ava'étk avátk,
kanyaa'íim,
"Xxx! xxx! xxx!" a'íik 'eta.
Alyashmáak 'eta.

Kwa'kútsəny iiwáanyts 'aláayəm,
ashmáa lya'ém,
nyaanymáam,
a'ávtəs,
viithík 'eta.

Viithíknyək,
viithíkəm áam,
'anyáayk viithíim áam,
amáan.

Amáan.
Nyaayúuts ava'étk vuunóom;
"Ava'étk 'ím 'ítsk 'etúm,"
'íik 'eta.

It sat up high,
and it was crying those (names).
"Paar'áak!
Paarxáan!
Aaah!
Aaah!
Paar'áak!
Paarxáan!"

"Hey!" he said,
and he got up, they say.
The younger one got up,
and he listened.
"(That's what) they say
(when) an important person passes by.
They say that," he said, they say.

"An important person passes by,
and they say that.
When a creature gets there,
you hear them say that it is alive."
That's what he was saying,
he said something,
and he made (the snoring sound) "Xxx! xxx! xxx!" they say.
He had gone back to sleep, they say.

The older one felt bad,
he didn't sleep,
and that's all,
he might have been listening,
(as) he lay here, they say.

He lay here,
and he lay here, and finally,
morning was coming, and finally,
they got up.

They got up.
The creature was (still) saying that;
"They're always saying that,"
he said, they say.

Nyáavi,
nyáavik viinayém viiwéts —
'atsémta.
Nyáavik viinayém siiwétsxa nyaa'ím,
nyáavik viiwéts nyama'íiny.

Tiimáa xuutsé a'ím uuv'óom,
axérk 'eta.
Tiimáa xuutsé uuv'óom;
axérək.
'Uunyévəts viithíkəm,
vathík tasháttk;
axérəkts,
aatkyéerək 'ét.

Vanyaawétsk a'íts,
nyáava 'iiwáa nyiipéttk,
viiyáa.
Kanáav.

Nyaawíim,
vathá axérək av'áwək,
nyáasi nyaawétsk.

"Makyí 'anyáats kaawíts nya'thóm,
pa'iipáa kwanyméts vathíik,
tiimáa xuutsé 'uuxíirəny ayúum.
Matxáyəm áamk,
vathá lyavíik,
wáayp wáayp wáayp.
' 'Áay!
pa'iipáats uuv'óosh!'
vathá a'ím vaa'íim,
ayúuxa.
***
Pa'iipáats —
'anyáats va'athúu aly'ém kwa'átsk nyiithómətəm,
vatháts vuuv'óom,
ayúu uuv'óom," a'íik 'eta.

At this (point),
at this (point) they left and went this way —
no, I made a mistake.
At this (point) they were about to leave,
at this (point) they were about to go this way.

(Things) called tiimáa xuutsé were standing there,
they had tied them up, they say.
Tiimáa xuutsé were standing there;
they had tied them up.
The road was here,
and they stood them up here;
they had tied them up,
(while) they were lying on their backs, they say.

They were going to go this way,
I forget this (part),
(but) they went.
They tell about it.

Then,
(the boys) stood there tying them up,
and (then) they went over there.

"Wherever we may be,
someone else (will) come along,
and he (will) see the tiimáa xuutsé we have tied up.
When the wind passes by,
(the tiimáa xuutsé will) go like this,
sway, sway, sway.
'Hey!
There are people standing here!'
this is what he (will) say,
(when) he sees them.
***
A person —
if nothing happens to us, just as they said,
these (things) will stand here,
they will stand here watching," he said, they say.

A'íim,
awíim,
tatsháattəm suuv'óom,
siiwétskitya.
Siiwéts.

*** *** ***

Nyaa'étk,
avnathíik 'eta.

Viithíim.
Takshé 'Aqwáas uu'íts nyáanyts,
nyaxuutsamáarəm a'ítya.

Nyaxuutsamáar awétkəm,
nyáa nyakóora nyiitapóoy a'étk,
'amátt axwély,
tsamíim,
viiwáak,
'atsawíim,
'amátt axwélyk viiwáak viiwáak a'ét.
Uuxakyíim,
viithík 'eta.

Viinthíikəm,
siiwétsk,
sanyaawéts sanyaawéts sanyaawéts sanyaawéts sanyaawéts,
awím,
'anyáa nyamayúush,
sanyaawéts.

'Amátt uuxwélyts avathíkəm,
katánəm —
arík a'íik 'eta.

Arík,
nyamáam,
uulyanáalyk 'eta.
Aalyáq,

So,
they did it,
they set (the tiimáa xuutsé) upright and there they were,
and (the boys) went along, they say.
They went along.

*** *** ***

Then,
they came along, they say.

They came along.
That one they call Yellow Gopher,
they were his children, they say.

They were his children, and so,
for a long time he had wanted to kill them;
he dug a hole in the ground,
and he put (something) down,
he went on,
he was doing things,
he went on and on digging in the ground, they say.
He laid a long object across (the hole),
and there it was, they say.

The boys came along,
they went along,
they went and went and went and went along,
and so,
it got to be afternoon,
as they went along.

The hole he had dug was there,
and they got there —
and it caved in, they say.

It caved in,
and that's all,
it made them fall in, they say.
They fell down,

alynáalya'ém.
Alysiitháw.
Alysiitháw,
tsuupámxats athótk siitháwətk —
uupóoyaləm siitháwəsáa,
avathótk:
apóoyəts athótəm.

Xantas'ílyts aváak 'eta.
Aváak awím.
Kaly'aaxwáay ta'úlyv,
tskwshámpat atáv awím,
atáv awét.
tatpóoyk 'eta.
Nyáasi.

Nyaattpóoy,
Xantas'ílyənyts,
avány nyiixwéttənyts áamk athótəm,
vathány vaawé alytathúun,
avány vaawé alytathúun,
a'éta.
Xantas'íly vathí atháw;
'axwéttəm,
mayúuxa.

Xantas'íly vatáyk uuváaxaya.
'Anyáak vathí uuváak uuváakitya.
Nyaany mayúm alyaskyíit.
'Atskaanáva vatháts:
vathí aváts 'axwétt,
nyiixwéttənyts.

Nyaathúum,
kanáavət.

Xatalwéts ayúuk,
aa'ár alyaavály a'étk,
viiyáak;
Kwanáw alyayémət.

they fell into it.
There they were, in there.
There they were, in there,
they were able to get out, over there —
it hadn't killed them, but
it happened:
they died (anyway).

Gila Monster came along, they say.
He came along.
He was carrying his war club,
he hit them right on the head,
he hit them,
and he killed them, they say.
Over there.

When he killed them,
Gila Monster,
their blood flowed,
and he dipped this (part) into it like this,
and he dipped that (part) into it like this,
they say.
(The marks) are right here on Gila Monster;
they are red,
you will see it.

That big Gila Monster is still around.
He is around here in the east, they say.
You can still see him.
This is the story:
he is red right here,
and it is (the boys') blood.

So,
they tell about it.

Coyote saw it,
and he dangled his tail in it,
and he went along;
he went to Kwanáw's (place).

"Móo,
nyáats 'tapúyk,
amáaməsh."
'Aayúu,
Paar'áak Paarxáan a'ét.

"Nyaaxwáy vatháts tapúyəs," a'étk 'eta.

Pa'iipáanyts xaltakóoyk,
"Áa-aa," a'ét.
Aatsxwáaar a'ét,
uupóoynya.
Pa'iipáa nyiixúuu a'ét.
Xaltakóoy.

Nyam mashxáy kwa'nóqənyts
'akór ayúuk siithíkəs 'et,
uupóoya.
Ayúuk siithíkt.

Nyiinyaatpóoyk awím,
Aashalyáam Kwanáw nyavály nyáasi awémkəm,
xuumáarəny alyúlyk 'eta.
Apáava awéta.

Paar'áak Paarxáan apáava.

Pa'iipáa tsáaməly apák
uumáavum.
Apáava.

Xuumáayvəny amáam,
nyatsasháak 'ashéntək áamp.
Yaaxuupóots athót.
Tsakwshá av'ótsk,
iisháaly 'ét.

Awím,
pa'iipáanyts xaltakóoyətk a'ím,
nyuunóok,

"Okay,
I've killed them,
that's all," (Yellow Gopher said).
Well,
he meant Paar'áak and Paarxáan.

"Perhaps my war club killed them," he said, they say.

The people rejoiced,
"Yes," they said.
They laughed,
about the death (of the boys).
People were all talking at once.
They were rejoicing.

The younger girl
might have seen it already,
the death (of the boys).
She lay there watching them.

He killed them, and so,
he went over there to Aashalyáam Kwanáw's house,
and he cooked the children, they say.
He roasted them.

He roasted Paar'áak and Paarxáan.

All the people came
to eat.
He roasted them.

He ate his sons,
and there was one bone left over.
It was a rib.
Their heads were there,
and their hands, they say.

So,
the people rejoiced, and so,
there they were,

àra'óoyk,
aaíim,
aatsxwáar a'étk vuunóot.

Tsakwshá kwara'óra
nyaayúu as'án 'ét.
As'án,
nyamkatsuu'ór avaawét.

Suunóot.
Iisháalyəny,
'atsnyamuumáav awét,
iisháalyəny.
Nyaawítsk,
kutsáar athúuk awíts:
nyamuumáav awét.

Yaaxuupóo vathá,
kaawítsəm kaawémk,
aatsuutáshk 'ét.

Awím,
'atsaatsxwáar,
kamaxánəts uuyóov.
"Óo,
mattkwiisháaytan," a'ét.

Pa'iipáanyts uuyóovət.
" 'Úux," aaly'étk awíts.

Athúm,
mashxáy,
kwa'nóqənyts,
kóra,
sa'áwv suuváakitya.
Nyáasi maxáyəly kwanóqəly aváamk.

Nyaaxavík uushmáam nyiimánək,
atúyv siiv97ányk,
'akór,
xuumárəts xamíi siivát.

they played games,
they did as they pleased,
and they were laughing.

Those round heads
were something to kick around, they say.
They kicked them around,
they played kickball with them like this.

There they were.
As for the hands,
they used them to eat with,
the hands.
When they used them,
they used them as if they were spoons:
they ate with them.

These ribs,
they did something with them,
they played shinny, they say.

So,
they were laughing about it,
and (the people) who enjoyed it were watching.
"Oh,
it's really wonderful," they said.

The people were watching.
"It serves them right," they thought.

So,
the young woman,
the younger one,
already,
she had had her baby, they say.
It had arrived (courtesy of) the younger boy over there.

It started when they slept together,
she became pregnant and there she was,
and after a while,
a child was born and there he was.

Nyaavák,
amáam,
nyakó apúy —
nyakórəly ayúuk siivát.
Xuumárənyts xamíi a'íi nyaavák.

Nyam nyakóny lyavíi,
nyakwas'uuthíinyts tsaanyíitəntim,
siivát.

Nyakór nyayúuk,
nyashuupáwk siivát.

Xuumárənyts viiyáak a'éta.
Kwasiithíiyapat,
atspéevəs athót.

Viiyáak aváam.
Nyakó iisháalyáa,
tsakwshánya nyaawétk,
katsuu'ór athúm vuunóom,
ayúuk siiv'áw a'étəm,
maxánək.

Aatsxwáar a'étəm,
ayúu alyav'áwk,
ayúuk siiv'áwtk.
Iiwáaly amét siiv'áwət.

Takavék,
viithíik aváat.

Xuumár aváts suuváam,
'anyáa kaathútsəm,
kwara'ák,
Aashalyáam Kwanáwəts,
"Xuumár avány,
matháw,
malyúlytsxa,
'anyáa kaathútsəm,"
a'íik 'eta,
xuumárək tsapéevany.

There he was,
and that's all,
his father was dead —
and he already had seen it happen.
The child was born and there he was.

He was like his father,
he had too much power,
there he was.

He had already seen it,
he knew about it.

The child went along, they say.
He had power too,
even though he was small.

He went along and got there.
(They were using) his father's hands,
and they were using his head,
they were playing kickball (with it),
and he stood there watching them, they say,
and they enjoyed it.

They laughed,
and he stood in (the group of people) watching,
he stood over there watching.
He stood over there, crying in his heart.

He went back,
he came (home) and got there.

This child was there,
and one day,
an old man,
Aashalyáam Kwanáw (said),
"This child,
you will take him,
and boil him,
some day,"
he said, they say,
(referring to) the little child.

"Mawítsxa,"
a'íik 'eta.

"Xóttk," a'ím;
pa'iipáanyts matt-tsanyóts siitháwət.
Saawítsxa.
'Anyáa kaathútsəm awíts.

'Anyáa tsakanáam,
saawíim.
Àra'óoyətk awím,
'anyáa atspák viithíi,
nyáanyəm saawétsk,
pa'iipáa uupóoy nyáany awétk —
nyatsasháak athúts,
atspáats athótəm,
àrtuu'óoyvi awét.
Mattamáarək vuunóot.

"Móo,
mamáarək," a'ét.
"Móo,
mamáarətsk," awét,
"Móo,
mamáarək," a'ét.
Vanyaawét,
aatsxwér,
"Áaaa!"

Pa'iipáanyts,
"Uupóoyəny 'úux," aaly'étk,
vaawétk;
vuunóok athót.

Nyam xuumáarənyts aváak;
maxánək nyuuváatk,
ayúut.
Nyakó tsakwshányáa,
iimény a'étk,
ayúut.

"You will do it,"
he said, they say.

"All right," they said;
the people agreed.
They would do that.
And one day they did it.

They decided on a day,
and they did that.
They played games,
and the sun came up,
and at that (point) they went along,
and they used those dead people —
it was their bones,
they had come out, and so,
they used them in games.
They were having a competition.

"Okay,
you've won," he said.
"Okay,
you've won," and so,
"Okay,
you've won," he said.
They did this,
and they laughed:
"Aaah!"

The people (thought),
"Dying serves them right," they thought,
and they did this;
here they were.

The child got there;
they were enjoying it,
and he saw them.
His father's head,
and his legs, they say,
he saw (these things).

"Móo!
Móo!
Nyam ma'ávətstəxa!" aaly'étk,
iiwáaly a'étk suuváat.

Sanyuuváam,
máam,
"Móo,
nyamáam,
xuumár avány nyamáamtəm,
'anóqəm,
malyúlytəxa," a'ét.
Suunóot.

Pa'iipáats aváam kanáts:
"Móo,
máam.
Kataráak!
Xá katapínyk!" a'íik 'eta.

"Xóttk,"
a'éta.
Taráak awím,
tashkyén tsaváwəts awím,
'axá tapíny.
Nyamtaráatan vuunóok,
kúur xuumár alytápk —
alyúlyú.

Nyam xuumárənyts kwas'iithíitiyum.
Nyamaamíny a'étəm áam,
'axány xantapáatsk avák athúuk 'eta.
Makyík alól aly'em.

Xuumár avák,
nyamaamíny a'étkəm áam,
nyakóny kwas'uuthíi lyavíitapatk a'ím,
nyamaamíny uu'ítsək,
amáam.

"Okay!
Okay!
You will feel (the consequences)!" he thought,
he was saying it in his heart.

There he was,
and finally,
"Okay,
that's all,
it's all over for that child,
he is small,
and you will boil him," they said.
There they were.

Someone got there and gave orders:
"Now,
that's all.
Light a fire!
Heat (some) water!" he said, they say.

"All right,"
they said.
They started a fire, and so,
they put a pot down, and so,
they heated water.
They really made (the fire) burn,
and in a little while they threw the child in —
they were going to boil him.

The child had power.
He was going to pass through it,
and he turned the water icy cold, they say.
It never did boil.

The child sat there,
he had passed through it,
he was like his father in (having great) power,
and he passed through it,
that's all.

Xány taxtsúur,
páq a'ét.
Aváts aráak,
kyérrrr awéts.

Ayáak,
vaawíim,
kaathúunyək a'ím,
'apíly a'ím,
kwaxatsúur viiváxayətá.

A'ét,
'a'íi nyáam aví atsét.
Taráat.

Nyaataráam,
xuumárənyts siiványk,
"Nyamáam,
'awíim 'a'ávəxa," a'ét.
Siivát.
Xuumárəts amáam.

Kwas'iithíi tsapéet vanyaavák.

" 'Ayáak aví 'ashathómp,
pa'iipáa tsuumpáp avkwatháwva nyáanyəm,
'atskuunáavxa," nyaa'ét.
Siiványk,
siiyáak 'eta.
Vathík shathómp siiyáat.
Takavék shathómp siiyáat.

Pa'iipáats viivám,
aváamək,
awéta.
Matxá Vàlyvály 'éta.

Matxá Vàlyvály 'ét,
siivám,
nakwíik:

He made the water cold,
it was freezing cold.
That (fire) was blazing,
they made it burst into flames.

He went along,
he went like this,
he did it somehow,
it was supposed to get hot,
but the coldness was still there.

So,
they put more in more wood.
And they lit it.

When they lit it,
the child sat there,
"Finally,
I will try to do it," he said.
He sat there.
The child (should have been) done for.

(But) he had great power.

"I (will) go along and head that way,
right through the four people who are there,
and I will tell him about it," he said.
He sat there, and then,
he went along, they say.
He headed this way and went along.
(Then) he went back and headed that way.

A person was there,
and (the child) got there,
he did.
(The person) was called Shifting Wind.

He was called Shifting Wind,
and there he was,
and (the boy) called him his mother's brother:

" 'Anakwíi," a'ét.
" 'Atskuunáav a'ím 'athósh."
"Móo."

" 'Anyáap vanyawítsk vuunóotəs,
   amáam.
Pa'iipáa tsáaməly,
nyamáam tsáam tan uunóot,
muutara'úy maavíir 'a'ím,
'athósh,"
a'íik 'eta.

"Piipáa tsáam matapóoya!" a'eta.

A'étəm,
iisháaly atháwk athósh a'étəm,
Matxá Vàlyvályts " 'Axóttk," a'íik 'eta.

"Nyaama'ím,
'anyáats,
Matxá Vàlyvály,
'anyáats xiipúk 'aváam,
vályavályavályavályavályavályavályavályavályavály 'a'ét,
pa'iipáanyts xaltakóoyxa,"
a'íik 'eta.

"Nyaaxaltakóoyəm,
Matxá Kaamalyíi a'ítsəm,
manakwíits athúuk,
vathík athík," a'íik 'eta.
" 'Anyáaly kayémək kayúuk anúut.
Matxá Kaamalyíi a'ét."

"Áa,
xóttk," 'ét,
nyaayáak aváamk,
nyaatayúuts.
" 'Anakwíi," a'ét.
"Nyaayúu,
miisháaly 'atháw vii'thíik 'athósh.

"Uncle," he said.
"I want to talk to you."
"Okay."

"This is what they did to me, but
  it's over with.
All the people,
  finally all of them are (here),
  and I want you get them taken care of,
  I do,"
  he said, they say.

"Kill everybody!" he said.

Then,
  he shook his hand, they say,
  and Shifting Wind said, "All right," they say.

"As you say,
  I (am the one),
  Shifting Wind,
  I will get there first,
  and I'll go gust-gust-gust-gust-gust-gust-gust-gust-gust-gust,
  and the people will rejoice,"
  he said, they say.

"While they are rejoicing,
  (the one) they call Storm Wind,
  he is your mother's brother,
  and he is right here," he said, they say.
"Go east and see him next.
  He is called Storm Wind."

"Yes,
  all right," said (the boy),
  and he went and got there,
  and he called him his relative.
"Uncle," he said.
"Well,
"I have come to shake your hand.

Pa'iipáats vaathótk vuunóom,
'awíim,
tsáaməly 'ashaaíim 'a'ím 'athósh,"
a'íik 'eta.
Xuumárənyts a'ím.

"Xótt,"
Matxá Kaamalyíits.
"Xóttk."

"Matxá Vàlyvályts xiipúk aváam,
'anyáats kúur aváam,
'anóqəm 'aspíiiir a'étxa,"
a'íik 'eta.
Matxánya.

Matxá Kaamalyíinyts.

Spíir a'ím,
nyaamatxáy 'ím,
Aashalyáam Kwanáwəts xalakúy,
'avá 'amáy akúlyk,
" 'Anyáats shamáats 'axóttk,
nyaayúu,
'atsaqwérək uuváam,"
a'étk awím.

Vaa'íim,
mataxáyk,
vályavályavály a'ím,
vaa'íim;
"Ma'ávúm,"
a'íik 'eta.
A'íim,
"Ma'ávxa," a'íik 'eta.
Xalakúy.

"Nyaa'íim,
Matxá Kwaspérənyts viithík,
nyamkwaxamók 'ím.

People are doing this,
and so,
I want to wipe them all out,"
he said, they say.
The child said it.

"All right,"
Storm Wind (said).
"All right."

"Shifting Wind will get there first,
and I will get there later,
and blow a little harder,"
he said, they say.
The wind (did).

Storm Wind (did).

He (blew) a little harder,
and when he blew,
Aashalyáam Kwanáw rejoiced,
he climbed up on top of his house (and said),
"I am lucky,
well,
I can make speeches from here,"
he said.

He said this,
and the wind blew,
it went gust-gust-gust,
like this;
"You might hear it,"
he said, they say.
And so,
"You will hear," he said, they say.
And he rejoiced.

"Then,
Strongest Wind is here,
he is the third one," he said;

Matxá Kwaspértanənyts avathík.
Nyáanya mayáaxa."
Nyaatskuunáav anót.

"Móo,"
a'étk,
nyaayáa,
Matxá Kwaspértan nyaaváam.
Nakwíi.

Nyaatskuunáav.
" 'Anyáats av'a'étk 'athósh.
Pa'iipáa tsáam vaathótk athúm,
'anyáats tsáam 'ashaaíim 'a'ím 'athósh,"
a'étəm;
" 'Axóttk," a'éta.

" 'Anyáats,
Matxá Kwaspérənyts nya'váam,
nyaayúu tsáam 'amáttəm 'atstútsxa,"
a'íik 'eta.
Aaíimət.
" 'Amatxáyk 'aspérət,
'aayúu 'akatsalyésh,"
aaíim.

" 'Awéxa,"
a'íik 'eta.

"Nyaawíim,
manakwíits avathíkəntik,
avík athík,
'Áw Aráats," a'íik 'eta.
"Nyaanymáam,
aváam,
nyáany tsáam tanəly aavíirúm,"
a'íik 'eta.

Avayáak,
'Áw Aráaly aváamtan.
Tayúutsəm.
" 'Axótt."

"Strongest Wind is there.
You will go to him (next)."
He told him about it next.

"Okay,"
he said,
and he went along,
and he got to Strongest Wind.
His mother's brother.

He told him about it.
"I have something in mind.
All these people did this, and so
I want to wipe them all out,"
he said;
"All right," said (Strongest Wind).

"I,
Strongest Wind, will get there,
and I will knock everything to the ground,"
he said, they say.
And he did as he pleased.
"I will blow hard,
I will break things," (he said),
and he did as he pleased.

"I will do it,"
he said, they say.

"Then,
there is another of your mother's brothers,
he is there,
he is Blazing Fire," he said, they say.
"Finally,
he will get there,
and he is going to finish everything,"
he said, they say.

He went along,
and he got to Blazing Fire.
He called him his relative.
"All right," (said Blazing Fire).

"Nyáa Matxá Kwaspérəny nyaaváam,
 nyaayúu tsáam katsalyéshk aavíir 'ím.
'Anyáats nyaamák 'ayém,
 tsáam tan shhhhhk 'awíim,
 nyaanyép a'íts,
 'iipáany,"
 a'íik 'eta.

" 'Awéxa," a'íik 'eta.

"Xótt-ta," nya'étk,
" 'Aváak,
 — ssssssss! —
'atkavék."
 Nyaaváanyəm,
 kwara'ákts nyavá 'amáy alyav'áw,
 nyaatsaqwérək athót.
"Shamáats 'a'axóttk,"
 a'étk,
 nyaayúu 'étəny vaa'étk.
"Mataxáyk,
 kany'évəly a'étəm,
 ma'ávətstəxa.

"Pa'iipáa ta'axán,
 nyaayúu tsuuqwérənyts vaa'íim nyaa'íiva," a'ét.
'Avá 'amáy alyav'áwk av'áwk 'eta.

Xuumár nyuuváak uuváat.
Nyaayúu xá tuupínyəm aamínytək,
 xányts xatsúur páq 'étk awét,
 alól alya'ém.

Nyam pa'iipáats nyuuváak,
 nyamkwalyúly alyapásk,
 a'ávəly —
'axáts xatsúurək nyiikwév.
Xatsúur viiváxay.

"When Strongest Wind gets here,
he is going to break everything.
I (will) go after him,
I (will) go whoosh over everything,
and they (will) be all gone,
those men,"
he said, they say.

"I will do it," he said, they say.

"All right," he said,
"I will get there,
— whoosh! —
and I will come back."
When he got there,
the old man was up on the roof,
making a speech.
"I am lucky,"
he said,
he said things like this.
"The wind is blowing,
so whatever I say to you,
you will hear it.

"(I am) a respected leader,
and what I have to say is this," he said.
He was standing up on top of the house, they say.

The child was there.
He passed through the heated water,
and he did (something to make) the water get freezing cold,
(so) it didn't boil.

A person was there,
and he touched what was supposed to be boiling (water),
he wanted to feel it —
and the water was impossibly cold.
It was still cold.

Vuunóoxayəm,
Matxá Valyvályts aváatk,
awítya.
Aváak 'eta.

Aváak,
vályvályvályvályvályvályvályvály.

Nyuunóony,
nyaamínyəm,
Matxá Kaamalyíits aváantik.
Nyaaváantik,
'anóqəm spíir 'ét,
'amátt llóp 'ét.

Nyaamíny amáam,
Matxá Kwaspértan nyaaváamtək,
amáam,
saawíik 'eta.
***
Uutsalyésh.

'Aayúu taskyén xáa tuupíny atháwət —
welawél a'és,
ta'áam.

Nyaawét,
amáam,
Matxá Kwaspértan nyáany nyaaváam,
nyaayúu tsáaməly nyaata'aaláayt.

Nyamáam,
'Áw Aráats nyam nyaathíik,
amáam.
Amáam,
amákəly,
'Áw Aráanya.

Nyaathíik,
amáam,

There he was, and suddenly
Shifting Wind got there,
he did.
He got there, they say.

He got there,
(going) gust-gust-gust-gust-gust-gust-gust-gust.

There he was,
and he passed through,
and Storm Wind got there in turn.
When he got there,
he (blew) a little harder,
and there was a sandstorm.

When he had passed through,
Strongest Wind got there,
and that's all,
he did that, they say.
***
He broke things.

He picked up the pot of heated water —
it rolled, but
he turned it upside down.

Then,
finally,
Strongest Wind got there,
and he destroyed everything.

Finally,
Blazing Fire came along,
that's all.
Finally,
after (Strongest Wind),
(came) Blazing Fire.

He came along,
and that's all,

'Áw Aráatan shhhhhh 'ím a'ém,
pa'iipáa kwuupóoyəny.

Pa'iipáats tsáaməly aamínyk 'ém,
"Wáaaa!" awét,
nyamáam.

Kwara'ákəts amám.
Apóm,
apúy.

Aváts tsáam,
apóm.

Nyaapúyəm,
nasíits 'ashént siivák 'eta.
Nasíiya.

"Nasíits," a'ím,
nyáany.
Nasíi atháw.
Vaawé 'étk.
'Avá vathí tsaváwkəm,
nyaayúu kwaskyíi 'amátt 'amáy ta'ám awét.

'Amáy nyaat'ám.
'Amáyəny tathíts uuv'óowk,
xatsúurək páq a'ím,
'amáyəny asíly,
púuuum,
nasíits maxák avák viivák 'eta.

Apúy aly'ém.

Nyaavám áam,
'Áw Kwaráany nyaamínyəm.

Nyamáam.
Vathány uutáq atháwk 'ét.
Apúyalyem.

Blazing Fire went whoosh,
and (he was) the one who killed people.

He passed by all the people,
and they went "Aaaah!"
and that was all.

The old man was done for.
He burned,
and he died.

All these (people),
they burned.

When they died,
his mother's older sister was the only one left, they say.
His mother's older sister.

"Aunt," he said,
to that (young woman).
He picked up his mother's older sister.
He went like this.
He made a house here,
he put a dish or something upside down on the ground.

He turned it upside down on top of her.
Hail fell from the sky,
it was freezing cold,
it dropped from the sky,
straight down,
and his mother's older sister sat under the dish, they say.

She didn't die.

She sat there,
and Blazing Fire passed through.

That was all.
He opened this (covering) and rescued her, they say.
She wasn't dead.

Xatsúurəm,
'amáyəny tathíts 'amáyk uuv'óowətəm,
apúy aly'ém viivát.

Viivám,
nyaatháwkəm áam.
Nyaashmán.
"Móo,
'anyáats,
pa'iipáa tsáam 'ar'ém!
'Anasíi,
máanyts mashénttan,
wanyakaváar 'avásh," a'íik 'eta.

Xuumáarənyts.
"Máany mashént waanyakaváarək nyaatháw.

" 'Awétsxa 'athík.
Kavéek 'anathóm 'awétsxá.
Nyaayúu nyuukuunáavəxa," a'íik 'eta.

Nyaatháwk vinthíik 'eta.

Nyaatháwk vinthíim,
xatspáats uuvák 'eta.
Xatspáats uuvám,
nyáany,
Xatalwéts nyaalyanályk,
apúy aly'émk,
'ashéntək áamk,
uuvák uuvák siivák,
Xatalwényts.

"Áa,
'alyshútsáa!
'Alyshútsáa!"
a'íik 'eta.

'Íis,
xuumárəts amáam masharáyt.
Nyakó apúyá.
Navíi avík uupóoy.

It was cold,
hail fell from the sky,
and here she was, not dead.

Here she was,
and he rescued her.
He woke her up.
"Okay,
as for me,
I curse all people!
Aunt,
you are the only one,
I care about you," he said, they say.

The child (said it).
"You are the only one I care about.

"We will do it.
We will head to the south and do it.
I have something to tell you," he said, they say.

He took her (by the hand) and they came along, they say.

He took her (by the hand) and they came along,
and there was a spring, they say.
There was a spring,
and that (spring),
Coyote had fallen into it,
and he didn't die,
he was alone in there,
he sat and sat and sat there,
Coyote (did).

"Oh,
little brother!
Little brother!"
he said, they say.

But,
the child was angry.
His father was dead.
His father's older brother had been killed there.

Máam masharáyt.
"Kaa'ém,
máany 'anamák 'aly'íts amáam."
Masharáyt 'étum.
Xatalwényts atspákəm,
ayáa uusúly uutsxavík,
alyaapáxk 'eta.

Nyaapáxk,
siiwétsk 'eta.
Nasíiny aaly'ák siiwéts.
Iiwáaly amét,
nyáasik siiyáat.

"Móo,
'Anasíi,
máam.
Nyaayúu,
'awíi av'ayémk'ash.
Máany miimáatt xáak 'awíim,
nyiitsóowxa,"
a'íik 'eta.
"Nyiitsóowəm,
nyaayúu muuváatxa,"
a'íik 'eta.

Nyaa'íim,
nyáasuuváak,
mattnamíilk,
iisháaly awét,
suuváam,
nyaayúu xashkyéevək awéta.

Kwashkyéevək uu'íts nyáany nyiitsóowk,
tawelawélk atápk viiwáak awím,
nyaayúu amátk,
"Wówówó" a'ét,
nyáava xaváatt.
Kaawíts amátk uuváak 'eta,
kwashkyéevək avats.

He was angry.
"Somehow,
we have decided to leave you behind," he said.
He was angry, they say.
Coyote came out,
and (the boy) went and ripped him into two pieces,
and he threw them down, they say.

He threw them,
and he went along, they say.
He had his mother's older sister with him and they went along.
He was weeping in his heart,
and he went along, over there.

"Okay,
Aunt,
that's all.
Well,
I am going to go ahead and do something.
I will do (something to make) your body different,
I will turn you into (something else),"
he said, they say.
"I will turn you into (something else),
and you will be (that) thing,"
he said, they say.

Then,
there he was,
he used his powers,
he did this with his hand,
there he was,
and he did (something to make her) a dove or something.

He turned her into what's called a dove,
he swung her and threw her, sending her this way, and so,
she ate things,
she went "Wówówó,"
and she scratched (in the ground) for something.
She was eating something, they say,
that dove.

Uuváam,
ayúuk siiv'áw,
" 'Ankáa,
'ansíi nyaayúu nyiitsóow sáa,
nyamayáalyeməsh.
'A'wíntixa," a'íik 'eta.

Awíntixa nyaa'étk,
avány vaawée nyaa'ét.

Siiv'áwkəm,
nyaawíntik,
tawelawélək atáp.
Kwalytéshq 'axwétt atsóowk 'eta.
Vathá lyavíik,
'axwétt kóx vathá lyavíik.

"Nyáanyts kwiisháayv," a'éta.
Ayérək,
'aayúu 'amáy anák,
'axwétt-tan kóx.

Nyamaaée,
kaawíts amátk,
kaathóm awét.

" 'Anasíi,
amáam 'axótt.
Nyáany mathótk,
nyaayúuk muuváatxa," a'ét.
"Kwalytéshq xwétt nyáany mathóxa," a'ét.

Nyaa'íim,
nyiinamák a'éta.

Nyaanamákəm,
ayérək a'étk uuváam,
'amáy avák.
Kwiisháaytank uuvát.

There she was,
and he stood there watching her.
"How about it,
I turned my aunt into something, but
I don't like it.
I will do it again," he said, they say.

He said he would do it again,
and that's what he did.

He stood there,
and he did it again,
he swung her and threw her.
He made a red wren, they say.
She was like this,
she was red and perfect, like this.

"That is wonderful," he said.
She flew,
and she perched on top of something,
and she was really red and perfect.

She moved around,
she ate something,
she did whatever it was.

"Aunt,
finally it is all right.
That is what you are,
and whenever I see you, you will be (that way)," he said.
"You will be that red wren," he said.

He said it,
and he left her there, they say.

When he left her,
she flew around,
and she perched up high.
She was really wonderful.

Nyaanamák,
siiyáak a'éta.
Xuumár,
"Amáam,
'ansíi nyáasi 'anamák."
Kwalytéshq 'axwétt atsóow,
nyiitsa'áttk namák.

Nyaamák,
nyaayáam,
kaathúum.
Nyakó nyáany —
nyiituupóoy nyáanyi aváamk,
ayúuk 'eta,
nyiituupóoya.

Nyáanyi aváamək,
ayúuk siiv'áw.
Amétk siiv'áwət.

Siiv'áwnyək,
siiyáatk,
aamínyk siiyáat.

Vanyaayáak,
'aayúu 'akanáavəm ma'ámək,
tiimáa xuutsé uuxíirənyts,
suuv'óok 'eta.

A'ím,
nyáany,
kór alyavám nyaayúuk awét.
Tiimáa xuutsényts suuv'óok a'éta.

Paar'áak Paarxáan uuxíiranyts.
Axíirtsəm,
"Xalyvím,
'anyáats nyaapóoy,
aváts suuv'óom,
'Pa'iipáats alynyaváy,

When he left her,
he went along, they say.
The child (said),
"Finally,
I have left my aunt over there."
He had made a red wren
and pushed her (away) and left her.

After that,
he went along,
and it happened.
His father —
he got to (the place) where (his father) had been killed,
and he looked, they say,
at (the place) where (his father) had been killed.

He got there,
and he stood there looking.
He stood there weeping.

He stood there, and then,
he went along,
he went passing through.

As he went along,
those things you heard me telling about,
the tiimáa xuutsé that had been tied up,
they were standing there, they say.

So,
as for them,
they were already there when (the boy) saw them.
The tiimáa xuutsé were standing there, they say.

They were (the ones) Paar'áak and Paarxáan had tied up.
They had tied them up, saying
"It is possible,
that when we die,
these will stand over there, and
'People live inside them,

piipáats suuv'óosh,'
nyiinya'éxa."

Awítya.
Nyaathúu kwa'áts,
suuv'óok athúum,
matxáyk awáayp.

Xuumárənyts ayúuk siiv'áwət.

Nyáanyi shaavártəntik:

> "Yaawaaypawaaaypaaaa,
> kawaaypawaaaypaaaa,
> kawaaypawaaaypaaaa,"

a'éta.

Shaavára.

Nyaayúuts wáaayp awáaayp awáaayp 'íikəta.
Nyáany aashváarək 'eta.

Nyáanyi viithíik 'eta.
Viithíik,
vanyaathíik,
aváak,
savám,
tiimáa xuutséts athótk;
uuv'óot.
"Áa," a'ét.
"Tiimáa xuutséts 'ím athúum,
'ayúush," a'étk 'eta.

" 'Ashuupóowəsh.
Tiimáa xuutséts athúm."

Nyáany aashváara:

> "Timaangáy xuusíii,
>   timaangay Kwapáaangk."

people are standing here,'
(is what) they will say about us."

They did it.
It happened, just as he had said,
they were standing there, and so,
they were swaying in the wind.

The child stood there watching them.

(Another song) is sung there:

    "Sway sway,
      sway sway,
      sway sway,"

(the song) says.

It's a song.

Those things were swaying back and forth.
That's what he sang about, they say.

He came along there, they say.
He came along,
he came along,
and he got there,
and over there,
there were the tiimáa xuutsé;
they were standing there.
"Yes," he said.
"They are what are called tiimáa xuutsé,
I see them," he said, they say.

"I know them.
They are tiimáa xuutsé."

This is what he sang:

    "Tiimáa xuutsé,
     Tiimáa Cocopa."

Ayúuny,
avathíi a'ét.

Tiimáa xuutséts suuv'óts athótk.
Nyáava aashváarət.

Nyaashváarəm,
nyaanamák,
nyáany,
tiimáa xuutsény,
uutanyék a'éta.
Xuuvíkəly.

Xuumár nyii'ényts athómtan.
A'avət.
'Uuqóləts iiwéey amáktsəm áam,
'uuqól a'éta,
ii'ény.

Xuumár nyakó apúy,
nyamáam.
Navíiəny apóoy,
amáam.
Iiwáany 'aláayəm,
tiimáa xuutsény uutanyékəm,
ii'ény alytathúunk 'eta.

Tathúun,
ii'éva tsáam apóm,
nyuupáyk amáam.
Qwalasháwəta.

A'ím,
***
apóm,
nyuupáyk amáam.
'Ora'órəts.
Qwalasháw,
ii'ée nyiirísh amáam.

He saw them,
and he came along, they say.

The tiimáa xuutsé were standing over there.
This is what he sang about.

He sang it,
and he quit,
and as for those (things),
the tiimáa xuutsé,
he cremated them, they say.
Both of them.

It might have been the child's hair.
He noticed it.
It was so long, it went below his hips,
it was so long, they say,
the hair.

The child's father was dead,
that's all.
His father's older brother had been killed too,
that's all.
He felt bad,
and when he had cremated the tiimáa xuutsé,
he dipped his hair into the fire, they say.

He dipped it in,
and all of his hair burned,
and it was completely gone.
He was bald, they say.

So,
***
it burned,
and it was all gone.
(His head) was round like a ball.
He was bald,
there was nothing left of his hair.

Siiv'áwət,
nyáany aashváarək a'éta.

Tsakwshá kwa'ola'óləny kanáavək.

"Kiituiinya iinya,
    kiitamuur amuur,"

a'íik 'eta.

Tsakwshá nyamáam,
'ola'ól a'ím,
mólal a'ím,
mólal a'ím,
mólal a'ím,
athúuk a'ím,
aashváar.

Nyaa'íim,
nyáany,
viithíkt amáam,
tsakwshányts 'ola'óləts siithíit.
Amétk viithíit.

Viithíi,
amáam.

Nyaathíik,
'aakóoy nyuuthík nyiiváak,
tsakwshány 'ola'ól viithíik.

'Atsayér nyakwaaíimts aví nyaváy,
viithíi.
Takúk a'ét.
'Axmá kwayéts a'étk,
kaawíts 'anyóoyəm nyaváyk mayúm.
Nyáany aashváarək viithíita.
Nyáam athíik ayúuk,
aashváarək viithíit.

He stood there,
and this is what he sang, they say.

He was talking about his round head.

   "Kiituiinya iinya,
    kiitamuur amuur,"

he said, they say.

It was his head, that's all,
it was round,
and wobbling,
and wobbling,
and wobbling,
it was, they say,
and he sang about it.

Then,
as for that,
he lay here,
and his round head came from the distance.
It came along weeping.

It came along,
that's all.

It came along,
and it got to the old woman's bed,
the round head came along.

All manner of birds lived there,
(as) he came along.
(One) was called a burrowing owl.
(One) was called a sparrow hawk,
and something ugly lived there, as you have seen.
(The boy) came along singing about that.
He saw them as he came along,
and he came along singing about them.

Viithíinyk,
viithíinyk,
viithíinyk,
'aakóoyəny,
aváata.
'Aakóoy nyaványi aváat.
'Aakóoy Sanyuuxáv nyaványa.

Xuumáar apóoyt amáam,
'aakóoyənyts 'ashéntək athúm,
viivát.

Vathík amáam,
pa'iipáa 'anyóoyəny nyavány tama'ór,
kángk a'ét a'ém.
Wilawíil atsét,
kaa'ém kaawíts nyiimátk,
aatsxwáaar a'ím,
nyaványa.

'Aakóoyənyts avathík kuu'éeytk viithík.

Xatalwéts kwaaxwíirəly wilawíil 'atsatsét.
Aatsxwáar a'étk,
'avány tama'órək uuvák 'eta.

Namáwkitya.
Alyaváam awítya,
xuumárəts.

Viiyáany,
nyaaváam,
nyaayúum,
tam'órtanava ayúut.

Vanyaavák,
'avá 'amáyvi mattaaxwílyk avathík 'eta,
xuumáarəts.
Kwas'iithíits,
'avá 'amáyk mattaaxwíly.

He came along,
he came along,
and he came along,
and as for the old woman,
he got there.
He got to the old woman's house.
Old Lady Sanyuuxáv's house.

Her children had died,
and the old woman was alone,
here she was.

He passed by here,
and there were unsavory people filling her house,
it might have been completely full.
They were playing flutes,
and they were dancing somehow,
and they were laughing,
at her house.

The old woman just lay there, poor thing.

Coyote was in a corner playing the flute.
They were laughing,
and they filled up the house, they say.

He called her his father's mother.
He went to her,
the child (did).

He went along,
and when he got there,
he looked,
and he saw that (the house) was full.

There he was,
and he hid himself at the top of the house, they say,
the child (did).
He was a powerful (person),
and he hid himself at the top of the house.

Tiinyáam aatsxwáar wilawíil atsétk,
kaawém awét.

Siithík.
Xuumárənyts amíim siithík,
iithonasányts tús anály.
Xatalwé vathí túsk,
Xatalwéts apák.

" 'Éey!
Kaawíts 'amáyk atús!
'Amáy thonalysáts," a'íik 'eta.
" 'Amáynyi."

"Talypó katspámək kayúuk," a'ím,
Talypóts avésh atspám.

Nyiirísh.
Makyík kwíi alya'ém,
nyiirísh.
"Qwalasháw kúuxaakúux 'éta,"
a'íik 'eta.

Nyiirísh.

" 'Ée" aaly'ét,
tama'órt siitháwəm.

Xuumár 'amáy athík siithík,
nyaayúu,
'avá kwanáw a'ím viithíkva.
Nyáany,
xwíip a'íik 'eta.

Xwíip,
'avány anám a'ét.

A'ím,
'aakóoyəny,
namáwəny,

At night they laughed and played flutes,
they did whatever it was.

He lay there.
The child lay there weeping,
and his tears dripped and fell.
They dripped onto Coyote here,
and Coyote came to a stop.

"Hey!
Something is dripping from up there!
It's little tears from the sky!" he said, they say.
"From the sky."

"Roadrunner, go out and look," he said,
and Roadrunner ran out.

There was nothing there.
It wasn't cloudy at all,
there was nothing there.
"It's perfectly clear,"
he said, they say.

There was nothing there.

"Oh," he thought,
and they filled the house.

The child was lying up at the top,
well,
he must have been lying on the center beam.
As for that (beam),
he jerked it, they say.

He jerked it,
and the house collapsed, they say.

So,
as for the old woman,
his father's mother,

xwíip 'ét —
atháw,
uutspám.

Talypóts alyavá nyamapúnyəq a'ím,
nyáavəts a'áv,
vathí aaqwáqəly.

Aaqwáq.
Nyaayúu tsáam.
***
Talypónya.

'Ashéets siiványk,
nyamapúnyəq atspám,
'atsamáa,
tsakwshávany uumpínyəq.
'Axwéttk.
***

Kór xalaqáw athótk,
'anóqəm awíita.
Aráav atsémtant,
uumpínyq atsémtək'əsh.
"Aqwáqám?" a'éta.
Nyakór xalaqáw athót,
'Ashéenya.

"Áa," a'ét.
" 'Anyáats av'a'étapat.
'Anóqəm vathí awíi atsém," a'ét.
Talypó nyakór aaqwáq,
vathí 'axwétt awíim,
nyaavák.

'Atskaanáav,
Talypónya kwaxwíttəva.

A'íts,
'Ashée nyaauumpínyq,

he jerked her (by the arm),
he took her,
and they went out.

Roadrunner was rushing around in there;
he felt it,
and he wanted to rip it apart here.

He ripped it apart.
Everything.
***
That Roadrunner (did).

Buzzard was there, and then,
he went rushing out,
and he ate things,
and he pinched his head.
It (turned) red.
***

He was already bald,
and he just did a little (damage).
It barely hurt him,
where he had almost pinched (his head) off.
"Is it ripped apart?" he said.
He was already bald,
Buzzard (was).

"Yes," he said.
"I would say so.
He almost did a little (damage) here," he said.
Roadrunner had already ripped him open,
he did (something to make) it red here,
(here) it is.

(That's) the story
of Roadrunner's red (mark).

So,
when he pinched Buzzard,

xalaqáw a'ét.
Xalaqáw,
uusúly.

***

Xatalwéts kaathómúm,
maxák nyáasily atspám awítya.

Tanám siivány,
axwílyk atspám,
Xatalwényənyts.

Nyáanyi amánək,
xuumáarənyts siiyáak a'éta.
Siiyáat.

Nyamáam,
iiwáanyts 'aláayətsəm.
'Aakóoyəny atháwk siiwéts.

Siiwéts amáam.
Xamaqtháshq siivák a'éta.
Xamaqtháshq nyaváytsəm,
nyamayémtəm;
" 'Éey!
Nyaayúu 'ashuuvíik va'uunóom,
mamáxa!"
a'íik 'eta.
"Kaváar,"
a'íik 'eta.
" 'Ats'amáaw 'a'íi aly'émək vi'ayémk va'thúu," a'íik 'eta.

Nyáanya amák,
xatakúlyts siitháwk.
" 'Atsatsuupíittk,
'atatpóoy," a'étk,
amáam,
kwatiinyáam nyiitsamíim,
tiinyáam tík a'étəm.

(Buzzard) was bald, they say.
He was bald —
and it tore (the skin of his bald head).

***

Coyote must have been (under the rubble) somehow,
and he got out from under it, over there.

It was pressing down on him,
and he dug (his way) out,
Coyote (did).

Starting there,
the child went on, they say.
He went on.

Finally,
he was feeling bad.
He took the old woman with him and they went on.

They went on.
Water Beetle was there, they say.
Water Beetle lived there,
and (the boy) went that way;
"Hey!
I am making gravy
for you to eat!"
(Water Beetle) said.
"No,"
(the boy) said, they say.
"I haven't come here to eat," he said, they say.

After that,
there were mountain lions.
"Let's trap him,
and kill him," they said,
and finally,
darkness fell,
and it was pitch dark.

Nyáava:
xatkúly alytháawk avatháwtk,
xuumáara tapúyá.

"Ée,
kaawíts maxwíivəm.
Mawétsk mathúum,
maxatakúlya.
nyiimakwév ammathúuk mathúum," a'étk;
siiyáat,
iiwáaly 'ét.

Kwatiinyáam tsamíim,
atháw 'étəm,
amákəly vaa'ée a'étəm,
amák alytsénək viiyém a'éta.
Kwas'iithíitk,
amák alytsén.

Viiyém,
nyáasi nyaav'áwk,
'aakóoyəny,
nyamáam,
'amátt ashék,
nyáasi uukathóm.
"Nyáasi muuváatk,
amáam,
samuuváatxa,"
a'étk,
nyaatayúutsk.

Nyaa'íim,
'Aakóoy Sanyuuxávəny atháw vanyuuváak,
xaasa'íly atóly atápəm athúuk 'eta.
'Avíits xaasa'íly atóly avák,
siiváxá.

'Uuyúulya'émts,
sáa
'atskanáav a'ét siivátəm.

This (was it):
the mountain lions waited there,
to kill the child.

"Oh,
you are not strong enough.
Whatever you do,
you mountain lions,
you (are going to) fail," he said;
he went along,
saying it in his heart.

Darkness fell,
and there there they were, they say,
and (the boy) went behind it like this,
he went down behind it and went away, they say.
He had powers,
and he went down behind it.

He went along,
and he stood over there,
and as for the old woman,
that's all,
he named a place,
and he directed her to it.
"You (shall) stay over there,
that's all,
you shall stay there,"
he said,
and he called her his relative.

Then,
he took Old Lady Sanyuuxáv,
and he put her down in the middle of the ocean, they say.
There was an island in the middle of the ocean,
and (that is where) she would be.

It's (something) I have never seen,
but
they talk about it.

'Aakóoy nyáasily aatsuunóoyk 'eta.
Xaasa'íly atóly.
'Aakóoy Sanyuuxáva.

Nyaatsuunóoyk,
xuumárəny.
Nyáasi av'áwk,
nyaakanáavək a'ím,
nyamáam,
Kwayáaxuumárəts athúuk 'eta,
amáam.
Xuumár axtáləts.
Kwayáaxuumár a'éta.

Vaathúum:
vanyaavák,
nyáavəts 'amáyk shathómpk 'éta.
Kuunáava.

" 'Amáy 'ashathómpək van'uuváak,"
saathúum.
'Akwíik uuv'ówk nyaathíim áam.
Uuqás,
kyérrrr a'éta!
Nyuutíish vaawíi awíim,
uuqásk a'íik 'eta.

Máam,
Kwayáaxuumárəts.

Kwayáaxuumárəts awíim,
nyaa'íiva 'ét,
nyaa nyuuqásk kyérrrrr a'ím!

Nyamáam.
Okay.

Nyamáam.

He abandoned the old woman over there, they say.
In the middle of the ocean.
Old Lady Sanyuuxáv.

He abandoned her,
the child (did).
He stood over there,
and he told about it,
and finally,
he became The One Who Acts Like a Child, they say,
finally.
The orphan.
He is called The One Who Acts Like a Child.

It happened like this:
here he was,
and he went up into the sky, they say.
(That's) the story.

"I will go up into the sky and stay there," he said,
and that (is what) he did.
Clouds and rain came.
It thundered,
it went crack!
He did this with his bow,
and it thundered, they say.

That's all,
it's The One Who Acts Like a Child.

The One Who Acts Like a Child is doing it,
they say this,
when thunder goes crack!

That's all.
Okay.

That's all.

6. 'Aavém Kwasám

Told by Tom Kelly

Translated by Millie Romero, Barbara Levy,
George Bryant, and Amy Miller

http://dx.doi.org/10.11647/OBP.0049.06

Tom Kelly told the story of *'Aavém Kwasám* to Abe Halpern twice: the first time on September 20, 1978, and the second time on October 2, 1978. The second version is presented here.

Notes and synopsis

This story begins with a race between *'Aavém Kwasám* and *Qal'iitáaq*. During the course of the race, *'Aavém Kwasám* sees and falls in love with a woman. (A discussion which takes place after the story is concluded suggests that the woman is actually the wife of *Qal'iitáaq*.) She agrees to marry *'Aavém Kwasám*, and they end up with two children.

Eventually Coyote hears of their marriage. (There is a suggestion in the post-story discussion that Coyote might actually be the vengeful *Qal'iitáaq*.) He beats *'Aavém Kwasám* unconscious and takes the woman to the home of his uncle, *Xóo Masée*. Introducing her as his sister-in-law, he tells his uncle, "Here I am, and I want this person so much that I am going to kill her." *Xóo Masée* knows a curse, and when Coyote uses the curse, the woman dies.

'Aavém Kwasám, distraught, decides to follow his wife into death. Cutting his hair — a sign of mourning — and leaving his two children behind, he goes off in a canoe. He sees the apparition of his wife, tries to embrace it, and drowns.

His body is carried along the river. Eventually two young buzzards find it rotting in a fish trap and take it home, intending to roast it. After four days of roasting, the body is recognizable as that of *'Aavém Kwasám*. The father of the two young buzzards instructs his younger daughter to fix the body up, presumably for cremation. She does so, making four trips underwater and enlisting the help of Beaver to restore hair to the corpse. She then returns home.

At this point, the telling of the story is interrupted. When the narrative continues, it focuses on *'Aavém Kwasam*'s children. After the death of their father, the two children are raised by their paternal grandmother. She makes small hunting bows for them and teaches them about the dangers they will face in the wider world. In spite of her warnings, the boys fall prey to Old Lady Flesh-Ripper. Flesh-Ripper carries them off in a sack on her back, intending to kill them. They manage to start a fire in the sack, and they escape while Flesh-Ripper burns to death. The boys then turn themselves into unfeathered arrows and go up into the four levels of heaven.

The person whom the boys encounter in the four levels of heaven is not their father but Old Lady Flesh-Ripper herself. Once again she tries to kill them — this time by secreting sharp objects in their food — and once again they escape. She herself swallows the sharp objects and dies. The boys return home to their grandmother.

Soon they set off again, one of them reluctantly and with difficulty, the other urging him on. They struggle through strong winds, blazing fire, and impenetrable rocks, and when finally they reach their destination in the east, they find two young women there. They marry, and the couples settle in a "colorful house" in the east. From these circumstances, the narrator explains, arises the song *'Axtá 'Amáyəly Aaée* ('Raise the Flute').

The second half of Tom Kelly's story of *'Aavém Kwasám* has much in common with the stories of *Kwayúu* in Chapter 4 and also with the stories of Old Lady *Sanyuuxáv* in Chapter 5. It leaves the reader with an entirely appropriate sense that many of the stories of Quechan oral literature are interconnected.

'Aavém Kwasám

Told by Tom Kelly

'Aavém Kwasám
Qal'iitáaqəm
asa'án matt-tsavakyévúm a'ím.

Viitháwm,
pa'iipáats mattaaéevək.
'Atsiimák,
shaavár uuxáyməs a'ét,
nyáanyi.

'Atsiimák vuunóom,
Xatalwéts alyuuváak,
tsáam shuupáwk uuváak.

'Aavém Kwasámts,
Xamashé Vatáyəny asa'ánək,
aváts —
'atapíly a'éta —
aváts 'amátt alyathík awím,
'atapíly nyáany nyiipáxapat.

Nyáany nyiisa'ánək athúm.

Viinathíik,
tsavakyévək viinathíim,
uutáp 'ashénti uuttáwk,
'Aavém Kwasáməts uuttáwk viinathíim.

Uutáp 'ashéntəm uuttáw,
avuuthíitsəm,
uuttáwk viiyám a'ím,
pa'iipáa —
sanya'ákts sanyuuváak —
"Xa 'ayáaw vanyaa'ayáak."
Xatsapáats ayúum,
alyaváam.

'Aavém Kwasám
and Qal'iitáaq
were going to have a kickball race.

There they were,
and people got together.
They danced,
even though they didn't know (many) songs, they say,
at that (time).

They went on dancing,
and Coyote was among them,
and he knew everything.

'Aavém Kwasam
kicked the Big Star forward;
and these things —
they're called cattails —
they were sticking out of the ground, and so,
he, in his turn, lost (the ball) in the cattails.

That's where he kicked it.

They came,
they came running,
and he was one length ahead,
'Aavém Kwasám was ahead as they came.

He was one length ahead,
and they brought it along,
and he went ahead intending to pass by here,
and a person —
there was a woman over there —
"I'm going to go get water," (she said).
There was a spring over there,
and she got there.

'Aavém Kwasám viitápk awím,
túlyəly a'ím,
paqátt nyaatháwk —
aavxáy iikwé a'ét —
avíly tsathúunəm.

"Kuuthíik!
'Uutáp 'ashént,
nyamáartsiyúm!"
Kuuthíik!"

"Kaváar!
Máanyts kathíik,
katháwk!"

"Áa,"
a'étk,
nyaayáak atháw.

"Móo,
nyatsúyk."

"Móo,
xótt."

Xatalwéts nyaa'ávək —
kór a'áv —
avány aaqwíttk vuunóony,
alythík,
apúyk viithík,
xweyamánək viithík.

Nyaaváak —
Xatalwéts uumáyk viiwém,
uunyíik a'ím,
avány antsénək a'í.

Viiwém.

'Avá kamém.

'Aavém Kwasám threw it,
and it went plop,
and she caught it —
there's a part of her dress —
she pushed it in there.

"Bring it back!
My one-length lead,
they might win it away from me!
Bring it back!" (he said).

"No!
You come
and get it!"

"All right,"
he said,
and he went and got it.

"Okay,
I'll marry you," (he said).

"Okay,
all right," (she said).

Coyote heard it —
later he heard about it —
and he beat him up,
and he lay there,
he lay here dying,
he lay here unconscious.

They got there —
Coyote invited her and they went,
and he called her his sister-in-law,
and he called her husband his older brother.

He took her there.

They got to the house.

Nyáanyi uuváash,
nyáanyts.
Vanyuuváak,
Xóo Masée a'étka.
Xóo Masée a'étk,
'axwíttk uuvám.

Nyáany,
iiwám mattkanáav:
" 'Anavíiya,"
a'ím.
"Ée,
'avétta,
kaawíts kamathúum?"
"Áa-á,
'athúum va'thúum va'thúum."

" 'Avák 'athúum,
pa'iipáany 'áartanək 'uuvák 'athósh.
'Atapúy 'a'ím a'ílya."
" 'Axótt."
"Sanya'áka."
" 'Axótt."

Nyaa'íim,
viinathíiik athúm,
'avám katán.
Nyamawítsk nyaayúu awíi vuunóok,
tawáam,
shuuvíi a'íim,
kaawíim.

Avány shuuvíi,
'axá alytsáam,
'axányts alól vaa'é a'ím,
nyamashtúum alytsáam:
"Áa,
kúur 'aavíirəm,
mamátsk mathútsxa."
a'ét.

There he was,
that (person).
There he was,
and he was called Xóo Masée.
He was called Xóo Masée,
and he was red.

That (person),
he told about himself:
"My father's older brother,"
he said.
"Well,
my younger brother's child,
what are you up to?"
"Well,
this is how I am and this is what I've done."

"(Here) I am,
and I want this person very much.
I want to kill her."
"All right."
"The woman."
"All right."

Then,
they came,
they got to the house.
She was doing things there,
she was grinding (grain),
she was going to make porridge,
and she was doing whatever it was.

She made that porridge,
she put in water,
and the water bubbled like this,
and she gathered (the ingredients) and put them in;
"Yes,
soon I will finish,
and you'll eat,"
she said.

"Áa,
 xótt," a'ím,
"A'íis,
 'amuuvílyk 'uunáam,
 'amuutsavíilyk 'uunáam av'athótǝm 'athúum."
"Maaíim."

" 'Awétk vi'atháwk," a'ítya.
 A'étǝm,
" 'Axótt."

A'étk a'ím,
 uupúuvǝk viiwétsk.

Avawétsk;
"Nyaayúu,
 'áw aráak kayúuk!"
 a'étǝm;
 vaa'ée ayúunyk,
 kaváar.

Viiwétsk viiwétsk,
 ava'íntik,
 xamók,
 nyamkwatsuumpápǝm,
" 'Áw aráanya,
 kayúuny!
 Maláwxa!"
 'A'áwǝnyts aráak,
 apómǝk viivám.

"Áa-á,
 ***,
 'Axótt."

A'ét.
"Nyaanyamáam,
 nyáanya.
 Nyaanyamáam,
 'ashént 'ashuupáwk,
 'awétǝm,
 nyáanyamáam."

"Yes,
 all right," he said,
"But
 I'm in a great hurry,
 (that is,) we are in a great hurry," (he said).
"Do as you please," (she said).

"I am doing it," she said.
 She said it;
"All right," (he said).

 He said it, and so,
 they went in and went along.

 They went along;
"Well,
 look at the fire blazing!"
 he said;
 she just glanced at it like this (without really looking),
 and nothing happened.

 They went on and on,
 and he said it again,
 three (times),
 and on the fourth (time),
"That blazing fire,
 look at it!
 You must turn your head!"
 The fire blazed up,
 it went on burning.

"Oh,
***
All right."

 She said it.
"That's all,
 that one.
 That's all,
 I (only) know one,
 and so,
 that's all."

Nyaa'étəm,
"Aváts nyaapúyk."
Sany'áakənyts tawáany av'áwəny;
" 'Iiwáats arávxá," a'étka'a.

Aa'áampət.
Apúyt.

Nyaapúyəm,
nyiinyaakwévəm,
'iipáa aváts vanyuuváak,
ii'ényts 'óook a'ím áam,
nyamaakyítt viiwáanyk viiwáany,
nyiikwévəm nyam.

***

Nyuupáyk,
vanyuuváak.
Nyaxuutsamáar xavíkəm,
uutsáam vuuváak awét.
'Aakóoyts nyiivántik athúm.

Áa,
Xatalwé nyuuváantika.

Iiwáam viiyém,
makyé ayémtək,
aváat.
Makyé ayémək uuváak,
nyáany awím,
'a'íi nyáany.

Áa,
alykyéttkitya.
Awíi vuunóok vuunóok,
'axaalyáak atséw,
uutara'úyk aavíir.

Viiyém a'ím.

When he said it,
"She will die," (he said).
The woman was standing there grinding grain;
"My heart hurts," she said.

She fell face down.
And she died.

She died,
that was the end of her,
and that man was there,
and his hair was long, down to here,
and he kept cutting it, on and on, until
there wasn't any left.

***

It was all gone,
and here he was.
There were two children,
and he was in charge of them.
There was an old woman there too.

Yes,
Coyote was there too.

(The man) went off by himself,
he went off somewhere,
and he got there.
He went off somewhere and there he was,
and he used that,
that wood.

Yes,
he cut down (a tree), they say.
He went on and on doing it,
he made a canoe,
he fixed it up and finished.

He wanted to go away.

Nyamkamáyk,
viiyémk apúy a'ím.

Nyamkanáav aly'émk uuváanyk,
viiyáam;
shatuupáawk viitháwk athúm,
nyaatuuqwíirək viiwéts.

"Kaváarək," a'étka.
"Avkuunóotsk.
Kaawíts 'ayáam,
'athúum,
'anymaatuuqwíir aly'ém.
Kuunóotk."

"Ma'axúutt muunóotəm ám."

"Ée'é,
'awítsapat 'a'étka.
'Athútsapat 'av'áwk 'aaly'éet," a'ét.

Matsats'étk vuuv'óom,
nyaayúuk,
"Ée'é,
kanéem,
vathány 'atsúutk," a'étk a'ím,
awíima.

Xalyamuutsáak awím,
"Ammawét vanyaathúm," a'étəm;
"Áa,
'axóttk,"
a'ét.

Uuv'óotəm awím,
tsúut nya'étk,
viiyém.

Xuumáarəts nyuuv'óok,
matsats'étk uuv'óok.

(He wanted) to go into exile,
he wanted to go away and die.

He didn't tell anyone,
he (just) went along;
they knew (what he was up to), and so,
they went along following him.

"No," he said.
"Stay there.
I'm going after something,
and so,
don't follow me.
Stay (there).

"You (two) are doing fine."

"Yes,
we want to do it too.
We think we'll do it too," they said.

They stood there crying,
and when he saw them,
"All right,
step back.
I'm going to launch this," he said, and so,
he did it.

He put it in the water, and so,
"Whatever you do, it will happen," he said;
"Yes,
all right,"
they said.

They stood there, and so,
he launched it,
and he left.

The children stood there,
they stood there crying.

Viiyáak,
viiyáak,
viiyáak,
viiyáak.

Vaa'éta:
" 'Axuumáy kwa'nóq 'anamák,"
a'ét.

    "Nuumáka,
    kwiiyáma,
    xuumáy kwiinóqa,"

a'étk.
"Aháaa,"
a'étk,
amétk viiyáak.

Nyáany ava'étk,
ava'étk,
viiyáam.

Nyaavée kwapúyənyts,
viiyám.

" 'Aavém Kwasáméey!"
a'étk,
iimáatt-ts atspáktək,
aathómptəm ayúuk,
viiyáak.

Nyamkwatsuumpápəm,
nyaavíirnyəm,
" 'Awém,
'atháwxa," 'aaly'étka,
nyaa'ét.

Nyaa'íntim,
"Manyuuwíts manyáaw,"
nyaa'ét a'ím,
taxmakyíp,
awíik aaly'ét.

He went,
and he went,
and he went,
and he went.

This is what he said:
"I'm leaving my little son,"
he said.

    "The one that's left behind,
     the one who goes,
     my little son,"

he said.
"Ohhhh!"
he said,
and he went along weeping.

That's what he was saying,
he was saying that,
as he went along.

His dead wife
passed by here.

" 'Aavém Kwasám!"
she said,
and her body appeared,
and he watched it change course,
and he went after it.

On the fourth (time),
when he finished,
"I can do it,
I can get her," he thought,
and he said so.

When he said it again,
"Go after your loved one,"
she said, and so,
he embraced her,
he thought that he did.

Ashváq a'étəm;
xalypám.

Apúyk a'ét.

Apúyk,
viiyáanyk,
viiyáanyk,
viiyáanyk,
viiyáany,
'axá — 'axá—
'aayúu —
'ataakwíily a'éta.
Xály avák;
'atáyk siivak.

Siivám.

Nyáaly axávək,
vanyaavák,
asháxk siivák,
apúyk asháx.

Siivám,
'ashée xarák,
vatstsáats xavík avuunóok.
'Amáttnya —
kavée 'anyaaxáapk vuunóok vuunóok vuunóom,
avawétsk,
nyaayúu,
'atsayér kwavatáts,
shat'ura'úurəny kwalyvíiny xalykwáatsk,
kaawíts apáavək amátsk,
kaawíts asháx awét.

Avathíkəm,
nyáava,
taxalykwéts av'áar vuunóok.
Vanyaawéts.

Suddenly there was peace;
he fell in the water.

He died, they say.

He died,
and (his body) went
and went
and went
and went, until
in the water — the water —
(there was) something —
it's called a fish trap.
It was in the water;
there were a lot of them there.

There it was.

He had gone in there,
and there he was,
he was rotting in there,
he was dead and rotting.

There he was,
and (there was) a kind of buzzard,
and his two daughters were there.
This place —
they were hanging around someplace in the southeast,
they did that,
well,
those big birds,
they hunt for things like eggs,
they roast something and eat it,
they use whatever is rotten.

He lay there,
and as for this,
and they went hunting as usual.
They went after (things).

Nyaayúuny ayúuxayəm,
viivák,
asháxk awím.

"Áa-á,
'ana'áy vathány a'éta!
Vathány a'íim;
vathány 'apáavəm amátxa,"
a'étka,
nyaayúu kwáarəny.

" 'Óo,
kaváar,
asháxk 'aláay!"

"Kanaqáməlyemk,
asháx;
nyaayúu 'uumáxats athúulyəm.
Nyaayúu shtar'úur avány 'awíim,
avány,
'aqwésxa."

A'ávəlyem.
"Kaváar.
Nyáava 'awíi 'a'ím 'a'ítya."
a'ét.
Nyaayúu xan'uuthíly a'étəm,
'a'íiny awíim,
nyaapítsk vuunóonyk vuunóony.
Nyaamáam.

Nyáava apáyk viinathíim,
"Áa,
asháxk,"
nyiixúu shapéttk,
amákəly athíik awím.
" 'Óo,
asháxk 'aláaytsəm."

They were looking around, and suddenly,
here he was,
he was rotting.

"Well,
my father said it was this one!
He said it was this one;
I'll roast this one and he'll eat it,"
she said,
the (sister) who wanted something.

"Oh,
no,
it's rotten and bad!" (said her sister).

"Let's not touch it,
it's rotten,
it's not the sort of thing we should eat.
We'll use these eggs and things,
these (things),
they'll turn brown."

(Her sister) didn't listen.
"No.
This is what I'm going to use,"
she said.
Something called a pallet,
she made it of branches,
and she went on slapping (the remains of the body) onto it.
That's all.

They came carrying this,
"Oh,
it's rotten," (said the older sister),
and she held her nose,
and she came along behind.
"Oh,
it's rotten and bad," she said.

Viinathíik,
viinathíik,
viinathíik,
viinathíik,
'avá katán,
awím,
"Áa,
nyáany 'a'épəm áam.
Kapáavət!"
apáav avuunóok.

Shamáts 'ashént,
'anyáa xavíkəm,
uutáqt ayúum;
uuvátəm,
ayúut.
Avawétk awétk,
kwatsuumpápənyəm,
nyamkwaxamókənyəm,
shuupáwk a'ím.
"Nyáanya.
Nyáany."
***
"Kaawíts uuvátəm athúm!
Ka'áv!" a'éta.

" 'Aavém Kwasáméey!" a'ét.
Aaksáatsk a'ím:
" 'Óo,"
a'ét.

A'áv,
ayáak uukanáavəm;
"Áa,
kuutara'úyk!
Kuutara'úyk,
avány kuutara'úyəm,
'axóttxa!
Vaathóxa."

They came,
and came,
and came,
and came,
and they got home,
and so,
"Yes,
that's what you heard me say.
Roast it!" (he said),
and she went about roasting it.

One night (passed),
and on the second day,
she opened it up and looked at it;
there it was,
and she looked at it.
She did it,
and the fourth (time),
(or) the third (time),
she recognized him, they say.
"That's him.
That's him."
***
"Something is there!
Listen!" she said.

" 'Aavém Kwasam!" she said.
He said it slowly:
"Oh,"
he said.

She listened,
and she went and told (her father) about it;
"Yes
fix it up!" (he said).
"Fix it up!
Fix that (body) up
(so that) it will be all right!
It will be like this."

A'étəm,
nyamawítsk,
uutara'úyk suunóom,
amákəny,
kwatsuumpáp,
atspák.

Avathótk:
xótt-təm ayúuts,
ii'ényənyts kaváarək athótk.
Vanyaavák.

"Nyaayúu,
ii'é 'awíyú 'avák,"
vanyaa'íim,
kaawíts 'axály atsénək a'úpk.

'Apén a'éta.
'Apénnya,
'aqwéshk viithíkəm,
kanáavəm:
"Ii'é 'atséwəm atspáa a'étka.
Kaváar."

A'étəm,
"Ka'úpəntik,
kaxávək!
Avík aviithíkəntik nyaavá.
'Apén vaathúts a'étəm,"
a'íik 'eta.

Aváam,
ii'é nyiitápkəm,
kaváartənti.

Aaxavík,
kwaxamók,
awíim,
kaváartəny a'ét.

He said it,
and she did it,
she went about fixing it up, over there,
and after (that),
on the fourth (time),
it came out.

This is how it was:
it looked all right, but
the hair was not (right).
There it was.

"Well,
I'm going to do something with the hair,"
she said,
and she dove down into the water for something.

It's called a beaver.
The beaver,
he was brown, lying there,
and she told him about it:
"I am trying to make his hair grow out.
It's not right (the way it is)."

She said it, and
"Dive in again,
go in!
There is another one there.
Beavers are like this, they say,"
he said, they say.

She got there,
and when she had put the hair there,
once again it wasn't right.

She did it twice,
and the third (time),
she did it,
and it still wasn't right, they say.

Nyamkwatsuumpápəm nyaaxávəntim,
ii'é ta'axán nyiitsaváw.

'Apén nyíilyts avathík awím,
nyáanyts awíima.
Ii'ény uutara'úyəm
nyíily,
aalywíishm,
'axótt-tanək atspák,
a'éta.

Nyaatspák,
viithíik,
'avá aváak;
"Nyaayúu,
'ats'amáaw," a'íim;
nyaayúu mathílyk,
"Vanythály muutsáawva,
'amáts 'athóxa.
Shuuvíi 'amátsú."

A'íim,
viivám.
Mashaxáy kwa'kúts nyaathúuva.
"Kaváarək" a'ét.

"Mana'áyəm kuutáarək," a'ét.

"Mana'áy kayém,
nyaayúu kawéeyk," a'ét.
Vaa'étk viiwáatk.

A'éta.

***

Nyáany a'étk,
xuumáarənyts
suunóok athúm,
alynyuuthútsk vanyuunóok —

When she went in again for the fourth (time),
she arranged the hair properly.

A black beaver was there, and so,
he is the one that did it.
He fixed up the hair
(so that) it was black,
and he twisted it,
and it came out really well,
they say.

When it came out,
she came,
she came to the house,
"Well,
let's eat something," she said;
(her sister) was making thick-mush corn bread,
"This little thing you are making,
we'll eat it.
Let's eat it as porridge."

And so,
here she was.
It was the older girl.
"No," she said.

"Share it with your father," she said.

"Go to your father,
and do something for him," she said.
She went on saying this.

So they say.

***

Anyway,
the children (of 'Aavém Kwasám)
were around over there,
and they were thinking —

uupúyts athótəm a'étk a'íim,
alynyuuthútsk vanyuunóok,
" 'Anyáats,
makyém 'uupúuvəxa?
'Aaly'íim,
'iiwáalyəm 'ayúus,"
vanyaathót.

Nyaayúu,
'aakóoyənyts ava'ét.

Xuumáar 'atskuunóom,
'uuntíish awéeytk,
iiwáanyi,
nyamáam,
nya'kúutsəm,
nyaayúu uukanáav a'ét.

"Nyaayúu,
uusóx,
nyaayúu 'aqwáaq,
pa'iipáa nyiikwanáam,
pa'iipáa 'axán uutssóots.
'Axánts —
pa'iipáa 'axán uutssóots athúuk a'ím.
***

"Nyamawítsk awíim,
tapúyk kamétk,
kaawíts awét.
Kaawíts awét.

" 'Aakóoy 'Amátt Shaxathúuk aví uuváak uuvák,
ava'étk,
pa'iipáa atháwk,
' 'Ashxthúk 'a'ávəlya,
'ashxthúk 'a'ét 'a'ávəlya,' a'étk,
a'etəs,
athúum!
Uuvám!

it was his death they were thinking about, and so,
they were thinking,
"As for us,
which way shall we go?
We (should) think about this,
and look into our hearts," (they said),
and this is what they did.

Well,
the old woman had something in mind.

The children were around here and there,
and she made little bows for them,
by herself,
and finally,
when they were older,
she explained things to them, they say.

"Well,
the (meat) that will be eaten,
a deer or something,
a creature worthy of respect,
(that's what) a proper person eats.
A proper (person) —
that's what a proper person eats, they say.
***

"He does it like that,
he kills it and brings it,
he does something.
He does something.

"Old Lady Flesh-Ripper is around here,
and so,
she takes people,
'I feel like ripping out his flesh,
I feel like ripping out his flesh,' she says,
or she might say,
and she does it!
She's around!

"Nyiimashtúum,
nyiimakwévəm!
Mashiithéevək athúm!"
"Áa,
ayóov awéts," a'ét,
viiwéts.

Athúm,
nyamathúts.
Siithíik,
"Pa'iipáa 'ashxathúk 'a'ávəlya!" a'ét.
***

Nyiishtúum,
amákəly aapáxk,
nyiithóshk siithíim.

Kwa'kútsənyts,
"Xwóott!
'Apóoyt a'ím!" a'étkəm,
mattkanáavəm a'ét.

A'étk,
awíim,
nyaayúuk.
'A'áw akyáam,
axtáttəly nyaatsavóowk,
karáy karáyts a'ím,
uutáaqsh,
uutspám.

'Aakóoy nyuuváks,
axtáttá,
vathá lyavíik.
***
Apúyk.
Apóm.

Nyáanyi atsénək,
viinathíik kanáav,
a'ét.

"If she catches you,
that (will be) the end of you!
She is dangerous!" (she said).
"Yes,
if we see her we will leave," they said,
and off they went.

And so,
that's how it happened.
She came along,
"I feel ripping somebody's flesh!" she said.
***

She caught them,
and she threw them behind her,
and she came along carrying them on her back.

The oldest one,
"Oh, my!
We're going to die!" he said,
and they discussed it among themselves.

And so,
they did it,
when they saw (an opportunity).
They started a fire (with bow and arrow),
and they set it on her back,
and she went hopping around,
and they jumped (out),
and they escaped.

The old woman was there,
and her back
was like this.
***
She died.
She burnt up.

They came down,
they came and told about it,
they say.

Nyaayúuny kanáavətsk:
"Vaathúum,"
a'ét.
Nyaany nyiikwanáam ashíittk uuváatəm;
"Áa,
nyáany 'awítsk," a'ét.

"Nyáany 'ayóovxa," a'ét.

A'étk,
nyamathúts.
" 'Iipá xash'étt matt'iitséw,
'amáy uutspámxa,"
a'ét.
Nyaayúu ayóov a'ét.
Xalyuukwéts,
aví vuunóok a'ét.
'Amáy uutspám,
athík aatsuumpápəly uutspám.

Pa'iipáanyts,
áa,
maawíi kwapúy,
áa,
matt-tsapéem ayóov.

Pa'iipáats vanyaavák,
uuvám,
katánəm.
Nyamathútsənyá,
awíts nyáts vuunóot.

'Aláaytanəm nyaa'ávək,
"Ka'athúts av'athú'əm?"
a'ím.

Nyaa'étəm,
nyiikwashtútsənyts,
avawétəm,
a'étəm,
"Ée-ee."

They told about the things (that had happened to them):
"It was like this,"
they said.
They listed the dangerous things (that they had done).
"Yes,
we did that," they said.

"We saw that," they said.

And so,
that's what happened.
"We will turn ourselves into unfeathered arrows,
and go up into the sky,"
they said.
They intended to see things.
They intended to look for their father,
as they were there.
They went up in the sky,
they went up into the four levels (of heaven).

The people,
yes,
their dead relatives,
yes,
they saw so many of them.

Someone was there,
there she was,
(when the boys) got there.
The (thing) that had happened to them,
the very (person) who had done it was there.

When they realized how bad (the situation) was,
"What shall we do?"
they said.

Then,
the one who had caught them,
she did something,
and they said,
"All right."

"Nyantamáatskəlyemtəm nyii'tháwk."
Kaathúts avatháwəm a'ím.
"Muuváak ma'ím."
"Ée-ee."

A'étkəm,
nyaayúu,
shuuvíi awíi vuunóok vuunóok.

"Makyény awítsk," a'étk.
"Nyatatapóoy a'ím," a'ítstəsáa,
uuxáyk,
amáatk,
xiipúk awíikəta.

Axúupt.
Nyaayúuk ayúuk,
vaa'éta.
Axúupk axúup.
Malyaqénya aakyíttk.

Apúyk aatkyéerk,
nyaayúuk,
natsénək, a'éta.

Natsénək,
viinathíik viinathíim,
'amáy athík aatsuumpápəm,
aatsavérək,
'avuumák uuv'óo.

Uuv'óom,
namáwənyts uuvám,
Xatalwényts nyuuváak,
***
alynyéxəmk uuvám áam.

Uuv'óok a'ét.
nyáanya,
nyaakatánəntik,

"I'm not going to let you go," (she said).
She intended them to stay where they were.
"You are going to stay there."
"All right."

And so,
well,
she went on and on making porridge.

"She's going to do it to someone," they said.
"She wants to kill us," they said, but
they knew (what she was up to),
and they ate the porridge,
they ate first, they say.

They gulped it down.
She was watching and watching,
and (then) she went like this.
She gulped it and gulped it.
It cut her throat.

She was lying dead, on her back,
and when they saw this,
they came (back) down (to earth), they say.

They came (back) down (to earth),
they came and came,
from the four levels of heaven,
and they finished,
and they stood there behind the house.

They stood there,
and their father's mother was there,
and Coyote was there,
***
and he was very restless.

They stood there, and so,
as for that,
when they got home again,

" 'Anyáanya,
'amáy 'anyáak,
'amáy 'anyáak 'anayém 'a'étk,
alynyi'athúutsəntik,"
a'ét.

Vuunóok athúm,
"Muuthóxats alyathóm.
Nyiikwanáam!"

"Áa,
'athútsəm 'a'ítya,"
a'ét.

Nyamathútsk.
Viiwétsk,
nyaayúu,
kwakútsənyts,
nyiikwévək,
uuthóxats athúm awét.

"Nyaayúu,
nyiikwanáam.
Matxá aspérək,"
a'ét.

" 'A'áw aráak,
nyiithík!"
a'étkəm;
"Kaawíts —
'aqwáaq matháwəm alyathík," a'étk.
" 'Avíits nyiitháwəm,
muuyémxats athúmk," a'ét.
Kanáavək vuunóok.
"Ée,
nyam'uupúuv aly'ém."

As'ílyəm,
a'ávəlyemk,
viiwétstək,

"The east,
up high in the east,
we are going to go up high in the east,
we think,"
they said.

There they were, and so,
"(That) is something that you must not do.
It's dangerous!" (she said).

"Yes,
we'll do it,"
they said.

That's how it happened.
They went,
well,
the older one,
he was no good at it,
(but) it was what he had to do and he did it.

"Well,
it is dangerous.
The wind is strong,"
he said.

"A fire is burning,
there it is!"
he said;
"(There is) something —
there is a deer in there for you to get," (his brother) said.
"There are rocks there,
and you will have to go through them," he said.
He went on telling him.
"Well,
we're not going through there."

He refused,
(but the younger brother) didn't listen,
and they went on,

avathúum,
viiwétsk,
aatsnyavárəm,
avawétk,
'amátt tsathóm tsathóm awét,
tsuumpápəm,
"Nyuukats'éeyk,"
tspáyk tspáyk a'ét,
uutspám.

A'étk,
nyáanya,
aashváarək ava'ét.
'Aashváarək ava'étəm,
nyaayúu,
" 'Iimé nyáanyts arávəm,"
a'ím.

A'ím,
"Xamanyéw nyáany," a'ét.

Nyaayúu,
nyamuuyémənya,
walytsaváamtəm,
nyaayúuk,
"Áa,
'anyxamnyéw," a'étk,
nyáanyəm,
"Kamawém,
athúuk təsaa
'axóttxa," a'ét.

"Ée'é,
máam,
kamawíim,
vi'nayémxa," nyaa'ét.

Nyamnayémk,
viiwétsk.

they did it somehow,
they went on,
(the older brother) was exhausted,
but they did it somehow,
they pressed on and pressed on, and so,
in four (days),
"I'll show you how," (he said),
and they held hands,
and they went out.

And so,
that song,
he sang it like that.
He sang it like that,
well,
"My feet hurt,"
he said.

And so,
"It's those shoes," he said.

Well,
that path,
he wasn't up to it,
but when he saw it,
"Yes,
it's my shoes," he said,
and at that point,
"You must be able to do something,
that's how it is, but
it will be better," he said.

"Well,
that's all,
you'll do something,
and we will go," he said.

Thus they went away,
they went.

Nyaayúuk:
'a'áw aráa a'étk,
awét,
'xá aspér a'étk.
***
Naxkyíik,
nyáanyi,
nyáayúu,
iimé nyáany arávək, a'étk,
kanáavək,
nyáanyi av'áwk:

    "Áaliiláalaláa,
     áaliiláalaláa,"

a'étk,
nyiiv'áwk a'ím,
xamanyéw,
xamanyéw uu'íts nyáanya,

    "'Anyxamarúy kaamawépətik aléel**ə**teee,"

a'ét.

Vaa'étk.

"Vany'uuváam,
'awéxa,"
a'étk,
nyáany awíim aavíirək,
viinayémək a'ét.

Nyamáam,
aapárv.
'Avíits lyavíik a'íikəm,
nyamuupúuvəm áam.
'Avíiny matt-takyév vaa'íim,
suuváam.

"Nyam'uupúuvxa,"
a'ét.

They saw it:
a fire was burning, they say,
and then,
the water was powerful, they say.
***
They went across;
and there,
well,
those feet of his hurt, he said,
and he told about it,
as he stood there:

"Fire is burning, burning,
    fire is burning, burning,"

he said,
and he stood there, they say,
and as for his shoes,
those things that they call shoes,

"What have you done with my shoes,"

he said.

He said it like this.

"I am here,
and I will do it,"
he said,
and he finished doing it,
and they went on, they say.

That's all,
it was the end.
The rocks were like this, they say,
and they went through them.
(Then) the rocks came together like this,
there they were.

"We'll go through it,"
(the younger brother) said.

Iisháaly tsapáyk,
amák nyiuutspám.

Ava'étk,
siiwétsk,
nyaayúu aatsxuukyáavk awím,
awím,
a'ávək.
Anáwəm,
matxály viithíim,
mashtxáats siitháwk,
a'áv.

A'étəm,
nyáanyi,
alytsénək awím,
sanyts'áakənyts viitháwəm,
tsakyévək,
aváts avány atháwk,
avány atháwk athúm.

Siitháwk a'étk,
nyaayúu,
'Axtá 'Amáyəly Aaée a'étk aashváarək,
nyáanyi atspáktəm.

Nyáanyi atspáktəm.
Kwatsáanənyts tsanyót,
'Axtá 'Amáyəly Aaéenya.

Vanyuu—
'avá kwanyór a'étəm,
nyáasi,
uupúuvətəm.

Nyáanyi atháwk,
'Axtá 'Amáyəly Aaée nyáanyi uuvák a'ét.
Nyáanyi atspák athúuk,
a'ím.

They held hands,
and they came out on the other side.

That's what they did,
they went on,
they crossed over something,
and so,
(someone) heard them.
They made noise,
and it was carried by the wind,
and there were some young women over there,
and they heard it.

So,
at that (point),
they went down, and so,
the women were over there,
and they paired off:
that one took that (boy),
and (the other one) took that (boy).

There they were, they say;
well,
they sang a song called Raise the Flute;
that's where it comes from.

That's where it comes from.
The Quechan (people) perform it,
the (song) Raise the Flute.

Then—
it was a colorful house, they say,
over there in the distance,
and they went inside.

There they were,
and Raise the Flute was there, they say.
It came from there,
they say.

Nyáany aashváarək viiyémkitya.
Kwatsáanənyts,
a'étəma.

Ava'étəm a'áv.

They go on singing that song, they say.
The Quechan (do),
they say.

I've heard them say so.

This book need not end here...

At Open Book Publishers, we are changing the nature of the traditional academic book. The title you have just read will not be left on a library shelf, but will be accessed online by hundreds of readers each month across the globe. We make all our books free to read online so that students, researchers and members of the public who can't afford a printed edition can still have access to the same ideas as you.

Our digital publishing model also allows us to produce online supplementary material, including extra chapters, reviews, links and other digital resources. Find *Stories from Quechan Oral Literature* on our website to access its online extras. Please check this page regularly for ongoing updates, and join the conversation by leaving your own comments:

http://www.openbookpublishers.com/isbn/9781909254855

If you enjoyed this book and feel that research like this should be available to all readers, regardless of their income, please think about donating to us. Our company is run entirely by academics, and our publishing decisions are based on intellectual merit and public value rather than on commercial viability. We do not operate for profit and all donations, as with all other revenue we generate, will be used to finance new Open Access publications.

For further information about what we do, how to donate to OBP, additional digital material related to our titles, or to order our books, please visit our website: www.openbookpublishers.com

OpenBook
Publishers
Knowledge is for sharing